LITTLE SAIGONS

LITTLE SAIGONS

Staying Vietnamese in America

Karin Aguilar–San Juan

University of Minnesota Press

Minneapolis

London

Published by the University of Minnesota Press
111 Third Avenue South, Suite 290
Minneapolis, MN 55401-2520
http://www.upress.umn.edu

Library of Congress Cataloging-in-Publication Data

Aguilar–San Juan, Karin, 1962-
    Little Saigons : staying Vietnamese in America / Karin Aguilar–San Juan.
        p. cm.
    Includes bibliographical references and index.
    ISBN 978-0-8166-5485-7 (hardcover : alk. paper) —
    ISBN 978-0-8166-5486-4 (pbk. : alk. paper)
    1. Vietnamese Americans—Ethnic identity—Case studies.
2. Vietnamese Americans—Social conditions—Case studies.
3. Community life—United States—Case studies. 4. Geographical
perception—United States—Case studies. 5. Place attachment—United
States—Case studies. 6. United States—Ethnic relations—Case studies.
7. Vietnamese Americans—California—Orange County—Social
conditions. 8. Vietnamese Americans—Massachusetts—Boston—Social
conditions. 9. Orange County (Calif.)—Ethnic relations—Case studies.
10. Boston (Mass.)—Ethnic relations—Case studies. I. Title.
    E184.V53A35 2009
    305.895'922073—dc22
                                        2009016774

Printed in the United States of America on acid-free paper

The University of Minnesota is an equal-opportunity educator and employer.

16 15 14 13 12 11 10   10 9 8 7 6 5 4 3 2

For the future of Vietnamese America

The stranger intends to stay,
although he cannot ever become a native.

—GEORG SIMMEL, "The Stranger,"
from *On Individuality and Social Forms* (1908)

Contents

Introduction   Where Does Viet Nam End and America Begin?

LITTLE SAIGONS EXAMINES THE ROLE OF PLACE in generating and supporting Vietnamese American community and identity. Because Vietnamese refugees fled their homeland and then immediately upon their arrival to U.S. shores in 1975 were purposefully dispersed across all fifty states by federal resettlement agencies, their subsequent congregation in just a few metropolitan regions poses many interesting questions about the relationship between place and community for refugees and immigrants.[1] I focus on Vietnamese American community-building and place-making in two distinct regions on opposite sides of the United States: Orange County, California and Boston, Massachusetts. In those places as in others, Vietnamese Americans—refugees, immigrants, and their U.S.-born children—have built distinct "enclaves" that to varying degrees and in varying ways contain, represent, and bolster their communities. But deep down inside, not all "Little Saigons" are the same.

This book underscores and elaborates upon the significance of place and the place-making process as integral and dynamic elements of community and community-building. In an era of massive transnational migration, global shifts in production, distribution, and consumption processes, and Internet communications, place as locality seems to have lost its purchase on most of our lives. We long for home, yet many of us are so busy moving from place to place that no single place appears to have much impact on us. "Home" has shrunken into a metaphor for belonging. As a result of our inattention to and apparent detachment from place, vital aspects of social life—in particular, certain mesolevel forms of community—suffer.[2] I hope to situate Vietnamese Americanness by emplacing Vietnamese culture and identity in specific U.S. sociospatial contexts. By highlighting the spatial and place-related dimensions of the Vietnamese American experience, this book focuses attention on the role of local contexts in shaping community and puts into play a series of scholarly discussions about identity and space, growth amidst globalization in an age of neoliberalism, and the Americanization process.

The idea that Viet Nam ends—and America begins—in Vietnamese American places is complex, loaded, and quite possibly incorrect. Why should we not look for Vietnamese America in Americanized places such as Viet Nam's Ho Chi Minh City, formerly Sai Gon? That question popped into my head over a decade ago when a student of mine, a Vietnamese refugee who was in his sixties, offered an unexpected response to an assignment I gave my class. Tell me about an Asian American place, I asked, and describe the people or activities that make it "Asian" and "American." I had already planned the responses in my head: they would write about Chinatown or a Vietnamese restaurant or a beauty pageant or a multicultural student organization. I was completely unprepared when Mr. Tuan, referring to his personal experience, wrote about the Tet Offensive of 1968.

"I am reminded of something that happened in my country years ago," he began. "On the first day of the Lunar New Year, we usually celebrate with firecrackers and family get-togethers. But on that day, we celebrated with fire and death. The North Vietnamese Army violated a truce on that day, and killed thousands of innocent civilians in my village in South Viet Nam. Many U.S. soldiers also died. I guess that is why you could call this an Asian American event in my country."

Mr. Tuan's framing of the 1968 Tet Offensive as an Asian American event took me by surprise because for a moment I had forgotten about all the ways that Asians, particularly Vietnamese, have had generations of contact with America through business, diplomacy, and war. Although migration paths often prompt images of a linear trajectory over time from one location to another, Viet Nam should not be treated as "prior" to America on a stage of history or cultural development. But even in Asian American studies that is sometimes how we treat Asia and America. Mr. Tuan prompted me to think in a new way about the social, historical, and spatial boundaries of Asian America and about the Americanization of the Vietnamese experience. In chapter 1, with these thoughts in mind, I elaborate on theories of space and place as they relate to Vietnamese America.[3]

Juxtaposing Orange County and Boston

An hour's drive south of Los Angeles and about an hour north of San Diego, Orange County encompasses over two dozen municipalities sprawling over six hundred square miles. On the west, coastal cities like Huntington Beach and Laguna Beach touch the Pacific Ocean. Landlocked cities in central and north Orange County have Disneyland as their major landmark. The southern tip of Orange County reaches down toward San Diego; farther south lies the U.S.-Mexico border. Throughout the region, relative sparseness accompanies sprawl: the county is home to 2.8 million, but there are only 3,608 people for every square mile.

A little more than a century ago this was Spanish and indigenous territory, but in a slow act of conquest, Anglos took over the rancho economy.[4] Agriculture has only a faint presence now on the flat, expansive landscape punctuated with big-box malls, industrial parks, golf courses, and residential enclaves and cul-de-sacs that claim to embody the American Dream. Nearly everyone drives—not owning a car is practically synonymous with poverty since without a car wage work, food shopping, and other basic activities fall out of reach—and the combination of ubiquitous freeways, relentless advertising, and constant travel makes it nearly impossible to resist fast-paced, individualistic, and superconsumer-oriented attitudes and values. Orange County provides the quintessential example of "post-suburbia," a region with an extreme spatial and cultural logic (Kling, Olin, and Poster 1991).

For the better part of a century, the towns and cities of Orange County did not diversify with the rest of the state of California or the Los Angeles region. From 1890 to 1950, Orange County hit the census as perfectly white; the region's controlling elite also embraced a John Birch–style ideology of white supremacy and small government.[5] Orange County changed significantly in the second half of the last century and continues to change now: this book tells a small piece of that story. Indeed, the arrival of new refugees and immigrants in the aftermath of the Vietnam War signaled a potential shift away from nearly everything that some people think Orange County still is: rich, white, and Republican. In 2000, only a handful of Orange County cities were still living up to the stereotype. For example, Laguna Niguel had a total population of approximately 62,000 of whom 83.5 percent were white. The median household income there was $80,733, nearly twice the median for the state of California. Orange County was still richer overall than Los Angeles County: in 2004, median household income was $58,605 behind the Orange Curtain, but only $43,518 in the land of Tinseltown. The region is still heavily Republican, but the succession of Loretta Sanchez over incumbent Robert Dornan to the U.S. Senate in 1998 was widely seen as the emergence of an "ethnic"-oriented Democratic vote that might give the Republicans a run for their money in future elections.

Like every U.S. metropolitan region, Orange County promotes and is also saddled with identities whose veracity shifts and morphs depending on the context and perspective. Perceptions from the outside such as mine inevitably fail to match perceptions from the inside, especially those of residents who by virtue of longevity or for other reasons are invested in improving or correcting the image of their places. That being said, Orange County's reputation among tourists and television audiences—as home to uber-rich whites with nothing to do but gossip and spend money, or more bluntly, as the epitome of an alienated suburb—has its corollary in scholarship on the character of the region and consequences of its decentralization, demography, and embrace of technology. For example, in the *Journal of Orange County Studies*, historian Spencer Olin conjectured that although place-oriented forms of community are not feasible in Orange County, other forms of community can and should be created to promote a "special quality of human relationships" (reprinted in Olin 1989). The journal collapsed after two issues, perhaps reflecting a lack of interest among regional scholars in studying, never mind cultivating, those relationships.

On the other coast, Boston provides a very different setting for Vietnamese American community-building and place-making. As the capital and major port city of Massachusetts, Boston plays an important hub role in New England's regional economy and social past. Where Orange County is a place apparently without much feeling for community or history, Boston has always been mired deeply in both. Boston is such an old place that the history of the entire nation is tied to many key events that took place here. Tourists who come to Boston are reminded of the midnight ride of Paul Revere, the Boston Tea Party rebellion, and the Underground Railroad, among other "American" things. In fact, Boston's tourist economy depends heavily on a particular take on history that emphasizes a national narrative and at the same time a left-of-center politics partial to diversity and multiculturalism. In some intellectual and activist corners, Boston's antislavery and anti-imperialist history is also underscored, giving Massachusetts its "socialist republic" nickname.[6] But despite what some see as political liberalism, for at least one writer, the Bay State to this day remains at a "racial ground zero," having not departed far enough from its tumultuous days of racist segregation and busing (Apidta 2003a, 3). If nothing else, these warring views of the city's past suggest strong attachments to history in this region.

The city itself is tiny, spanning only forty-seven square miles on land once recovered from the sea. Although Boston appears at first glance just like any traditional city, in fact spatial decentralization and subsequent growth in the in-between spaces of industry turned the city early on into a "dense web of urban villages networked together by mass transit and highways" (Bluestone and Stevenson 2000, 77). Those villages include the establishment of white ethnic immigrant neighborhoods, the growth of a Chinatown that now serves as a "pan-Asian ethnic crossing," and the concomitant segregation of poor blacks in public housing projects (T. Chung 1995; Gans 1982; King 1981). Boston reached its peak population of just over 800,000 in the 1950s. Since then, the city has seen a net loss in its inhabitants for the most part due to the economic change. Today, Boston is home to slightly over half a million people. As the region's demographics and economic foundations shifted and changed in the last three decades of the twentieth century, so Boston experienced marked differences in the shape and character of its neighborhoods.

In Orange County and in Boston, the post-1975 waves of Vietnamese refugees and immigrants resulted in Vietnamese American places and communities that share some notable features but overall differ greatly. On the west coast, Orange County's Little Saigon is a huge and vibrant business and residential district consisting of approximately two thousand businesses, including restaurants, groceries, nail and beauty salons, professional offices, and social services. A large shopping complex with a bilingual name, Asian Garden Mall/Phuoc Loc Tho, anchors Little Saigon at the intersection of Magnolia and Brookhurst Avenues. Inside, you can have beef noodle soup for lunch, get your haircut, buy a pair of shoes, and get food to take home for dinner. Better yet, you can do it all in Vietnamese. For very old people whose main activity is reminiscing with friends, this mall is a popular, safe, all-day-long, and all-Vietnamese destination.

The unique identity of Little Saigon is signaled to outsiders by bilingual Vietnamese-English street signs and generic Asian architectural elements such as sloped, pagoda-style roofs and life-size sculptures of tigers and dragons. Little Saigon spreads out into Garden Grove, Santa Ana, Fountain Valley, and Anaheim, four other adjacent cities. Shoppers can access Little Saigon off its own exit via the Garden Grove or the San Diego freeways, and residents can head out north to Los Angeles or south to San Diego in under two hours.

Orange County's Vietnamese business district revitalized the economy of a city and region that was in decline in the 1970s. At that time, the city of Westminster was primarily a white, working-class town devoted to light manufacturing and family farms. Some of those farms are still hanging on;

I met one Japanese American whose third-generation strawberry farm was still nestled amid working-class trailer parks and pseudosuburban cul-de-sacs. Elsewhere, the Vietnamese business district has made possible other kinds of global enterprise more commonly seen in bustling, urban areas: the appearance of a Starbucks along Brookhurst Avenue south of Magnolia, for example, or other big-box retail stores lodged near the major freeways. A journalist who often played his guitar there once told me that the Brookhurst Starbucks has the atmosphere of a Parisian/Vietnamese café, suggesting the immense power of Little Saigon to reshape an otherwise cultureless and placeless franchise.

The city of Westminster has been affected in unique ways by Vietnamese Americans, not only by their affluence and their businesses but also by their memories. The Westminster War Memorial is a phenomenal structure complete with an eternal flaming torch and two soldiers, American and Vietnamese, posed as heroes of equal physical stature. The monument is practically an extension of Westminster city hall—it occupies a park next door named Freedom on a street called All American Way. Without the economic and political clout of Little Saigon, this monument might have never seen the light of day.

Far away on the other coast, Boston's Vietnamese Americans struggled through the 1990s to arrive only recently at a modicum of recognition and respect. A small and less-than-affluent population dispersed throughout at least four nonadjacent neighborhoods made the early waves of refugees and immigrants feel more like isolated strangers than welcomed heroes. Another part of the problem is that Boston had a Chinatown for about one century before the Vietnamese refugees arrived and tried to make their own place and community. Bostonians, with their attachments to the past, have been a little slow to take notice. Add to that lines that blur. Chinatown, easy to reach via public transit, offers everything you need, and many of the vendors came from Viet Nam. If even non-Asians do know the differences between Chinese and Vietnamese people, it is not always clear why those differences should matter.

After a decade of moving back and forth between Chinatown and other neighborhoods, Vietnamese began to gravitate toward Fields Corner. They set up shop and bought homes to live in or rent out. Step by step, this pocket-sized village in South Dorchester became a Vietnamese town complete with a couple of restaurants, bakeries, groceries, hair and nail salons, travel agents, a dentist, and a doctor. Dorchester Avenue, with many of its intersections already staked out in the mid-1980s as minimonuments to the Dorchester residents who gave their lives in the Viet Nam War, eventually became a Vietnamese "Main Street."

In 2002, Vietnamese Americans stamped Fields Corner as their place by building a new, two-story community center that serves first and foremost Vietnamese but of necessity must also serve the other racialized minorities in the area: Puerto Ricans, Cape Verdeans, Haitians. The center replaced an old gas station, just a stone's throw from the Fields Corner subway and bus stop. This strategic location further solidified the area's Vietnamese identity because getting off the train or bus one is immediately surrounded by Vietnamese-looking people and shops. Yet Boston's Vietnamese American leadership understands that a "neighborhood" does not necessarily equal a "community," especially as upwardly mobile Vietnamese move to outer-ring suburbs, as have other Asian ethnic groups. The majority of Boston's Vietnamese do not live in Fields Corner. In the end, what confirms the identity of Fields Corner as a Vietnamese town—that is, a mini–Little Saigon—is the symbolism and clout that Vietnamese American leaders, residents, and city hall have attached to the place.

In truth, exploring the features of any single instance of Vietnamese American community would have enabled an interesting discussion about what community looks like in certain places, and why. But juxtaposing Little Saigon and Fields Corner raises particular questions that are fundamental to community and place. Putting a post–World War II California hypersuburb and an old New England city next to each other highlights the significance of population size, geographic centralization, regional histories and contexts—and also brings up much more perplexing factors such as racial formations, war memories, and ethnic entrepreneurship in an age of presumed color blindness and claims to small government. This provocative comparison requires elaborate description and an even more elaborate set of explanations. Ultimately, the Orange County-versus-Boston framework sets the stage for my findings on how and why some Americans stay Vietnamese despite conventional signs of "becoming American": speaking English, participating in local politics, and living in the suburbs.

Orientalism, Suburbanization, and Community

By treating Vietnamese American community-building and place-making as a sociological issue, I appeal to ongoing conversations about race and ethnicity, suburbanization as a form of assimilation, and the perilously vague matter of community. Vietnamese America is Asian and therefore not white. Theories about what happens to Asian ethnic groups if and when they leave their "ethnic enclaves" for places that are presumably less "Asian" and more "American" drip with bias. Furthermore, most of those theories do not deal with whiteness or Asian American racial formations. Since racial formation theory has not come to full grip with current ideas about space and place, thinking about the suburbs and spatial mobility is only loosely connected if at all to racialized ethnic group identities such as "Vietnameseness." With a deeper and sharper understanding of race, space, and place with regard to Vietnamese Americans, we can better identify the place-related dimensions of community and what it really means to "stay Vietnamese."

Sociology's Oriental Problem

Despite a strong and growing presence of sociologists and other social scientists who specialize in the Asian American experience, mainstream sociology in the United States still suffers from what I will boldly call an "Oriental" problem, in the hopes that I exaggerate and overestimate it. By this I mean that many misconceptions about Asian Americans still shape the social sciences, including assumptions about Asia as the true originating point for Asian American culture and history, about the marginal role of Asian Americans in U.S. history and social life, and about stereotypes of Asian Americans as model minorities and perpetual foreigners. I write this not to claim "victim" status for Asian Americans or to suggest that there are or should be easy alliances between Asian Americans and other racialized minorities. Indeed, I name this problem out loud only to foreground what I see as some basic obstacles to the proper sociological framing of Vietnamese American community life.

Orientalism reifies the relationship between the United States and Asia, viewing them "as cultural polarities defined by (real or imagined) distance" (R. Lee 1999, 28). The Chicago School of sociology's Orientalism not only embraced the idea that East and West were opposites but actually elevated itself into a "theory" of race, space, and identity.[7] This pseudotheory still often informs contemporary sociology's approach to Asian American communities and places.

Little Saigons is no Orientalist text. I do not assume that Vietnamese spaces are "foreign" or somehow close to Viet Nam, nor do I jump to conclude that once Vietnamese people leave those spaces they suddenly clamor to become "honorary" white Americans. To combat Orientalism, I adopt a race-cognizant approach. Armed with classic and emerging theories of racial difference, racial oppression, and racial justice, I treat Vietnamese

American community-building and place-making as part of the larger historical process of U.S. racial formations. I see this process as led by the racial state and challenged from below by social movements. More, I fully acknowledge the racialized circumstances surrounding my relationship vis-à-vis my subject and the production of scholarship about this subject: I am simultaneously "inside" as an Asian American and "outside" as a non-Vietnamese. This book escapes the pigeonhole of Orientalism because it redefines the racialized terrain upon which knowledge about Vietnamese Americans, and Americans more generally, should be framed.

Suburbs and Assimilation

Even though many of today's suburbs are no longer the bastions of race and class privilege that they once were, in many people's minds suburbanization is still linked to the idea of assimilation. Indeed, spatial-assimilation theory equates "suburbanization" to "Americanization"—and might even be interpreted as a formula for "deracinating" immigrants.[8] On a good day, this is how the theory goes: Immigrants congregate in ethnic enclaves close to the center city, where they support each other through ethnic associations and institutions that preserve their languages, religions, cuisine, and traditions. Then, over a period of generations, they abandon their crowded enclaves in favor of the sparsely populated cul-de-sacs of suburbia. Once safely tucked into suburbs, the descendants of immigrants learn to speak English, to worship in Christian churches, to eat hamburgers and apple pie, and to make themselves an integral part of "mainstream" (read: white) society. Their ethnic ties become decorative options rather than substantial or necessary resource connections.

This suburban-oriented model of immigrant incorporation is based on the experience of Europeans who arrived in the United States at the dawn of the twentieth century. The model is not an accurate portrayal of the European American experience. European Americans traveled a roundabout path from a hodgepodge of cultures and histories into a homogeneous category called "white." This path demanded alliances between ethnic and national groups who did not look upon each other with particular fondness (for example, British and Germans), forced poor and working-class Europeans to abandon their "colored" peers, and required multiple interventions by the state in the form of English-Only policies, discriminatory lending and hiring practices, and restrictive covenants, to mention just a few. In other words, moving to suburbs and becoming white is neither inevitable nor straightforward, even for European immigrants.

Spatial-assimilation theory suffers from a racial blind spot. Whiteness remains unmarked and unexplained.[9] Instead of seeing suburbanization as part and parcel of the historical construction of the social and spatial privileges of whiteness, this theory promotes a notion of suburbs as devoid of race, ethnicity, or culture. We therefore expect people who move into them to have disposed of their group-oriented perspectives and traditions. In fact, until recently we did not have a way to think about the role special places like Little Saigon or Fields Corner might have in allowing suburbanized communities to hang onto their identities. But this book shows that place can and does operate as an anchor, a platform, and an organizing device—regardless of the residential, suburbanized status of a population.

What Makes a Strong Community?

From the perspective of those who seek the benefits and resources that community can offer, neither a lot of people nor a densely packed group of people guarantees its most sought-after feature: a sense of "solidarity and significance" (Clark 1973, 404). When the architects of U.S. refugee resettlement policy decided that forced dispersal would be the best way to push Vietnamese and other Southeast Asian refugees to join U.S. society, obviously they anticipated and perhaps feared the consequences of refugees sticking in one place together over a prolonged period. At that time, of course, the example of anti-Castro Cubans establishing Little Havana in Miami had set a precedent that policy makers, for any number of reasons, wanted to avoid.

Yet as secondary and chain migration patterns reveal, people will insist on physical proximity in order to access information, support, and protection from xenophobia. To the extent that "Little Saigons" across the United States served as racial safety zones, especially as anti-Asian hostility and violence peaked in the 1980s, being close to others provided needed comfort and validation. The need was heightened by the linguistic and cultural strangeness that the new Vietnamese population represented to "host" neighborhoods and regions. While Cubans and Soviet Jews seeking political refuge had the possibility of being received by Americans who shared key aspects of their language and culture, at least in the beginning, Vietnamese had none.

Information about well-paying jobs and adequate housing is also among the most valued aspects of community life. Whether and for how long people must cluster together in order to have access to jobs and housing depends in part on how quickly they can find a way into the primary labor market. The ethnic enclave/ethnic economy debate, carried on for years in the pages of social scientific books and journals, emphasized the lack of access on the part of post–World War II immigrants to these jobs and thus the importance of the "ethnic entrepreneur" in creating a secondary path for themselves and presumably for their "co-ethnics" into the local and national economy.[10]

That debate, meticulous as it was, left largely untouched the problem of an unequal and uneven distribution of power and resources within refugee and immigrant populations. For the most part scholars assumed that a strong merchant class would boost the whole community; therefore, the bulk of the research concentrated on the precise mechanisms of entrepreneurial advancement within ethnic communities. Was it the strength of trust among immigrants? Was it the fact of the physical proximity of immigrant residences to ethnic-owned business? Was it the ties to financial and social capital in the homeland? Surely, in the absence of an economic infrastructure that could provide the kind of upward mobility available to workers before World War II—and in the midst of a neoliberal agenda that had yet to unfold fully in the United States and throughout the world—ethnic entrepreneurship had many promises.

Only a few scholars addressed the divisions within refugee or immigrant communities. Among them, Peter Kwong (1996) studied and revealed the cleavages between "Uptown" and "Downtown" Chinese in New York's Chinatown. In his exposé, the sweat and blood of Downtowners, mostly desperate and illegal immigrants, create the advantages that eventually accrue to greedy and merciless Uptown business owners. Because outsiders assume that Chinatown either has no problems or should deal with those problems without asking for help, bribery and corruption rule: such is the legacy of the bootstraps narrative for immigrant communities.

To say that the strength of a community is defined at the get-go by its ethnic economy is to shrink the meaning of community and to overlook other sources of power and clout. Jan Lin (1998) also studied Chinatown and, in addition to the impact of globalization on the multitiered ethnic economy, he notes the significance of place. As metropolitan regions vie for corporate investment to fill the void once occupied by government funding, one of the things they hope will make them shine is their cultural and symbolic landscape. Creating tourist zones or polishing up old heritage sites boosts the uniqueness of place and attracts new business. Thus, a mostly unspoken accomplishment of ethnic entrepreneurs is to spiff up blighted areas of a city, making it financially possible for developers with much bigger budgets to come in and repackage places as desirable destinations for those with money to spend in them.

Meanwhile, ordinary people—residents and working people, and the refugees and immigrants among them—have few choices but to live or work in the environments that elites and experts have already designed and created. This is not to say that individuals cannot make places their own in smaller ways, for example, by attaching emotional or psychological significance to certain routes or landmarks. But the fact is that when poor neighborhoods or sacred monuments are razed to the ground to open space for freeways, big-box malls, or luxury condominiums, then the power of the neighborhood as a community is clearly diminished. In this important context, place buttresses community; place amenities and services such as clean and well-lit streets, trash removal, parking lots, baseball fields or basketball courts, green spaces, traffic control, and public pathways all help to improve community life in ways that are sometimes in conflict with "expert" and elite development agendas.

Neoliberalism—the call to deregulate the economy and to privatize formerly public goods and services—makes it easy to scoff at the place-related components of community. Capital flows mostly without regard to territorial boundaries, and rich people dismiss their attachments to particular places as they brag about "global citizenship." Especially for the most privileged globe-trotters, place hardly qualifies as a topic worthy of inquiry— except as a marketable commodity. Because place in every other sense is seen as negligible, "those caught in the maelstrom of urban decay" are now subject to a politics of "contempt and neglect," as David Harvey so sharply notes (1996, 407). Some of those people are Vietnamese American.

One thing that makes a community strong, then, is the capacity to determine its own spatial fate. Shaping and organizing place so that the communities they represent are materially supported as well as politically recognized and respected absorbs a great deal of energy among the Vietnamese American leaders I interviewed. In the examples that follow, struggles around actual physical structures and the resources and narratives associated with them reveal the urgency and complexity of each community's investments in place.

A Bridge Named Harmony and a Community Center

Ideas about Asia and America as opposites, about suburbanization as a deracializing process, and about communities existing without place all enhance our potential *mis*understanding of Vietnamese American community-building and place-making. Two examples illustrate this. In 1996, Little Saigon's premier developer, Frank Jao, proposed a suspended bridge/shopping mall called Harmony Bridge. The bridge never happened, but the controversy around it had lasting consequences. In 2002, Fields Corner became the site of a nonprofit, Vietnamese owned and operated community center. The new building represents the culmination of many years of planning and strategizing by Viet-AID (Vietnamese American Initiative for Development), a community development corporation formed by younger Vietnamese American leaders. In both cases, community leaders pushed for a Vietnamese identity within a local and American political context.

If Frank Jao had had his way, Harmony Bridge would have consisted of a pedestrian minimall contained inside a bridge suspended over Bolsa Avenue, Little Saigon's main street. The bridge would channel shoppers from Jao's Asian Garden Mall, the center of the business district, to his Asian Village. At the time, Asian Village consisted of a strip mall, Ranch 88 (a Taiwanese-owned supergrocery chain), a California-style flea market called New Saigon, and a unique outdoor Cultural Court featuring a dozen white plaster sculptures of Confucious and his disciples. The flea market and the courtyard have since given way to residential developments. Jao's bridge project drew acrimony when Mai Cong, the president/CEO of the Vietnamese Community of Orange County (VNCOC, an Orange County–based social service agency for Vietnamese) organized an anti–Harmony Bridge campaign she took directly to Westminster's city hall. According to her, Jao should be stopped because he is really Chinese, and the bridge would finalize his scheme to turn Little Saigon, a Vietnamese place, into Little Cho Lon—a reference to Chinatown in Sai Gon, now Ho Chi Minh City. This scheme was supposedly already apparent in the names "Asian" Garden Mall and "Asian" Village as opposed to Vietnamese Village.

Jao never built the bridge. But the lasting impact of the controversy has been to raise the question of Little Saigon's true meaning as a Vietnamese—not a Chinese—place. Saying this, I do not mean to suggest that authenticity is either a feasible or measureable goal for Vietnamese American place-making.[11] Certainly the creation of an authentic Vietnamese culture in any American "Little Saigon" (with or without its references to one thousand years of Chinese colonialism) is made more difficult by the fact that U.S.–Viet Nam travel—though increasingly common since the normalization of relations between the two countries in 1994—remains a social taboo.

Furthermore, in the case of Orange County's Little Saigon, nearly half of the ethnic economy is run by Chinese-Vietnamese, ethnic Chinese with origins in Viet Nam. The presence of ethnic Chinese as a merchant class in Orange County is a both a legacy of Vietnamese history and a reflection of the specific context in which Little Saigon developed as a Vietnamese American tourist/business district. I describe this history in greater detail in chapter 1 and explore the implications of the Chinese presence for the identity of the place in chapter 4. Authenticity is an issue that will only worsen with globalization.

Jao's plan to build Harmony Bridge set off a series of fiery discussions about Little Saigon's ethnic identity that extended well past the intersection of Bolsa and Magnolia. At the University of California, Irvine, Vietnamese American students wrote papers exploring and denouncing the Harmony Bridge project.[12] Boston's Vietnamese American leaders asked me what I knew about Harmony Bridge and then told me that Little Saigon "shouldn't become Chinatown." They care about authenticity too, but unlike Orange County, Boston's Vietnamese American community does not depend on ethnic Chinese for their entrepreneurship or leadership abilities.

Indeed, Boston's Vietnamese Americans have different kinds of worries. In a city where neighborhoods historically have been synonymous with race or ethnicity, Fields Corner is a multicultural, multiracial residential area populated by Cape Verdeans, Haitians, Latinos, and whites, along with Vietnamese. Boston's Vietnamese Americans are not the majority population here, and they reside or own businesses in many other neighborhoods. Opening the new two-story building in Fields Corner in November 2002 marked an important physical and conceptual accomplishment for Boston's Vietnamese American community. The new center branded Fields Corner as the city's "Little Saigon" and made Vietnamese Americans the neighborhood's politically dominant group.

Ironically, the new center came to being just as the more comfortable middle-class Vietnamese Americans had begun moving out of Fields Corner or bypassing it altogether for the outer-ring cities of Quincy, Milton, and Randolph.[13] Even among the staff of Viet-AID, whose services and programs are intended to serve Fields Corner residents, less than one-half lived in Fields Corner at the time the building went up. Meanwhile, Viet-AID staff felt pressure to deal with and to some extent represent the needs of Cape Verdean and Latino residents, who are not represented by their own community development corporations.

How do we engage with the neighborhood? Do we become multiethnic?

If not, how can we speak for everyone in Fields Corner? The questions facing the staff suggest that place is much more than a location, and that place-making is hardly reducible to simply residing in a neighborhood. Even stamping Fields Corner as "Vietnamese" does not close off for good the many other possible uses and meanings of the neighborhood. Instead, the project of creating an actual edifice that represents the Vietnamese American community put forth one set of options for Fields Corner to which neighborhood residents, leaders in other communities, and Boston's city hall have responded. While Vietnamese Americans are politically strengthened by the physical presence of the center in Fields Corner—mostly because Bostonians are in the habit of linking place and community—the location of the center also heightens an existing tension between competing definitions of the community as "Fields Corner" or as "Vietnamese."

Defining and Emphasizing Place and "Platial"

The Harmony Bridge controversy in Little Saigon and the new Vietnamese American center in Fields Corner illustrate the multiple ways that Vietnamese American community-building takes place somewhere, rather than nowhere, with observable and tangible results.

I found the word "spatial" an overgeneralized, vague, and thus ineffective descriptor for the place-based processes of Vietnamese American community-building. As I wrestled with the puzzle of spatial relationships, locality, meaning, and the physical form of community for particular sites in Orange County and Boston, it made sense to utilize the word "platial" as an adjective that would accompany not only the noun place, but especially and more importantly—as I will detail in chapter 1—the action of "place-making."

To tell the truth, I am not the first to favor "platial" over "spatial" as a way to describe and engage with place-related phenomenon. And, for reasons this book should make clear, I believe the word will push its way into our everyday-speak soon, because it has common-sense resonance. But for now, "platial" is still a relatively unknown term that is batted around by philosophers, academic geographers, and self-proclaimed "neogeographers."[14] The obscurity of "platial" owes something to the fact that place itself is in contestation—why worry about describing place-related things if the relevance of place to our globalized lives will fade?[15]

This book argues that place is not diminishing: for Vietnamese Americans as a displaced and exiled population, place and place-making hold great—and perhaps increasing—value. Indeed, "platial" is necessary to get at the specific instances in which Vietnamese Americans are investing particular spaces (that is, places) with their personal and community narratives. The act of making place—rather than simply, passively inhabiting it—requires its own adjective, "platial."

The platial aspects of community involve its location, its physical or "built" form, and the narratives or identities that surround and generate place itself.[16] In my view, many forms of community are not substantively platial because they do not suffer if people are dispersed, buildings torn down, or homes relocated—consider, for example, professional associations, business networks, cyberfriends, or virtual chat lines. To speak platially is to bring into view the elements of community that are often overlooked when a population is considered marginal or powerless. To "platialize" community or race—which I argue we should do—is to acknowledge and understand the significance of place, placefulness, and platiality in the production of communities and racial formations.

I emphasize the place-related dimensions of community partly to expose the fact that place-based communities depend upon ever-shrinking resources. As metropolitan regions constantly redevelop themselves to accommodate capitalism's uneven agenda, poor people's homes and communities are moved or discarded. Yet, few people can afford to find another place to live because geographic mobility is a scarce resource. What happens in "Little Saigon" has extrastrong consequences for those people. They lack the money and the connections to move, and they require and depend upon Vietnamese-oriented goods and services, twenty-four hours a day, seven days a week.

What It Means to "Stay Vietnamese"

In this book I show how and why community-building and place-making help people to "stay Vietnamese." The phrase evokes an image of Vietnamese culture and identity that is frozen in time and space, but what I intend to describe instead is a shifting and changeable condition whose very instabilities have generated this study.[17] In promoting the notion that something important remains the same as Vietnamese people construct new lives in America, I must first make a crucial series of caveats. I do not mean to treat Vietnameseness as an essential or fixed quality that somehow got transported across the ocean in a single, solid piece.[18] I understand that the Vietnamese American community has many internal divisions, and I acknowledge the fact that not everyone belongs equally to this, or to any, community. The last thing I want to do is to reanimate a stock morality tale about model minorities who make the "American Dream" come alive through their careful preservation of Confucian-type collectivist values regarding filial piety, duty, obligation, or sacrifice. Nor do I want to invigorate the all-too-common view of the Vietnamese refugee as a tragic elder struck by grief and trapped in the past. Though there may be small grains of truth in these widely held views of the Vietnamese American experience—indeed, many of the people I interviewed for this book have been portrayed in the English-language media as the living embodiment of these ideas—here I strive to contextualize the issue of "staying Vietnamese" in a social and spatial setting rather than a personal or psychological one; to reveal the multidimensionality, changeability, and sometimes ambiguous nature of Vietnameseness; and to render Vietnamese American people as conscious agents of their destinies rather than as passive or traumatized victims of history.

In fact, staying Vietnamese is not an act of constancy but of purposeful, and ultimately strategic, shifting and changing in order to arrive at new ways of being Vietnamese in a U.S. context. This thoughtful and deliberate recalibration of culture and identity allows Vietnamese Americans in Orange County and Boston to find a new "equilibrium state" in which Vietnameseness is redefined so as to serve a myriad of simultaneous and sometimes contradictory social and historical functions.[19] I think of this equilibrium state as an evolving sociospatial condition that requires adjustments not only inside the Vietnamese American community in any given region but also across the U.S. nation as a whole.

Vietnamese Americans need to stay Vietnamese so that they have some connection to themselves, their histories, and their cultures.[20] For the older generation, most of whom are refugees, this means "keeping our roots." Mai Cong is an elder, first-wave refugee who in 1995 was employed as a mental health counselor and president/CEO of the VNCOC. Writing in the *Los Angeles Times* for a column called "Orange County Voices," she uses the metaphor of America's "cultural tapestry" to explain and justify the refugee's need to hang onto Vietnameseness:

> Like plants that are transplanted to new soil, however fertile, we have to keep our roots in order to grow and to thrive. In order to take up the new, we may have to get rid of certain old things, but we don't get rid of our own selves. To move fast into the mainstream, we have to maintain our cultural identity. And in maintaining our cultural identity, we will be contributing to the rich tapestry of cultures that is America. (Cong 1995)

This statement defends the preservation of Vietnamese identity against a regional and national culture that is ambivalent about nonwhite immigrants.

Mrs. Mai is a professional representative of the refugee community. But this is not to say that the ordinary individuals on whose behalf she presumably speaks are also concerned with identity issues per se. Duong Nguyen was a recent graduate of UCLA and an employee of Mrs. Mai's agency in Little Saigon when I interviewed him in 1996. As he put it,

> When I was growing up . . . we never asked, "What does it mean to be Vietnamese American?" That's a very, I always thought that is a very luxurious question, or very esoteric.

In Duong's view, the chores of everyday living made thoughts about identity in the abstract seem a luxury, at least when he was a child and the community as a whole was new to this country. Timothy Le, a Chinese Vietnamese entrepreneur in Little Saigon in his mid-30s, was even blunter with me: "It costs money to look for your roots." Staying Vietnamese is a collective issue of community-building and place-making rather than a problem of individual adaptation. All of these views, though seemingly in conflict, can be true simultaneously. Especially for place-dependent Vietnamese—those people who cannot leave Vietnamese American places such as Little Saigon or Fields Corner because they depend on the community and its goods and services there, or because they cannot afford the cost of moving away—staying Vietnamese could simply entail working or living in a place that is identifiable to outsiders as "Vietnamese." Indeed, at the microlevel of everyday living, most people are probably not really trying to stay Vietnamese. But at a larger mesolevel of community they are, and the job for leaders is to provide a legitimate story for place dependency that can be understood and accepted by non-Vietnamese. This is not to overlook the less magnanimous motives that elites might have for taking on leadership roles in the community, or the fact that leadership itself is a contested category. I discuss the notion of leadership and my rationale for interviewing leaders later in this chapter.

Points of Departure: Studying Little Saigon and Fields Corner

In 1993, Professor Peter Nien-chu Kiang, an Asian American studies professor and community activist, suggested I visit Fields Corner, an area of Dorchester with a growing presence of Vietnamese refugees and immigrants. Dorchester is Boston's oldest neighborhood. I was born in Boston and raised in Connecticut by Filipino immigrant professors, and after graduating from college, I moved back to Boston to work as an editor and writer. I considered myself to be a well-informed member of the Asian American community. Despite living and working in Boston for about a decade, I had never heard of Fields Corner, nor had I ever visited any Vietnamese American place in the city. I spent a few months introducing myself to people in Fields Corner and soon I felt compelled to investigate its platial dimensions. In 1996, I moved to southern California. Buried deep in Orange County, Little Saigon easily engulfs its residents and visitors in Vietnamese American social life. How do Fields Corner and Little Saigon compare? That question bothered me for months and became the engine for this book. To the untrained eye, they look the same: pedestrians, shops, street signage, and public events keep alive a distinctly Vietnamese culture that is widely recognized as such by tourists and local residents alike. Had I been without a sense of the larger context in which "ethnic enclaves" like Little Saigon emerge, I would have had nothing else to think about. But it seemed to me that many things needed exploration and explanation. Among them: Did Little Saigon serve as Orange County's Chinatown? If so, how did Fields Corner, its counterpart in Boston, deal with its Asian American "competitor," Boston's Chinatown neighborhood? Was Little Saigon a complete world, meaning that someone could be born, go to kindergarten, learn to walk and talk and read and write, and die there—as a Vietnamese person? If so, what made that "institutional completeness" possible in Orange County and not in Boston, where it was clear even at first glance that Fields Corner did not support a full social life for its Vietnamese residents?[21] Was Fields Corner just a baby version of Little Saigon, and if so, what would happen to all the non-Vietnamese once Fields Corner grew up into a full-fledged Vietnamese place? Finally, I wondered, who makes these places happen, and what is their final goal?

Eventually what initially appeared to me merely as "differences" between two places developed into a striking conceptual paradox: a strong ethnic community in a quintessential suburb, and a weaker ethnic community in an old immigrant city. Slowly, I saw that in order to explain the differences between Little Saigon and Fields Corner as Vietnamese American places, I would have to know more about the surrounding contexts. My realization that this paradox required some deep thinking about "community" and "place" led me to step back to view the larger picture in which Orange County and Boston operate as places in and of themselves. At this bigger scale I began to find clues as to how race, memory, and the commodification of culture function in each region. Seeking to explain a relatively small issue made it more and more important to understand a much bigger scenario in which multiple social actors lay their claims on community and place. One person I have interviewed in Boston since 1996 noted approvingly in 2005 that my questions were no longer focused narrowly on Vietnamese Americans. Jokingly, she said I should title one chapter of this book "God and Cosmos in Fields Corner."

As I gained familiarity with the regional cultures and histories of Orange County and Boston by living and doing research there, I became convinced that community and place are not lifeless, bloodless concepts. I no longer liked the idea of viewing the city and suburb as "social laboratories" in the old-fashioned terminology of the Chicago School. It was clear to me, having met and talked with people with a wide range of practical and ideological investments in Vietnamese America, that community and place were alive, in process, and on the move.

By focusing on community-*building* and place-*making*, I mean to heed the warnings issued decades ago by Elena Yu and William Liu (1986) regarding research on Vietnamese refugees. Describing refugees as a "deprived and captive" population, these authors declare that professional research agendas rarely take into account the perspectives of the refugees themselves. Thus I declined to treat community and place only as "givens," that is, as things that are already accomplished and complete, needing merely to be analyzed and measured by objective experts. Instead, I approached community and place as works in progress whose final form should be approached as topics of controversy and struggle among the people most invested in shaping them.

I was not disappointed. To get a handle on the complex relationships between community and place, I conducted long interviews in English with fifty-two Vietnamese American leaders and twenty outside experts in Boston and Orange County, and I reinterviewed a handful of those individuals multiple times over the ensuing years. I worked in Boston from 1994 to 1995, again during four months in Spring 2002, and once more over one week in Spring 2005; and in Orange County from 1996 to 1999 and again in two-week-long visits in 2000, 2002, and 2005. I made these contacts using a variety of techniques: reputational, snowball, and quota (see the Appendix for sample questions and characteristics of the informants). The people I spoke with represent first-wave refugees, ethnic Chinese, former political detainees, immigrants, and U.S.-born Vietnamese. They include a retired general and other former military officers, clergy, an ob/gyn doctor, a grocery-chain owner, elected and appointed government officials, businesspeople, bankers, lawyers, social workers, a sex-education teacher, delegates to the Democratic and GOP conventions, and several recent university graduates. They embodied generational, occupational, and gender diversity. Their opinions on and attachments to Viet Nam varied so widely that for my own safety, to protect my reputation as an unbiased researcher, and so as not to inflame ongoing conflicts within the community, I have kept my connections secret. Throughout this book, I guard my interviewees' anonymity by using pseudonyms unless I am quoting from a public source such as a newspaper.

The term "leader" is obviously a contested one. More than one person I spoke to told me "there are too many chiefs and not enough Indians" or that leaders are like "a lot of crabs in a barrel," indicating that leadership in the Vietnamese American community, as with many other groups, is often disputed and challenged from within. For my purposes, although they may have too many enemies and not enough followers, what is important to me is that the people I interviewed are often asked to represent their community to the outside non-Vietnamese world, and that they are able to mobilize their constituencies to respond to issues and concerns in that world. Often, they have acted as place makers by altering the shape and character of the places they occupy, for example by creating physical establishments or public events that are recognizable as Vietnamese.

I do not intend to ignore the very real conflicts among leaders, or to downplay the ways in which some leaders may indulge in romanticism or opportunism or take advantage of fear and paranoia within the community to achieve their own ends. But because of their English-language ability and familiarity with American ways of conducting business, many leaders have pull with Americans who are not Vietnamese, especially powerful individuals in city hall or the chamber of commerce. Leaders have the ability to shape the issues for their community and to influence what outsiders know or think they know about Vietnamese Americans. Understanding how and why leaders approach the tasks of community-building and place-making is an important key to resolving the paradox of Fields Corner and Little Saigon.

Being invested in community-building and place-making gives the individuals I spoke with an interesting edge on the issues I explore here. I am well aware that they are by and large elites, more privileged than ordinary people for whom residence in Little Saigon or Fields Corner is not a choice. In many instances, these elites "manage" and "supervise" community and place from a distance, with their own families safely ensconced in more affluent nearby neighborhoods. Like the "Uptown" Chinese Peter Kwong excoriates, perhaps some of the individuals I interviewed here could be considered "Uptown" Vietnamese.

To put these interviews in their proper context, I did extensive field research. I tried to achieve for myself an "experience of place," a feeling for the special characteristics of each region (Hiss 1990). I tried to hone my sensitivity to the peculiarities and textures of Boston and Southern California. In between interviews with leaders, I examined census statistics, news clippings, and organizational documents. I attended community events. I also created my own maps and photographs to help me interpret what I observed.[22]

These sources lead me to argue that Vietnamese American communities are trying to stay Vietnamese by establishing places that engender and embody Vietnamese hopes and dreams. The distinct patterns of community-building and place-making in Orange County and Boston reflect the distinct regional contexts in which leaders work. Instead of finding that Vietnamese are losing their attachments to community and place in order to become American, I discovered that Vietnamese American leaders in Orange County and Boston are engaged in an active, place-based process of creating and claiming a group identity as "Vietnamese." Neither community nor place is a finished product; both are always "underway" and their dimensions and boundaries are thus constantly "up for grabs." Looking at Vietnamese America in this way challenges strictly positivist notions of community and place as discrete things that exist separately from our ideas about them. This is not to do away completely with tangible observations and measurements of community and place such as census data and maps. But it is to recognize the centrality of meaning and discourse in the "structuration" of community and place (Giddens 1984).

The take-home message of *Little Saigons* is not only that place is central to community, but also that Vietnamese Americans—especially though not exclusively the individuals who occupy elite positions of leaders or spokepersons—play an active and strategic role in shaping place and community. Their strategies for place-making and community-building respond in complex ways to the specific environmental and social contexts that Orange County and Boston present. The strategies also reflect the internal composition and concerns of the population itself. At the end of the day, staying Vietnamese is about finding new ways to be Vietnamese in America and, through community-building and place-making, projecting those ways into the future.

Chapter 1   Producing and Constructing
Vietnamese America

BECAUSE OF THE STRONG INTERESTS of the U.S. government in receiving and resettling Vietnamese refugees, there is no shortage of raw statistics or other social scientific data about their migration and settlement patterns, nor is there a paucity of social scientific commentary on the nature and pace of their assimilation into the American mainstream. In this chapter I cull the key facts about the end of the war and the implementation of refugee programs, patterns of migration and settlement within the United States, and the emergence of—and diversity within—various communities. I frame these facts in terms of a metaphor about the "architecture" of Vietnamese American community and identity as a way to suggest that community and identity have structures that are not random or accidental, but purposefully built. This is not to say there has been a single "master plan" imposed upon Vietnamese Americans from above; however, many simultaneous and sometimes contradictory agendas had been at play long before the end of the war in 1975 that since then have conspired and collaborated to make Vietnamese America. From the inside and the outside, many "architects" have been working and continue to work at multiple levels of social and spatial scale to produce and construct Vietnamese American community and identity. They include the engineers of U.S. foreign and military policy in Viet Nam; the U.S. agencies and organizations at all levels of government that organized the resettlement of refugees after the war ended; the policy makers for the Socialist Republic of Viet Nam, including those specializing in trade and normalization of relations with the United States; the local U.S. state, including governors and mayors, private corporations, philanthropic foundations, nonprofit organizations, real estate developers, urban and regional planners, and city boosters; Vietnamese American leaders, whether elected or self-appointed, "sparkplugs" or "mouthpieces"; university and college students organized into Vietnamese

1

Student Associations; and poor and elderly Vietnamese residents of places such as Little Saigon, whose daily efforts merely to survive reinforce the identity of the community and the place. The people I interviewed for this book come from a midsection of Vietnamese American place makers; made up primarily of community elites, they are neither very powerful state actors nor members of the embattled masses. They are, nevertheless, effective middle-level architects of community and place whose words and actions shed light on the cultivation of Vietnamese America.

I adopt the inelegant terms of "producing and constructing" Vietnamese America because the more elegant possibilities fail to capture an important distinction between the material and the discursive aspects of community and place. Here I draw my cues from anthropologist Setha Low, whose innovative study of the Costa Rican plaza as an example of urban public space necessarily distinguishes between the material/historical/political-economy dimensions of the plaza—which she refers to as "produced"—and its symbolic/phenomenological dimensions, which she calls "constructed" (2000, 128). Similarly, when this chapter refers to the production of Vietnamese America, I mean to reference the material and historical aspects of community and place, such as population migration or real estate development. On the other hand, the construction of Vietnamese America is a gesture to the symbolic or perceived aspects of community and place that are often embedded in complex ideological narratives, such as the notion of Little Saigon as the capital not just of Vietnamese America, but of the Vietnamese "free world." Although analytically the material and discursive aspects of community and place are separate, in reality these aspects are closely interwoven and interdependent.

The comparison between Vietnamese Americans in Orange County and Boston is intriguing in part because those are places for which most readers will have some preformed mental images. Naturally, those images fall somewhere between fact and fiction, fed by personal experiences and media hype. This chapter fills in the gaps by presenting Orange County and Boston as regions each with its own unique demographics, history, "personality," and traditions. Harvey Molotch, William Freudenburg, and Krista E. Paulsen (2000) write about places as "rolling inertia," meaning that the character of places, especially cities, accumulates over time via a series of overlapping events; these include economic development, changes in political regimes, and population shifts. Reviewing some of those key events helps to portray Orange County and Boston as distinct and "rolling" contexts for the production and construction of Vietnamese America.

Vietnamese American leaders in Little Saigon and in Fields Corner share the same general goals: to create a sense of "solidarity and significance" among the local Vietnamese population; to support and sustain Vietnamese networks, organizations, and resources; and to establish a central place that will stay Vietnamese even after the population has dispersed. In addition, they seek positive recognition for their former role as U.S. allies during the war in part to counter the effects of xenophobia and racism that even the most successfully assimilated Vietnamese Americans have faced. Yet due to the divergent sociospatial contexts that Orange County and Boston comprise, Vietnamese American community-building and place-making in Little Saigon and Fields Corner take very different turns. Where Vietnamese Americans in Orange County have a strong say in the shape of Asian American politics, their counterparts in Boston often have to go with the flow of long-established Asian American networks and organizations, many of which are based in Boston's Chinatown neighborhood. Where Orange County's Vietnamese have put up their own monument representing the war, Boston's Vietnamese tiptoe carefully around old monuments that show the war from a non-Vietnamese perspective. Whereas Little Saigon is primarily a Vietnamese business/tourist district, Fields Corner is a multi-cultural, multiracial neighborhood. In the end, Fields Corner is not merely a mini–Little Saigon but comprises its own individual version of a Vietnamese American place. In Orange County and Boston, Vietnamese American community-building and place-making pull resources together in such a way that Vietnamese Americans in Little Saigon and Fields Corner each have their own complex tales to tell.

Community and Place Revisited

The experiences of Vietnamese Americans bring together the concepts of "community" and "place" in new ways that make it necessary to revisit and revise our understanding of those concepts. This is not to ignore the continuing usefulness of classical approaches to, and definitions of, community and place. For sociologists and geographers, these concepts are so basic and fundamental that entire books have been written solely to explore them.[1] I am choosing selectively from this vast literature and also from a rapidly expanding list of interdisciplinary books and articles on "space."[2]

In colloquial usage, "community" is often an intangible, ineffable feeling of connection we have to others. Community is something most Americans say they want and need, and yet something that in our time of mass consumption and dispersed, suburban living seems rapidly to be disappearing.[3]

Janet Abu-Lughod observed that "the concept of community occupies a privileged place in the romantic symbolic lexicon of America, as significant as mother, apple pie, and democracy" (1991, 209).

A few years into my fieldwork, I was told that in the Vietnamese language, one word for "community" can also refer to "communism" and thus brings to mind a closed bureaucratic process rather than an open democracy. For example, the word "cong" in *cong dong Viet* (Vietnamese community) is the same word as in *Viet Nam Cong San*, usually shortened to *Viet Cong*, the name of the armed insurgents of North Viet Nam. Despite this conflation of meanings, I found that most people I interviewed took my questions about community and community-building outside of the context of communism.

In conventional social science, "community" refers to a place, a set of common ties, or a field of social interaction. With regard to refugees and immigrants, community often means the creation and adaptation of place-based institutional structures that serve their specific needs. Perhaps the most concrete definition of community is represented by the idea of "institutional completeness." Raymond Breton defined institutional completeness for ethnic groups as "a state of social organization in which the ethnic community could perform all the services required by its members" (1964, 194). These would include mutual aid associations, radio and newspapers, groceries and restaurants, health clinics and legal services, churches, temples, and schools. In addition to supporting these material aspects of community, Vietnamese American community-building emerges as a social process that concerns language, ideas, and symbols.

Raymond Plant argued that "[t]here is always going to be some normative and ideological engagement" (1978, 106), meaning that we will always conceptualize community according to what we think ought to be rather than according to what actually is. Indeed, David Clark declared that community research ought to start with sentiment because that is "where people stand," (1973, 410) not where researchers believe people should stand. He went on to assert that the two most essential features of community are *solidarity* and *significance*. According to Clark, "[s]olidarity . . . encompasses all those sentiments which draw people together (sympathy, courtesy, gratitude, trust and so on)" while significance refers to a sense of "achievement" or "fulfillment" (404). In this chapter and throughout this book, community represents a perpetual striving toward the terms of solidarity and significance.

Viewing community as a perpetual striving also invokes a contemporary feminist approach to community as a social process. Nancy Naples asks:

Is community a geographic and identifiable site or a collective process through which individuals come to represent themselves in relation to others with whom they perceive share similar experiences and viewpoints? (2003, 79)

By counterpoising community as a "geographic and identifiable site" to community as a "process" of self-representation, this question prioritizes the collective and discursive dimensions of community-building. Importantly, in this definition the place aspect of community drops out of the picture, making it necessary to incorporate a spatial analysis.

Community-building and place-making push for a sense of social and spatial solidarity and significance among the various constituencies of Vietnamese American leaders in Orange County and Boston. These efforts comprise an ongoing and contested activity whose outcomes pose certain challenges to the status quo. By insisting for example that certain forgotten memories of the U.S. War in Viet Nam need to be commemorated, Vietnamese American community-building puts into question conventional ideas of U.S. national identity and racial formation. By organizing around place, Vietnamese American place-making further defies conventional notions of spatial assimilation.

Since the time of Robert Park, the sociologists of the Chicago School have been concerned with place, especially the city. Because of the city's population density, Park, Burgess, and McKenzie saw it as a unique social space that "shows the good and evil in human nature in excess" (1968, 46). Although urban sociology presumably takes the city as its object of study, much ink has been spilled debating the uniqueness of cities and, ultimately, the usefulness of spatial analysis.[4] Peter Saunders takes that debate to the extreme, arguing not only against the city as a unique space, but against a focus on space—which he describes as "futile and diversionary" (1986, 11).[5] Mark Gottdiener and Ray Hutchison (2000) also reject the notion that cities are unique social spaces. But rather than reject space, they forward a theory of urbanism that gives spatial factors—that is, location, the built environment, and the social meanings attached to place— equal billing with social factors such as population size and composition. In applying their "sociospatial approach," I treat space not only as a container for Vietnamese American community, but also as an active element in the community-building process.

Neil Smith and Cindi Katz warn that spatial metaphors are "out of control," and that their unexamined use threatens to impose a hegemonic discourse about space as natural or absolute (1993, 80).[6] So as not to contribute to this problem, I hold that spatial formations are contested rather than empty or devoid of social relations of power and inequality.[7] I distinguish between *space* — as a broad gesture to the geographical dimension of social life, what Robert David Sack (1997) calls "homo geographicus"—and *place*, a specific instance of space, one imbued with purpose, identity, or meaning. The kind of place that this book considers has three, interrelated core elements: location, physical form, and the attached narratives that generate identity and significance for place. In other words, an area bounded by four streets is not a place, nor are the walls and roof of a building in and of themselves a place. "Somewhere" and "nowhere" are locations, but they are not places. To qualify as a place, all of these elements must be simultaneously engaged. A place, then, is a "lived world" that draws together territory, culture, history, and individual perceptions. "Thick" places are heavy with meaning, overlapping purposes, or contested histories; conversely, "thin" places exist for more narrow uses, indicating that people are less likely to interact and more likely to become alienated from one another (Sack 1997). As people begin to shape space into thick or thin places that serve certain uses as opposed to others, places grow into contested terrain. A political-economy approach holds that this contestation is inevitable.

I insist that place is a persistent component of Vietnamese American community-building. Yet, there are many valid forms of Vietnamese American community that do not depend upon place as I have defined it here: included among these are alumni and professional associations; networks based in cyberspace; and poetic, figurative, or "imagined communities."[8] While all of these examples of community have spatial dimensions, they do not require the three place elements of location, physical form, and narration. Consequently, community-building in those often more privileged social contexts often neither encounters nor challenges existing formulations of place.[9] Communities that depend on the three elements of place for their sustenance are weakened when those elements are removed. When poor, minority neighborhoods are razed to the ground to make way for luxury offices and condominiums, the social relations among the people who lived in those neighborhoods are drastically altered. Herbert Gans (1982) and Hillel Levine and Lawrence Harmon (1992) both wrote about white ethnic communities that were dismantled as a consequence of Boston's urban renewal in the 1960s and 1970s. On the other hand, when people leave a neighborhood in great numbers by choice, the place that remains can also decline. Grace Lee Boggs writes about "place-conciousness," by which she means an awareness of common, local experiences and a drive to organize around them.[10] Through documentary photographs and sociological text, Camilo José Vergara (1997) documents the "new American ghetto," the belt of inner-city enclaves across the nation that have been left behind by industry and the working families they once supported. Meanwhile, the exclusive gated suburbs and "privatopias" to which the nation's most affluent families have retreated—severely regulated miniworlds in which the preservation of property values is a top priority—have become the only definition of community or place that many middle- and upper-class people know.[11]

Vietnamese American community-building and place-making occurs against a backdrop that is heavily littered with complex questions about the creation and preservation of community boundaries, the relationship between community and the various elements of place, and the equation of community with public spaces versus private property. As a collective project, staying Vietnamese bumps against the prevailing expectations that Vietnamese refugees and immigrants become American by letting go of both community and place. Instead of letting go, in many instances Vietnamese Americans have fortified their ties to both community and place.

The Power and Experience of Place

In early January 2005, grateful for a few glimpses of sun after days and days of pounding rain, I climbed into my rental car outside a friend's apartment in the San Fernando Valley and embarked onto the Ventura freeway. I headed south through Los Angeles, switching to the Glendale and the Santa Ana freeways, cruising past Disneyland. After about an hour and a half, I drove across the "Orange Curtain"[12] and entered Little Saigon. My destination was Phuoc Loc Tho, a site known more commonly to English-language speakers as the Asian Garden Mall.

When I arrived, pedestrian and automobile traffic were at their height. Finding no better space, I parked at the farthest possible end of the several-city-blocks-long lot and then joined throngs of working people—along with their parents, children, friends, and colleagues—in a lunchtime stroll around the mall. A blind Buddhist monk, barefoot and wrapped in a bright orange robe, stood absolutely motionless just outside the entrance. Most of us slowed to look at him, as if to check for a pulse, before entering the mall.

Suddenly, a plethora of distinctive sights, sounds, and smells enveloped us, re-creating perhaps for some visitors a semblance of life in Viet Nam, pre-1975. A freestanding cart displayed lucky bamboo plants, tiny Buddha trinkets, and assorted curios in fake gold and jade. From a restaurant and nearby bakery flowed the steam of beef noodle soup and the sugary scent of crusty French pastries. Nonstop videos danced on a gigantic flat-screen television at one of several music shops, accompanied by what sounded like unbearably tragic love songs. Amid the din, shoppers and vendors eyed one another, haggled, and exchanged money. At the central food court, old men sat alone sipping dark sweet coffee; their sad and distant gazes seemed full of memories.

As an architectural anchor and geographic focal point of the tourist/business district, Phuoc Loc Tho/Asian Garden Mall is unique. This is not an ordinary California-style strip mall, although Little Saigon is replete with those. Its symbolism is huge, not only for the visitors who seek a connection to Vietnameseness. Several leaders told me that the mall represents the "center" and the "heart" of the Vietnamese American community. Despite the fact that the mall's intended use is commercial and therefore it is essentially a private, exclusive, and highly regulated space, its role in generating and shaping Vietnamese American community life is significant.

The Asian Garden Mall is one of those structures whose symbolism exceeds its physical stature.[13] This symbolism is the outcome of efforts by various social actors to transform the place from a mere collection of storefronts to a cultural and political zone spanning the Vietnamese American community, city, county, state, nation, and globe. The mall is often a target for politicians hoping to collect the Vietnamese American vote. For example, on September 13, 2000, a crowd of mostly Vietnamese Americans awaited presidential candidate George W. Bush in the parking lot of the mall. Bush was nearly two hours late. To keep spirits high in the scorching heat, Republican leaders offered their chants, pledges, and prayers. "Welcome to America's most Republican county!" beamed the local party chairman. "This is Bush country!" yelled a state assemblyman. When Bush finally appeared, he made an immediate gesture to the racial demographics of his audience: "I love the wonderful fabric of this state." Then, prompted by a campaign aide, he continued, "You can move to England and not be an Englishman. You can move to France and not be a Frenchman. But if you move to America, you're an American." Sixteen minutes later, people cheered, confetti flew in the air—yellow and red, the colors of the flag of South Viet Nam—and Bush was gone. In that brief and simple moment, the soon-to-be president of the United States turned Phuoc Loc Tho/Asian Garden Mall, and Little Saigon in general, into Republican territory and also into an exemplar of the nation's social and spatial mobility. The actual complexity of activities inside the mall and elsewhere disappeared, and with the turn of a phrase, Little Saigon became instant "proof" of the nation's presumed commitment to diversity, freedom, and democracy (Moxley 2000).

The mall is a site of multiple individual and collective histories and visions. Places like this mall are powerful because they generate an infinitely complex range of experiences and social, cultural, or political meanings. For example, through the arrangement of people's movement and action, the multilingual signage and other audiovisual references to language and culture, and the constant surveillance of hidden cameras and armed security guards, the mall ensures a regular flow of shoppers. Meanwhile, the mall is also a site of social activity. I have seen adults dropping off their aging parents here to let them spend the day sipping coffee and chatting with other elders. I have seen men in their fifties and sixties while away the hours playing Chinese chess on tables in front of the mall. Despite rules around loitering, these noncommercial uses of the mall seem to be tolerated by the security patrol. For my own friends, I have designated the mall as an initial meeting spot before we go to an event or another restaurant elsewhere in Little Saigon. Because of its easy access and recognizability, the mall functions as an orienting device. Several of the leaders I interviewed describe this mall as the "heart" of the Vietnamese American community, but then go on to explain that they try to avoid coming here because of the crowds and the constant "fender benders" in the parking lot. In this sense, the mall has become a mental destination whose meaning is possibly even bigger than if it were just a shopping venue.

Tony Hiss (1990) and Winifred Gallagher (1993) describe the emotional and psychological dimensions of the environment, pointing out the ability of place to affect our innermost thoughts. Hiss observes that places organize our senses into moments of "simultaneous perception," and he argues that as public citizens we have a responsibility to create places that enhance those moments. However, as an urban sociologist I am less interested in making a deep analysis of these sorts of personal perceptions than I am able to describe and explain the impact of place on public, social, especially community, life. I have spoken at length with people who are much more familiar and invested in these places than I am. Certainly I am in no position to describe either everyday life in southern California or a Vietnamese American's insider experience of Little Saigon. The point is not, after all, to explain what it feels like to be Vietnamese American living in these spaces; instead, we are exploring the manner in which place bolsters community by eliciting a sense of group identity and belonging among Vietnamese refugees and immigrants in the United States. I am particularly interested in the collective thoughts and feelings behind efforts to make place as a foundation for community. To the extent that place becomes a resource in and of itself—a self-contained universe, a lived world, a symbol of Vietnameseness—place and place-making turn out to be crucial and persistent elements of Vietnamese American community and community-building.

Place-Making and Place Makers

When the first Vietnamese refugees arrived, they did so into places whose purposes and meaning had already been defined. Their place-making involves taking apart the existing elements of place and reformulating them so as to engage and promote certain forms of Vietnamese American community. In Little Saigon and Fields Corner, I identify three distinct kinds of place-making activities: territorializing, regulating, and symbolizing.

Territorializing means establishing the scale, boundaries, and "imageability" of place. For example, in his classic study *The Image of the City*, Kevin Lynch (1960) pointed out that each city acquires its image through a different use of physical structures including paths, districts, edges, nodes, and landmarks. Territorializing creates regions within space to which purpose and meaning may then be attached. While city planners are obviously paid to design these regions, city residents may develop their own understanding and perceptions of the regionalization of the built environment. Thus, territorializing is not only a professional activity but can be the work of ordinary people. Sanjoy Mazumdar et al. study the quiet, individual acts of territorialization among ordinary Vietnamese Americans who "make pilgrimages" to Orange County's Little Saigon (2000, 328); Joseph Wood focuses on suburban Vietnamese Americans who have "configured a labyrinthine geography for themselves" in northern Virginia (1997, 70). But in this book, territorialization is a public act by Vietnamese American business and community leaders who want to make the scope and purpose of their places clear not only to accommodate Vietnamese American social life but also to gain clout and recognition not just for themselves but also for their constituencies in city hall. Turning the Asian Garden Mall into a spot on George W. Bush's 2000 campaign trail also territorializes Orange County's Little Saigon, enlarging its scale from a local to a national site for the Vietnamese American vote.

Regulating sets up rules for who belongs and who does not belong in a particular place. Regulating is a hegemonic activity that seeks to maintain the status quo of a place. The state monitors and controls the movement of people across the boundaries of public and private places—parks, hotel lobbies, government offices, corporate plazas, shopping malls, residential neighborhoods—through its lawmakers, the police, trained security guards, and the court system. For example, requiring special identification tags or fingerprint scans for entry into a corporate or government workplace regulates traffic in and out of place.

Regulating can also be an informal activity. In her classic defense of urban neighborhoods and street life, Jane Jacobs (1961) reminds us of how city streets are sometimes safer than suburbs because neighbors often know each other and can look out for one another. When people are excluded and marginalized from a place, they can attempt to counterregulate. Neil Smith (1993) offers the example of an artist's invention of a vehicle that would allow a homeless person to sleep, wash, store belongings, and avoid bad weather. The artist's point was practical and political: designed in collaboration with homeless men and women, the vehicle made a wider range of movement more visible, thus "retaliating" against efforts to make a disturbing social reality invisible. Obviously this retaliation comes from a place of relative powerlessness, but the fact that even homeless people can oppose state regulations is an important aspect of place-making.

In the Vietnamese American context, the most powerful acts of regulation happened before, during, and shortly after the war. But at a more recent and smaller local scale, Vietnamese American community leaders also help to regulate the boundaries of place through commerce and through political ideology, namely anticommunism. My earlier discussion of the Asian Garden Mall in Little Saigon illustrates some ways that "public" activities in a privately owned shopping area are controlled and monitored by security guards and by social norms about other acceptable activities, for example, playing chess in the outside courtyard. The rules of mass consumerism and the acquisition of private property mesh neatly with the rules of political ideology. The Hi-Tek incident of 1999 provides a memorable instance in which Vietnamese Americans in Orange County took to the streets in the hundreds of thousands to regulate the political boundaries of place by ousting a shopkeeper who insisted on displaying an image of Ho Chi Minh in his store. Vietnamese Americans in Boston have not had opportunities of the same scale to publicize their hatred of communism, although I have been told that a reign of fear keeps people from vocalizing political opinions that might be misconstrued as "communist."

Symbolization gives meaning to place through the attachment of symbols, metaphors, memories, and even myths. Putting up monuments is the quintessential act of symbolization, casting into stone the history and identity of a group or nation (N. Johnson 1995). Just as the writing of history is a contested act, so making monuments to honor certain heroes or events—and not others—can be interpreted as an act of power (Harvey 1979). Because they are physical objects, monuments that symbolize also act as landmarks that enhance the territorialization of place.

The built environment is fraught with contested memories and other ideological messages (Boyer 1996; Wright and Hutchison 1997). David Hummon (1992) elaborates upon the ways that community residents use place imagery to define "self" and "other." Usually, otherizing involves some kind of moral or political commentary. For example, in the symbolization of West Hollywood, California as a place representing gay men, Benjamin Forrest (1995) notes that place is also tied to a narrative about gay men as good citizens who should not be stigmatized or marginalized. So, too, the symbolization of Vietnamese American places emphasizes the perilous journey of refugees to America, and their positive economic and cultural contributions once settled here. This narrative counters prevailing ideas of Vietnamese as gangsters, welfare cheats, or violent and obsessed war veterans.

A crucial impulse toward place-making in Vietnamese America comes from the transition from mutual assistance associations (MAAs) focused on social services for refugees to community-based organizations focused on jobs, housing, and economic development. This transition was made necessary by the decline in federal and local funding for refugee services and the changing needs of their growing communities. But whether or not place-making is seen as a practical or useful activity depends on your perspective.

Lincoln Le arrived in New Jersey in 1975 when he was just out of his teens. His family moved to Florida and then Boston a year later. By flipping through the phone book, he discovered there were about thirty Vietnamese already in the greater Boston area. He called one of the numbers and ended up living with the person who answered for six months. A few weeks later, he moved to Chinatown. He spent many years teaching bilingual Vietnamese classes in the Boston public schools then became a lawyer. I interviewed him in 1997, just as the Vietnamese American community was beginning to make this shift from services to community-building.

LINCOLN LE: Most Vietnamese communities in the United States have a so-called, what is that? Vietnamese community of Massachusetts, Inc.?

A CBO?

LINCOLN LE: Right. Most of the communities have that official social system that are supposed to gear their activities toward creating coalition, political awareness, advocating for services, things of that nature. But these CBOs are not very effective since their inception. Just pick Massachusetts. What has that organization done to help the community? I haven't seen nothing.

Well, they have commemorative events against the war, and those kinds of things.

LINCOLN LE: You think those are practical? May have some cultural values behind it. But in terms of providing some iota of security of members of the community—there's none.

You don't think even the symbolic significance is important?

LINCOLN LE: It's important. Once the people is self-sufficient. You cannot live on symbols. You have to live on rice and vegetables. The majority of those Southeast Asian CBOs have been focusing on symbolic events: April 30, Tet, cultural events. But the real social support, the real educational support are not there. . . . How do you call that? The organizing drive to make sure the ability and the interest somehow merge into action is not there.

What Mr. Lincoln identifies as a lack of ability and interest merging into action was in fact a broader issue facing MAAs nationwide. In 1992, the Southeast Asia Resource Action Center (SEARAC) launched a year-long "MAA-Sparkplug Leadership Training" project to help shift the focus of Cambodian, Laotian, and Vietnamese MAAs from a service-oriented approach to organizational development and leadership team-building. The project, funded by the W. R. Kellogg Foundation, promoted "intergenerational and inter-cultural leadership mentoring" and established three-person teams consisting of the executive director of the MAA, a board member of the MAA, and a community resource person designated as a "sparkplug."[14]

Whether leaders function as professional "sparkplugs" in the fashion of this foundation-sponsored project or as mere "mouthpieces" for various factions within the community, their efforts to territorialize, regulate, and symbolize place have important ramifications for community-building. Through the 1990s, Vietnamese Americans in Boston struggled to make this shift from refugee services to community development and to do so without alienating an older generation whose views about place would be outmoded. I interviewed Hoa Nguyen several times over the years from 1994 to 2005, during which he held a number of influential positions in Vietnamese American community organizations. Mr. Hoa is still considered one of the younger leaders in the community. In one conversation, we spoke about how difficult it is to define "community," and with some exasperation Mr. Hoa listed for me all the community organizations he could think of.

HOA NGUYEN: Let me tell you about the national community. Each city or state have its own Vietnamese "community" that not classify as CBO [community-based organization]. They have their own elections. They have the Vietnamese Community of Springfield, the Vietnamese Community of Worcester, the Vietnamese Community of Boston, the Vietnamese Community of Massachussetts. Of Northeast region, West, and Northwest, and then the whole entire country! And then they have their own conventions, their own conference every number of years. They reach over to Europe to unite with France, England, Switzerland. Whatever. Their interest is to have an umbrella community. Sooner or later, they're going to call the Earth: Vietnamese Community of Outside Viet Nam. But what is it for? Not the purpose to help Vietnamese life, but to deal with Viet Nam. That's the interest. It's all exile community. I'm not saying it's a waste of time. But we can learn lessons from that. People should have seen a long time ago whether this kind of thing is doable or leads us anywhere.

Seen through the lens of exile, community-building requires claiming bigger and bigger territories that can ultimately cover the entire globe. The desire on the part of displaced exiles to "jump scale" from the city to the planet makes sense if one frames one's entire sense of self and community on the loss of homeland.[15] When Mr. Hoa suggests that this approach to community is not doable and does not lead anywhere, he speaks out of a professional viewpoint that values realistic options. Given the parameters of community-building and place-making in Boston, he has accepted the project of staying Vietnamese within an American context.

Placing Vietnamese America

Until recently, the concept of place has been taken for granted and thus has been severely undertheorized with regard to Vietnamese Americans—despite what seem to be obvious references to the need for a critical spatial analysis of the forced exile and resettlement of refugee populations. The very notion of a refugee, after all, represents the "tragic phenomenon of displacement," a phenomenon that is not new but which multiplied beyond all historical precedent in the last century (Smyser 1987). Drawing from sociology, geography, and other fields, this chapter brings into plain view the centrality and power of place in everyday life, thus setting the stage for a critical and in-depth discussion of the relationship between community and place in Vietnamese America.

This book joins a long tradition of examining spatially bounded Asian American communities; it is certainly not the first time anyone has "placed" an Asian ethnic group in a specific urban or suburban location, or alongside another racialized group. Chinatown, of course, has received the most scholarly attention, and continues to be the basis for excellent scholarship on class conflict, globalization, and suburbanization.[16] Koreans in New York and Los Angeles have provided fascinating, if somewhat disturbing, analyses of the origins of conflict and cooperation within the Korean community, or with blacks and Jews.[17] In all of these recent works, scholars make us think about U.S.-based Asian ethnic groups not just as wannabe-citizens but as key players in larger regional and national formations. Asian ethnic groups exist in relation to others, and in the existing scholarship those relationships are often expressed in specific terms of geography, territory, region, or location: in other words, place. But as far as I know, no scholar has yet taken an Asian American community as the basis for formulating a critical theory of space or place.

This discussion of community and place in Vietnamese America needs to be "critical" in the sense that spatial assumptions need to be surfaced and examined; in fact, these assumptions influence social scientific scholarship regarding the Vietnamese American experience. When scholars do address space, they rarely explain how space itself—that is, the spatial arrangement of populations but also the creation of spatial scale that results in boundaries between and among neighborhood, community, and nation—is actually the outcome of sustained struggle and conflict between and among various social actors, social institutions, and the state. Where things are in space, including the location of particular neighborhoods, is not just the random effect of individual actions. A critical, or active, approach to space attends to this complex, and always ongoing, process.

To think "platially" adds another level of inquiry to spatial theory. Now, not only are we asking questions about the wide geographic implications of social life—that is, what Henri Lefebvre called the "production of space"—but we are also attending to the "humanistic epistemology" that is attached to place-making.[18] Platial theory requires that we ask about the interweaving of meaningful narratives to spatial forms, the very act of which turns space into place. By moving analytically from space to place, we make possible a tricky shift from an outsider/objective analysis to a participatory/experiential one. It is not so much that anyone loses objectivity but that as researchers and as people in the world, we gain "positionality" by acknowledging and validating specific experiences and relationships.

Spatial-assimilation is the central theory that mainstream social scientists employ to think about where immigrants live and work and why location affects them. In this theory, "space" refers simply to location, a point on a map, a specific place that if devoid of the people and objects currently in it would be described as "empty." In thinking of space this way, we are not asked to consider the complex social and historical processes that had to occur prior to our moment of observation in order for these areas to evolve into the places we now see. Nor are we meant to think about the experience of actually being in these places; the perceptions and sensory aspects of place are not important, so that one place ends up the same as any other, except for its location on the map. Space in the spatial-assimilation theoretical framework is by and large a reference to distance and proximity between and among people and community resources.

In observing and measuring the residential integration of immigrants, spatial-assimilation theorists are reminding us that the location of one's home indicates, and to some degree determines, one's access to material resources such as jobs, services, or public amenities. Their explicit assumption is that the more that immigrant settlement patterns resemble those of middle-class whites, and the more immigrants are integrated into white neighborhoods, the more incorporated they will become into mainstream society. The movement of whites from inner-city ghettos to outer-ring suburbs is taken as normative and as a given rather than as an uneven historical process involving the state. Thus, spatial-assimilation theory as it is applied to immigrants conceals from view many assumptions about the racialization of metropolitan space in general and about the construction of white privilege specifically.

The closer one remains to an economically disadvantaged neighborhood, of course, the more difficult it is to escape the long-term impact of those disadvantages: poorly funded public schools, drugs and crime leading to street violence, and exposure to pollution and toxic wastes are the examples that come instantly to mind. For those reasons, living in a wealthy suburb is surely better in many ways than living in a poor area of a city. Unfortunately, the development of metropolitan regions creates inequality, so that what appear to be the separate fates of the suburbs and the cities are in fact linked and interdependent. In truth, the advantages enjoyed by people in rich places are carved out of the disadvantages suffered by people in poor places.

The association of suburbs with whiteness is neither accidental nor the result solely of hard work and a desire to assimilate on the part of whites. Nor is it entirely accurate as middle- and working-class people of color, including immigrants, also suburbanize. In *Place Matters: Metropolitics for the Twenty-first Century*, Peter Dreier, John Mollenkopf, and Todd Swanstrom explain how a series of "stealth urban policies" created the suburbs as enclaves for privileged whites while the abandoned inner cities became home to native-born and immigrant minorities (2001, 102). Stealth urban policies have been the primary engine behind the settlement patterns of whites, yet spatial-assimilation theory frames immigrant residential patterns outside of the context of such policies by focusing instead on the characteristics of immigrant populations themselves.

The emergence and growth of Vietnamese America as a "community" depends on, and in many ways constitutes, the production and construction of places such as Little Saigon and Fields Corner. Vietnamese American place-making is not only a matter of Vietnamese American people congregating in particular spots on the map; indeed, in certain cases, the actual number of people located in a place is irrelevant to the social significance attached to a place. Moreover, Vietnamese American place-making must contend with the features of already existing places, rearranging and reformulating them to meet Vietnamese American community needs. The challenges and opportunities of staying Vietnamese in Orange County versus Boston are distinct not only because of the different characteristics of the Vietnamese American population, but also because Orange County and Boston are different places to begin with.

The Architecture of Vietnamese America

Borrowing terms from other disciplines is always a risky business. I use the term "architecture" full well knowing that readers who expect a full-blown, professional analysis of the built environment, in this chapter or elsewhere in the book, will be disappointed. Unfortunately, from the perspective of physical geographers and architects, my gestures toward the physical form of place will seem half-baked, even as they pose a more serious challenge to sociologists and others who are unaccustomed to giving space their unswerving attention. In applying a sociospatial lens to the problem of staying Vietnamese, I walk a fine line between these disciplinary approaches. But the risk of disappointing some is worth the possibility of convincing others that the spatial dimension of the Vietnamese American experience needs to be taken seriously. In the passages below, I describe the social and historical context for Vietnamese American community-building and place-making. Then, I compare Orange County and Boston as contrasting settings for the production and construction of Vietnamese America. In all of this, the already existing architecture with which Vietnamese Americans must deal is understood also to be a production and construction rather than a set of naturalized facts.

The End of the War

Vu Pham (2003) presents a historiography of the thousands of Vietnamese students and professionals who lived and worked in the United States from 1945 to 1975. This historiography challenges the idea of 1975 as the birth year of Vietnamese America, and also questions the conception of Vietnamese Americans only as forced exiles whose primary concern was to adapt to U.S. society and become Americans. South Vietnamese students and advanced scholars, for example, were financed and supported by the U.S. government in the hopes that later they would advance U.S. foreign interests through their American-based education. At the end of 1974, nearly fifteen thousand Vietnamese were already living in the United States.[19] Of these, some did not return to Viet Nam as planned, becoming instead "silent refugees" in the United States.

Thus, even before April 30, 1975—the date to which exiled Vietnamese refer as their "Day of Mourning"—the U.S. federal government and its military attachés in Viet Nam had already earmarked spaces, materially and discursively, for Vietnamese Americans as political refugees who would serve as a "showcase for U.S. democracy."[20] In the last weeks of the war, the communists gained territory and thousands of people moved toward the shrinking, U.S. government–controlled areas. The reasons for moving were surely complex. A *New York Times* reporter found that fear of crossfire, not fear of communism, motivated the flow:

> When people are asked why they join the human tide, abandoning home, possessions, and livelihood, the typical reply was "Because everyone else is going." . . . Not one said it was because he or she feared or hated Communism.[21]

In the mainstream media coverage about the flight from Viet Nam, refugees were often portrayed as "voting with their feet" against communism, but what is often overlooked is that "forced-draft urbanization" was a U.S. military strategy that encouraged massive population displacement from the countryside as a way to degrade the Viet Cong. As Richard Nixon put it, "The enemy will be denied all but the most limited and furtive access to the people."[22]

In the first weeks of April 1975, the Ford administration's plans to rescue the eighteen thousand orphans remaining in South Viet Nam most certainly represented a political maneuver on the part of the United States, not a children's vote against communism. Operation Babylift was denounced by the communists as "kidnapping on a vast scale."[23] Observers around the world saw Operation Babylift as an illustration of American hubris. For example, an editorial in England's *Manchester Guardian Weekly* stated:

The evacuation of Vietnamese orphans, while emotionally understandable, can rightly be described as cradle-snatching. But its real significance, so far as Americans are concerned, is that *it starkly reveals how many Americans still implicitly believe it is better for Vietnamese to become Americans that [sic] to remain Vietnamese,* as is their birthright, if it means living under a government which America does not like. (italics added)[24]

The idea that Vietnamese refugees in the United States should become American rather than stay Vietnamese—an idea wrapped up in complex layers of political and cultural assumptions—serves as the most basic fodder for this book.

Even within the U.S. Congress, Operation Babylift had its detractors, some of whom described the evacuation of the first two thousand babies as a "guilt trip" that saved the children but failed to end the war. One black administrative aide pointed out the irony that while blacks had not yet been accepted as full citizens in this country, the U.S. government was trying to rescue Vietnamese children and make them into Americans.[25]

Bill Ong Hing notes that although many policy makers saw refugee parole as a humanitarian endeavor, between 1948 and 1979, "the ideological bias of refugee policy [was] to accommodate refugees fleeing Communist countries" (1993, 124). Between April and December 1975 alone, about 125,000 Vietnamese were paroled into the United States by the discretionary authority of the attorney general. From 1975 to 1979, an additional 169,000 Vietnamese entered the country. Between 1975 and 1980, over 400,000 Southeast Asian refugees were thus "paroled" into the United States; the vast majority of these were Vietnamese. Hing states, "These figures betray any claim that refugee policy was based solely on humanitarian considerations" (124).

At this time, some U.S. lawmakers expressed anxiety about the potential social instability caused by the influx of refugees, but restrictions on refugee admissions were seen as "morally treacherous" given the political controversies surrounding U.S. actions in Viet Nam (Hing 1993). The Refugee Act of 1980 came about partly as a response to widespread dissatisfaction with the ad hoc nature of discretionary parole. The act defined a refugee as someone with a "well-founded fear of persecution." In practice, persecution was most often taken to mean persecution by communist regimes.[26] Between 1980 and 1990, about 307,000 Vietnamese came to the United States, the majority of them officially designated by the act as "refugees."

Three other programs ushered in the rest of the Vietnamese who came to the United States in that period: the Orderly Departure Program (ODP), the Amerasian Homecoming Program, and the Special Released Reeducation Center Detainee Resettlement Program (more commonly referred to as "HO"). ODP was established in 1979 by the United Nations High Commissioner for Refugees (UNHCR) in order to facilitate the migration and permanent resettlement of the individuals and families who were fleeing their homelands. The Amerasian Homecoming Program, enacted by Congress in 1988, allowed children of Vietnamese mothers and U.S. soldiers into the country. Many of these children hoped to find fathers who had abandoned them.[27] The HO program was implemented in 1989 to enable former political prisoners and their families to enter the United States. Many of these individuals had served prison sentences of anywhere from eight to fifteen years because they had worked for the South Vietnamese government or military and were unable to flee when the war ended. In the future, new immigration is not likely to play much of a role in the growth of the Vietnamese American population.

The 2000 census lists 1,122,528 Vietnamese in the United States, making Vietnamese the fifth largest U.S. Asian ethnic group. This is nearly double the figure of 614,547 listed on the 1990 census. The increase was due to new refugees, to new immigrants coming to be reunited with their families, as well as to U.S.-born children (Table 1). Steven Gold (1992) describes three subgroups within the Vietnamese American population that correspond roughly to three "waves" of refugees: the pre-1975 elite, the boat people, and the ethnic Chinese. Each of these waves has had different patterns of assimilation and acculturation based on the economic and political circumstances in which they left Viet Nam and arrived in the United States. Amerasians and ex–political detainees did not come in a separate wave although they represent two additional subgroups within the population. There are, of course, many other ways to describe the composition of the Vietnamese American population; throughout the following chapters, community-building and place-making reflects and enacts these various divisions and perspectives.

Migration and Settlement

Richard Alba and Victor Nee note that the geographic concentration of immigrants is guided primarily by social networks, whereas for refugees, at least upon arrival, their original destination is determined by government agencies and private sponsorship (2003, 248–60). In the first few years of U.S. resettlement, federal agencies purposefully dispersed Vietnamese refugees across all fifty states. The intent of this "scatter policy" appears to be a

Table 1. Refugees and immigrants from Viet Nam, 1951–2001

FISCAL YEAR	REFUGEES	IMMIGRANTS
1951–70		4,675
1971		2,038
1972		3,412
1973		4,569
1974		3,192
1975	125,000	3,039
1976	3,200	4,230
1977	1,900	4,629
1978	11,100	2,892
1979	44,500	2,065
1980	95,200	4,510
1981	65,279	2,238
1982	27,396	3,030
1983	22,819	3,275
1984	24,856	5,203
1985	25,222	5,120
1986	21,700	15,256
1987	19,656	11,489
1988	17,571	14,231
1989	21,924	25,957
1990	27,797	37,773
1991	28,396	43,939
1992	26,795	45,580
1993	31,401	29,365
1994	34,110	14,027
1995	32,250	13,157
1996	16,107	12,367
1997	6,612	16,222
1998	10,266	12,728
1999	9,622	15,890
2000	2,839	21,171
2001	3,109	25,180
Total	756,627	412,449

Source: South Asian American Statistical Profile 2004, published by Southeast Asia Resource Action Center, http://www.searac.org.

matter of interpretation: some analysts insist that dispersal was intended to facilitate assimilation, lessening the burden on small municipalities whose resources might be easily drained (Ascher 1981; Le 1994). According to one urban planner, the point was to "avoid another Miami," a reference to the concentration of Cuban refugees in Florida (Rumbaut 1995, 242). Whether the wish to prevent a second Miami was motivated by a benevolent desire to help refugees integrate into U.S. society, by a negative xenophobic impulse, or by a desire to forestall the emergence of a right-wing interest group are all plausible explanations. Hing notes "the persistent impulse to control the presence of Asians" within U.S. borders (1993, 16). Indeed, policies of parole and dispersal of Vietnamese refugees strike a recurrent theme in immigrant history that may be unique to Asian Americans: white fears of Asian inassimilability combined with a desire to hasten their assimilation by preventing them from sticking together. In this larger historical sense, dispersal—and the spatial-assimilation theory that guided dispersal policy— might be construed as a formula for the "domestication" and "deracination" of Vietnamese refugees.[28]

Once purposefully scattered, the first wave of Vietnamese refugees quickly migrated toward other regions of the country. Subsequent arrivals followed them. Among the many causes of these patterns of "secondary migration" and "chain migration" are a desire to reunite with family members for emotional and financial support, greater access to employment, cheaper rents, higher public benefits, Vietnamese-specific social services, and warmer weather. In many cases, voluntary agencies ("volags") encouraged more established Vietnamese refugees to assist brand-new arrivals by picking them up from the airport, teaching them basic survival skills, and providing temporary housing. MAAs were formed out of those networks. Thus, an ad hoc resettlement policy emerged that required face-to-face contact and that facilitates ethnic ties, in contrast to the original intent to separate and isolate the population.

The U.S. government set up four receiving centers for refugees: Camp Pendleton in California, Fort Chaffee in Arkansas, Eglin Air Force Base in Florida, and Indiantown Gap in Pennsylvania.[29] Within a decade, Vietnamese developed visible areas of population concentration around the nation. For instance, 34.3 percent of the Southeast Asian refugee population (the majority of whom were Vietnamese) lived in California in 1981. By 1989 that figure rose to 39.6 percent, and by 2000 it had risen only slightly to 39.8 percent.

"Propinquity," in this case meaning a condition of physical proximity, continues to be an important but not necessary feature of Vietnamese American community-building and place-making.[30] In 1990, more than three-quarters of the entire Vietnamese American population resided in only ten states. By 2000, despite a near doubling overall, those same ten states still held nearly three-quarters of the total. For example, California's Vietnamese population went from 280,223 in 1990 to 484,023 in 2000. Texas increased from 69,634 in 1990 to 143,352 in 2000. Massachusetts went from 15,449 in 1990 to 36,685 in 2000. Alba and Nee (2003, 252) note that through the 1980s and 1990s segregation did not increase for Asian Americans even though the population grew rapidly. At least at the state level, new Vietnamese immigrants and refugees reinforced the established settlement patterns presumably because the already existing Vietnamese American communities and places provided things they needed but could not access elsewhere: jobs, housing, and social services in Vietnamese. Obviously, the new arrivals help to refuel enclave economies by providing both their labor and their purchasing power.

At smaller levels of spatial scale, we can see where the biggest concentrations of population lie (see Table 2). CMSAs, or consolidated metropolitan statistical areas, capture the regions in which people both live and work. By far, southern California is the favorite destination: in the Los Angeles–Riverside–Orange County area, there were 233,573 Vietnamese in 2000.[31] The reputation of Orange County is so strong that supposedly some people in Viet Nam know of only one destination in the United States: "Orange *Country*." California's San Francisco–Oakland–San Jose CMSA comes in second with 146,613, and in Texas, the Houston–Galveston–Brazoria CMSA is third with 63,924. San Jose and Houston are also well-known sites for Vietnamese American community. On the East Coast, the Washington D.C./Virginia/Maryland/West Virginia PMSA, or primary metropolitan statistical area, which includes Fairfax County, holds 43,709 Vietnamese Americans. Falls Church, Virginia serves a wealthy, suburbanized Vietnamese American community.[32]

Table 2. Ten largest Vietnamese populations by metropolitan area, 2000

STATE	METROPOLITAN AREA	POPULATION
California	Los Angeles–Riverside–Orange County (CMSA)	233,573
California	San Francisco–Oakland–San Jose (CMSA)	146,613
Texas	Houston–Galveston–Brazoria (CMSA)	63,924
Texas	Dallas–Fort Worth (CMSA)	47,090
mid-Atlantic	Washington, D.C./Virginia/Maryland/West Virginia (PMSA)	43,709
Washington	Seattle–Tacoma–Bremerton (CMSA)	40,001
California	San Diego (MSA)	33,504
Massachusetts	Boston–Worcester–Lawrence (CMSA)	31,325
mid-Atlantic	Philadelphia–Wilmington–Atlantic City (CMSA)	24,779
Georgia	Atlanta (MSA)	23,996

Source: National Congress of Vietnamese Americans, http://www.ncvaonline.org/archive/census_population10VNMSA.shtml.

Changing Identities, Building Community

A number of key measures of socioeconomic status—naturalization, education levels, housing, income, and employment—suggest the extent to which Vietnamese Americans have become part of U.S. society. These measures are commonly taken as the end result of assimilation, but I present them here instead as indicators of the social context for the subsequent efforts to build community and establish place.

According to the 2000 census, of the total Vietnamese American population, 58.2 percent are naturalized citizens compared to 40.3 percent for the general U.S. population.[33] The number of U.S.-born Vietnamese is 332,362, a figure four to five times greater than that of Cambodians, Laotians, or Hmong.[34] The Vietnamese population tends to be slightly older, more educated, and have higher incomes than that of other Southeast Asians. While 43.5 percent of the general U.S. population is between the ages of twenty and forty-nine, a slightly larger proportion of 51.6 percent of Vietnamese are in that same age bracket, and 31.3 percent are under twenty years old. In contrast, for the Hmong 60.3 percent are under twenty years old, while 32.5 percent are between twenty and forty-nine years old. Among Vietnamese aged twenty-five and over, 17 percent were college graduates. This rate is comparable to the general U.S. population (21 percent) but far under the Asian American rate of 38 percent. Meanwhile, for Cambodians, Laotians, or Hmong in that same age group, college graduates numbered between 3 and 7 percent. Not all Vietnamese are so fortunate however; 8 percent of Vietnamese had no formal schooling (for women this is even higher) compared to only 1.4 percent of the general U.S. population.

Despite relatively high levels of formal schooling, many Vietnamese Americans speak Vietnamese at home. Linguistically isolated households are those in which no one over the age of fourteen speaks English fluently. Among all Asians, 24.7 percent were linguistically isolated, compared to 45.0 percent for Vietnamese. Linguistic isolation is usually an indication of lack of access to mainstream resources, but in the case of Vietnamese Americans may indicate a preference for Vietnamese over English. Alba and Nee note that among the five largest Asian ethnic groups, Vietnamese have the lowest propensity to speak only English at home, even among U.S.-born Vietnamese between the ages of twenty-five and forty-four years old (2003, 223). They offer no social, cultural, or spatial explanation for this trend, but quite possibly this suggests that even among Vietnamese who speak

English at work or at school, preserving the Vietnamese language at home or using it in places such as Little Saigon is one way to stay Vietnamese.

The distribution of Vietnamese people across occupational categories is skewed toward service (19.4 percent) and production/transportation/material moving (28.1 percent) compared to 14.9 percent and 14.6 percent for the general U.S. population. While 43.2 percent of Asian Americans hold management and professional positions, only 27.0 percent of Vietnamese do. The median household income for Asian Americans was $57,874 in 1999, topping the U.S. general population's median household income of $50,046. Meanwhile, the median household income for Vietnamese was $46,929. Only 10.2 percent of Vietnamese households received public assistance, compared to 30.2 percent for Hmong. For the general U.S. population, 12.4 percent live below the federal poverty line, while for Vietnamese, 16.0 percent did. Like other Asian Americans, Vietnamese tend to live in cities: 97.9 percent of Vietnamese lived in urban areas, compared to 79.2 percent for the general U.S. population. About half (52.8 percent) live in owner-occupied homes, compared to 66.2 percent for the general U.S. population. Vietnamese households are often larger than those of the general U.S. population and even that of Asian Americans: 51.8 percent of Vietnamese households had four or more people, compared to 25.0 percent for the general U.S. population and 37.1 percent for Asian Americans. Among households with unmarried partners, the percentage of households led by same-sex partners is 14.4 percent for Vietnamese, 15.4 percent for Asian Americans, and 12.6 percent for the general U.S. population.

Small business ownership among Vietnamese rose from 25,761 total firms in 1987 to 97,764 in 1997. In 1997, there were 18,948 Vietnamese-owned firms with 79,035 paid employees.[35] But the actual impact of ethnic entrepreneurship on Vietnamese American community-building and place-making is difficult to assess because of the division between ethnic Chinese and the rest of the Vietnamese American population. This division is maintained through language, formal business practices, informal networks, and organizational affiliations. For example, Gold (1994) treats Chinese-Vietnamese business ownership as integral to the Vietnamese American community in Orange County though he describes the community as "multiethnic." He points out that while up to 40 percent of the businesses belong to ethnic Chinese and some of the most successful entrepreneurs in Little Saigon are ethnic Chinese, nevertheless ethnic Chinese often face considerable social and economic difficulties.

These data help to position Vietnamese Americans vis-à-vis other refugees, other Asian Americans, and the general U.S. population. They help to show that Vietnamese America is not a monolith, and while these numbers do suggest broad patterns of adaptation and social life they do not necessarily reveal the many important differences in migration experience, political outlook, social status, and family background that strongly influence the stances people eventually take regarding community and place. These differences will become more relevant in the context of local community-building and place-making activities in Orange County and Boston.

In a polemical article on immigration and race, Stephen Steinberg (2005) observed that when immigrants come to America, one of the first things they learn is that black people are on the bottom of the totem pole. To put it another way, in a society whose national history and identity is based on a deeply entrenched system of white privilege, "disidentifying" with native-born blacks is an obvious requirement of acceptance in white society.[36] Precisely for that reason, scholarship investigating racialization— the social, historical, and spatial processes by which dozens of national, ethnic, and cultural groups from all over Asia are constructed and produced into one "Asian" category—is indispensable. Becoming racialized as "Asian American" is one of the very fundamental changes in identity that Vietnamese refugees and immigrants deal with, yet the category of race is disturbingly absent from all of the major social scientific studies of Vietnamese so far, except as a reference to the persistent disadvantages of being black in America.[37] Chapter 2 examines Vietnamese American community-building and place-making in the context of racialization and racial projects. Unlike Steinberg, I do not assume that all Asian immigrants or Asian Americans accept or participate in white racism against blacks.

The conventional approach to the "changing identities" of Vietnamese is to assume a trajectory from "refugee" to "citizen" that takes as given "white" as an unmarked position of freedom and full citizenship and "black" as the negation of whiteness. To avoid seeming racist, immigration scholarship ignores this background, taking cover under what Christopher Doob calls "cultural camouflage" (1999, 16) and others term race-blind liberalism; in other words, the question of inequality is not framed by race but by culture. Robin D. G. Kelley (1997) makes the astute observation that social science has conflated "culture" with "behavior" with regard to native-born, urban blacks. The other side of that conflation is that immigrants are thought to succeed, sometimes despite the color of their skin, because of their presumed values, social capital, community ties, and attitudes toward authority.

The driving idea for this book, that people actively endeavor to stay Vietnamese, is not incompatible with the idea that Vietnamese refugees also have had to change in substantive ways in order to make a living today and to ensure a range of possibilities for future generations. By looking at various indices of socioeconomic change, we can see the extent to which Vietnamese Americans have accommodated themselves to the key institutions of American life. At the same time, the pervasiveness of a stock morality tale about immigrants that extols their inherent virtues and, by implication, puts down the ostensibly deficient cultures of native-born minorities makes it necessary to point out that the individual efforts of Vietnamese to survive and thrive in the United States have been bolstered not only by refugee policy but also by other kinds of industrial, employment, health, and housing policies that are themselves the result of a long history of popular and grassroots movements to secure better living and working conditions for poor people and people of color. The irony is that while white supremacy forces a disidentification with black people, post-1965 immigrants benefit from struggles for social and economic justice waged by and on behalf of black Americans and other non-whites. In fact, in the case of Orange County and Boston, Vietnamese Americans were preceded by Chinese and Japanese whose efforts to create community and place in the late 1800s and early 1900s also required collective struggles as laborers and immigrants. The racialization of Asian Americans has been a historical process that has also shaped the meaning of whiteness and blackness.[38]

The Vietnamese American story has much in common with that of other cold war refugees. Comparing the early community formations of Vietnamese and Soviet Jews, Stephen Gold found that "distinct, localized networks" (1992, 229) played a central role in refugee survival. Comparing Vietnamese to Cuban Americans or to Central American refugees would surely reveal other dimensions of identity—political, linguistic, cultural—that are transformed through community-building and place-making.

Comparing Orange County and Boston

Orange County and Boston serve as two different settings for Vietnamese America, and they also represent two "ideal types" of places: a postsuburban outgrowth of a sprawling West Coast metropolis and a crowded, nineteenth-century industrial city on the East Coast, long an entry port for immigrants. Putting Orange County and Boston side by side brings to the foreground a paradox regarding community and place that requires a sociospatial explanation. Each with its own distinctive image, culture, and history,

Orange County and Boston present a contrasting series of challenges and opportunities for Vietnamese Americans.

The epitome of white suburbia and the former headquarters of the John Birch Society, Orange County got its start after World War II as a planned extension of Los Angeles. Los Angeles earned a reputation as a social dystopia from Ridley Scott's film *Blade Runner*, and that reputation was reborn (at least for the popular media) with the uprisings of 1992. But Orange County promotes itself as a place that is suburban, safe, modern, and cultured.[39] A typical tourist magazine boasts: "[S]uburban sprawl mixes easily with sleek, stainless steel-and-glass high-rises. Where bean fields and orange orchards once flourished now proliferate high-powered corporate concerns—and the arts."[40]

The key to Orange County's distinction is partly geographic: its eight hundred square miles encompass twenty-seven municipalities with deep canyons, curving hills, a spectacular coastline, and a relatively sparse population of only three million people. But affluence and political conservatism is Orange County's real niche. Described alternatively as "postsuburb," "hypersuburb," and "global suburb," Orange County takes suburban preferences for privatization and exclusivity to an extreme.[41] The result is a "cookie-cutter civilization" and, oddly enough, "suburban blight."[42]

Despite recent demographic change and a longstanding Mexican population in the north, Orange County's rich, conservative, and lily-white image persists. From 1890 to 1950, as the rest of California, particularly Los Angeles, became racially diverse, Orange County stayed nearly all white. Rambling tracts of undeveloped land served as a kind of inland frontier for white, middle-class families seeking "refuge" from the perils of urban sprawl. The bedroom communities were secluded from the problems of the city, but they also could not claim to offer any of the necessary or more exciting amenities of a contemporary metropolis.

Then, the Irvine Company took upon itself the task of transforming Orange County into a model community based on gated residential enclaves and specialty zones catering to for-profit enterprise.[43] From 1950 onward, Orange County became a place no Chicago School theorist would have recognized: a decentered, multinucleated region of sprawling and highly planned townships and neighborhoods. With their homes organized into areas technically defined as cities but more reminiscent of a maze of cul-de-sacs inhabited by the Stepford wives, Orange County residents ensconced themselves behind gates and walls designed to protect private property and also to put forth an image of desirability and prestige.

Orange County takes the southern California culture of living in your car and driving everywhere, even to destinations only a few blocks away, and thus never interacting with strangers, to a new height. Ubiquitous freeways and carefully planned communities allow for a region full of "thin" places with single functions, unlike the "thick" places of a traditional city whose many purposes overlap. The social and spatial boundaries for shopping malls, government offices, parks, and residential neighborhoods are sharply drawn, keeping the purposes of each space distinct and channeling social activity in specific ways. For example, the lack of pedestrian walkways inhibits casual encounters among neighbors on the sidewalk—what Jane Jacobs (1961) saw as a benefit of urban life. This is just one indication that unplanned events are not meant to happen here.

Despite an aversion to big government and public spending so strong that it famously went bankrupt in the late 1990s, Orange County's intensely regimented social and spatial structure lends itself easily to the regulation of spheres of life that in many other regions of the country still would be considered off-limits to the state.[44] One impact of these regulations is to preserve and proliferate social inequities even in the midst of intense physical proximity. Kristin Hill Maher (2004) finds that in an exclusive gated community in Irvine, affluent white residents interact daily with working-class Latinos as gardeners, nannies, and housekeepers. The intimacy of this cross-racial and cross-class contact does not lead to greater equality between the groups because of the residents' complex discourse around safety and crime, along with their strongly enforced rules about who can enter the gates when and what comprises proper behavior once inside the compound. The community-building and place-making activities of Maher's Orange County white suburbanites offer a very important illustration of how social barriers may persist and proliferate despite spatial assimilation in a postsuburban setting.

Originally a string of "streetcar suburbs" (Warner 1982), Boston now consists of sixteen officially designated Neighborhood Planning Districts. While other cities expanded from an inner core or central business district into outer-ring suburbs, Boston grew in a patchwork pattern to produce an intricate web of villages connected by federally subsidized highways and a public transit system. Oscar Handlin (1991/1969) made Boston famous as a site of the acculturation of European immigrants. Decades later, Herbert Gans (1982) documented the bonds within a working-class Italian community in Boston's West End, while Hillel Levine and Lawrence Harmon (1992) eulogized the Jewish community that once occupied Roxbury. Both communities were destroyed as a result of urban redevelopment, emphasizing in retrospect the significance of place for early immigrant communities.

In contrast to Orange County, Boston is an old-world city that holds a widely revered spot in the nation's historical and sociological imagination. References to the first Thanksgiving, for example, contribute to Boston's image as a site of the nation's history and culture. The entire state of Massachusetts—and indeed the whole New England region—has played a central part in the production of a national mythology. As Richard Brown and Jack Tager put it, "Settled by the English almost four hundred years ago, Massachusetts and the experiences of its people have been emblematic of larger themes in American history in every subsequent era" (2000, vii).

However, being emblematic of a national history and mythology does not exempt Boston or Massachusetts from a social or political critique of white supremacy. Tingba Apidta (2003a; 2003b) has written two popular histories of Massachusetts from a black, Afro-centric perspective intended as a corrective to dominant accounts of the history of the "Bay State":

> Though Massachusetts has tried to tuck itself away from the racial cauldron that has always inflamed America, a close inspection of the historical record shows the Bay State to be a racial Ground Zero. (2003a, 3)

Boston's "racial Ground Zero" is etched in many people's minds perhaps most notably by the violent era of segregation and court-ordered busing.[45] This era is still a fresh and painful memory for Bostonians of all races. One of my outside informants is a third-generation Irish Bostonian originally from Dorchester and a former school bus driver in the 1980s, several years after busing ended. As we drove down Morrissey Boulevard toward South High School one afternoon, she recalled vivid images from earlier years when school buses carrying black children were dramatically escorted down the boulevard by the National Guard to protect them from bricks and Molotov cocktails heaved at them by angry white residents. She told me that in those days the Irish shamrock displayed on doors throughout South Boston was understood as an antibusing—and therefore a racist and anti-black—symbol. I do not know if the shamrock still carries that message in Southie today.

The spatial and social segregation of black Bostonians fueled the emergence of a black consciousness and political movement. Mel King (1981) tells the story of the poor black ghetto, attending to the evolution of black community development in its three critical stages: the social service stage, the organizing stage, and the institution-building stage. These stages may parallel the development of Boston's Vietnamese American community. Making an important distinction between community as "the people" and neighborhood as "the real estate," the late Mauricio Gastón and Marie Kennedy (1987) argue that Roxbury's blighted condition was the outcome of a national program of urban renewal and highway construction. Consequently, as blacks and Latinos in Roxbury fought to save their homes, they came up against the much more powerful forces of city hall and corporate investors. Occasionally, the community won: the Dudley Street Initiative is an uplifting example of a grassroots-led public-private partnership to revive this area of Roxbury (Medoff and Sklar 1994).

Like blacks, Chinese were also forced into separate areas of the city. In the 1890s, Chinese laborers arrived in Ping-On Alley, pitching tents in the center of what is now Chinatown. In the decades after the Chinese Revolution of 1949, Boston's Chinese immigrant population increased to three times its original size but also lost nine acres of land due to urban renewal. Through the 1990s to the present, Chinatown community activists have pushed for the welfare of residents against the demands of the tourist industry and the shrinking geography of the neighborhood. Michael Liu (1999) chronicles grassroots political mobilization and neighborhood development in Chinatown from the 1970s to 2000, highlighting the role of neighborhood activists in the growth of community. Tom Chung (1995) observes that in roughly the same period, Chinatown has served as an "Asian ethnic crossing" for post-1965 Asian immigrants and refugees. While the old Chinese were shoved into Chinatown, new Asian groups clearly have other final destinations—including the wealthy suburbs—depending mostly on the conditions of their arrival and their integration into the labor market.

As contrasting settings for the emergence of Vietnamese America, Orange County and Boston exemplify features and trends shared by other regions across the nation. For instance, suburban sprawl in New Jersey, Florida, Colorado, and Texas offers similar challenges of privatization and regulation as Orange County. Subject in other ways to the regime of neoliberalism, manufacturing-based cities such as New York, Chicago, and San Francisco display many of the intense neighborhood boundaries that characterize Boston. Juxtaposing Orange County and Boston brings out important themes in space, race, culture, and history that have important ramifications for Vietnamese American community-building and place-making in other regions of the country.

A Tale of Two Communities

To the untrained eye, Little Saigon and Fields Corner look the same: lots of restaurants and gift shops; doctors, dentists, and lawyers all catering to Vietnamese clientele; pedestrian and bicycle traffic; people with Asian features milling the streets; Vietnamese-language signage; imagery, music, and interactions between people that convey another world. But upon closer inspection, and given some hints about the geographic and cultural landscape of each region, the two places are wildly dissimilar and give rise to two very different types of Vietnamese American community. In Orange County, a large Vietnamese population is highly concentrated across the borders of five adjacent cities: Westminster, Garden Grove, Santa Ana, Anaheim, and Fountain Valley. In the most densely populated census tracts, 60 percent of the residents are Vietnamese. But in Boston, a much smaller Vietnamese population is dispersed into four neighborhoods, two of them not attached to the others: Allston-Brighton, East Boston, and North and South Dorchester. In South Dorchester, in an area called Fields Corner, the most densely populated census tracts are only 35 percent Vietnamese.

These contrasting patterns of settlement each contradict the general patterns in their region. Orange County, a super suburb, is made up of hyperplanned communities that are designed specifically to prevent urban/ethnic formations such as Little Saigon. Heavy pedestrian and bicycle traffic is a frequent sight here, but an anomaly in other parts of Orange County. Place is thick in Little Saigon, with certain places serving many different functions unlike the single-use places throughout the rest of the county. On the other hand, Boston is a neighborhood-oriented city, and a visit to Fields Corner on a summer evening would confirm the feel of a neighborhood: people of all ages walking home from subway and bus stops; narrow streets lined by triple-deckers out of whose windows radios blare; people washing their cars and sitting out on their porches. In the case of Boston it is not that Vietnamese have made Fields Corner into an unusual place. Instead, Fields Corner is surprisingly not as much of an intensely Vietnamese neighborhood as Boston's history of immigrant neighborhoods would lead us to expect.

A very interesting factor in the differences between Little Saigon and Fields Corner is the presence and strength of the Chinese-Vietnamese ethnic economy. Little Saigon's ethnic economy is the primary force behind the clout and recognizability of Orange County's Vietnamese American community. Some of the most prominent entrepreneurs here are Chinese

Vietnamese; however, the influence of Chinese culture on Vietnamese American social life is a matter of great controversy among non-Chinese Vietnamese. For example, they point to the word Asian as in "Asian Village" as a corruption of Little Saigon's authenticity as a Vietnamese place and denigrate the premier developer of Little Saigon for having a secret plan to turn the place into "Chinatown."

Fields Corner has a semblance of an ethnic economy—dozens of shops that line Dorchester Avenue, helping to mark the neighborhood as a Vietnamese place—but in truth those shops do not sustain the city's Vietnamese American population in terms of either jobs or goods and services. Fields Corner cannot compete with Chinatown, a century-old neighborhood, for its recognizability and reputation as Boston's Asian ethnic enclave. In fact, while Chinatown has lost space due to downtown development, it has also been revitalized by the influx of Chinese-Vietnamese entrepreneurship which for a variety of reasons could not establish Fields Corner as the city's second Chinatown.

Orange County's Chinese population has a history that dates back to the days of the transpacific railroad. A small Chinatown in Santa Ana was burned down after news of a case of leprosy.[46] In 2000, people who identify as Chinese on the census, including Chinese Vietnamese, were widely dispersed throughout Orange County. They are not concentrated in Little Saigon. This suggests that the majority of Little Saigon's Chinese-Vietnamese entrepreneurs probably live in neighborhoods with other Chinese rather than in Little Saigon with Vietnamese. Boston's Chinese population is scattered throughout the city, especially Allston-Brighton, with the densest tracts in Chinatown. Census tracts show very little overlap between the Chinese population and the areas recognized as "Vietnamese."

Comparing the Vietnamese American places of Orange County and Boston according to particular features underscores the differences between the outcomes of and contexts for community-building and place-making in each region. Table 3 summarizes these differences. The strength of Little Saigon's community—meaning institutional completeness—is reflected in the presence of ethnic-specific social services; mutual aid associations; radio, TV, and print media; recreational activities; groceries and pharmacies; places of worship; and other kinds of institutions. Little Saigon is perhaps the only Vietnamese American place that has elected Vietnamese American representation in two cities (Westminster and Garden Grove). Significantly, in November 2004 a prominent lawyer from Orange County named Van Tran joined the California State Assembly. Tran is the first Vietnamese American elected to a state legislature.

In terms of institutional completeness, Fields Corner appears to be a mere shadow of Little Saigon. Vietnamese American community-building and place-making in Boston, while it shares some major goals with Orange County, has to deal with a very different set of pre-existing circumstances. In this sense, population size and composition alone are necessary but not sufficient explanations for the contrasting features of Little Saigon and Fields Corner.

Treating community and place only as givens puts out of sight the complex negotiations and struggles that people go through in order to achieve a sense of, and real connections to, community and place. This is not to say that community and place are just about feelings or perceptions, nor is it necessary to ignore the very tangible and measurable aspects of community and place. What is crucial to take away from this chapter is that the architecture of Vietnamese America—its structure, character, identity, and reputation—is the result of much more than mere migration and settlement.

Table 3. Comparison of Little Saigon and Fields Corner

PLACE FEATURE	LITTLE SAIGON	FIELDS CORNER
Vietnamese American population, 2000	233,572	31,325
Composition of population	33% refugee, 33% ethnic Chinese, 33% immigrant	70% refugee, 10% ethnic Chinese, 20% immigrant
Residential concentration	four adjacent cities	four nonadjacent neighborhoods
Highest externally recognized official	Westminster City Council (elected)	mayor's community liaison (appointed)
Size of business district	2,000 businesses in Westminster 1,000 businesses in Orange County	30 businesses in Fields Corner, dozens in Chinatown, more in greater Boston
Lingua franca	Vietnamese, Chinese, English	English, Vietnamese
Religious places	$3 million Catholic Center Dozens of Buddhist and other temples	Catholic mass held in existing parishes 3 Buddhist temples
Year city or neighborhood incorporated	Westminster, 1957	Dorchester, 1822

Sources: 2000 census; interviews; organizational documents. The Vietnamese American population figure represents the population of Los Angeles–Riverside–Orange County and of Boston–Worcester–Lawrence (CMSAs).

To argue that place is an essential component of community is to bring a sociospatial analysis to bear on the process of community-building. Now, not only are Vietnamese Americans building communities in two different regions of the country, they are also *making place*: territorializing, regulating, and symbolizing in order to give each place a distinct set of boundaries, functions, and identities. Place-making boosts community. In the chapters that follow, Vietnamese Americans wrestle with and through place so that their communities may respond to racialization, the production and construction of dominant memories, and marketplace multiculturalism.

Chapter 2   Q: Nationality? A: Asian.

STAYING VIETNAMESE occurs on, and against, racialized terrain. In this chapter I focus on themes of race and racialization—and, by implication, the unmarked norm of whiteness—as they impact Vietnamese American social life. By making "race" an explicit component of my analysis and interpretation of Vietnamese American community-building and place-making in Orange County and Boston, I bring to the foreground issues that have not been analyzed in prior scholarship on Vietnamese Americans: among these are the racialization of the war in Viet Nam, the impact of the presence of ethnic Chinese in Vietnamese American places, and the relationship between race and place-making. As racialized minorities, Vietnamese are not considered "white" either on the official U.S. census or in social scientific discourse. Indeed, my fieldwork suggests that their inclusion into U.S. society requires that, collectively, they stay Vietnamese. Being "Vietnamese" qualifies their Americanness, signifying both racial and ethnic distinction. This chapter emphasizes the impact of racial formations not only on individual perspectives on community and identity but also on the contrasting patterns of Vietnamese American community-building and place-making between Orange County and Boston.

The Racialization of Ethnic Places

Treating Vietnamese American community and place in racial rather than ethnic terms requires a thoughtful and deliberate departure from sociological convention. Many influential mainstream social scientists still embrace ethnicity and the bootstrap model of upward mobility that accompanies the ethnic framework. Meanwhile, they relegate the concept of race to a physical/heritable component of ethnicity, reject race as an idea with popular resonance but no scientific merit, or reserve race as a topic concerning only African Americans.[1] If America is racist, they might argue, it is so only for the "darkest" Americans; as a U.S. minority group that at this historical juncture is understood to be better-than-black but not-quite-white, Asians are thought to be somehow beyond racism.[2] Consequently, putting the terms "race" and "place" together brings to mind black ghettos and Latino barrios, but never Asian ethnic enclaves. This social scientific reticence to deal with the broad empirical realities of race is buttressed by political discourse, where a false logic of egalitarianism paraded by neoconservatives of color has convinced the larger public that racism is a thing of the distant past.[3] Importantly, the idea that Asian Americans epitomize the nation's model minority often serves as "proof" that racism is over.[4] To some readers, therefore, the application of a racial frame to Vietnamese American place-making and community-building probably appears not only unnecessary, but ideologically biased and therefore without scientific merit.

Yet decades of respected scholarship in the interdisciplinary fields of African American studies, Asian American studies, and recently, American studies underscore the centrality of race for U.S. social life and the construction of a U.S. national identity, in both the past and the present.[5] What is race?[6] In this chapter, "race" refers to a produced and constructed category that marks one group of human bodies apart from another. Race turns into racism when those bodily markings are treated as signs of innate inferiority or superiority and serve as the justification for discursive and material practices of exclusion at successively larger scales of social space: families, communities, cities, the nation. The origins of race and racism as we know them today in the United States go back to the transatlantic slave trade of the fourteenth century.[7] Racism is observable today not only in empirical patterns of racial segregation, but also at a more fundamental level, where U.S. collective notions of citizenship, freedom, and humanity still reflect a deeply racialized understanding of the world.[8]

A basic assumption of this chapter is that while we prefer to blame race and racism on a handful of ignorant and prejudiced people, race and racism are perhaps more meaningfully described as entrenched social and historical facts, generated and preserved by complex interactions among the global economy, the nation-state, and social movements based in civil society. Put another way, the production and construction of racial categories in the United States may be seen as a consequence of shifts in global markets, war, annexation, and colonization, and as the outcome of policies regarding citizenship, immigration, property ownership, miscegenation, prisons, jobs, schools and housing, families, and reproductive rights.[9]

Simultaneously, race is also produced and constructed by groups of individuals in civil society, for example through organized attempts to secure protection against discrimination in jobs, housing, or schools, or through basic programs such as voter registration, bilingual education, or hate crimes legislation. Whether these efforts originate at the level of the state or of civil society, Winant (1995) refers to the efforts to assign meaning to race, and to redistribute resources along racial lines, as "racial projects."

In pushing race forward as an analytical category for the Vietnamese American experience, I underscore the extent to which Vietnamese American community-building and place-making involve, or respond to, racial projects. However, I do not mean to do away with ethnicity, or to disregard the many critical insights provided by an ethnic framework. Indeed, ideas about ethnicity—a reference to "shared beliefs, norms, values, preferences, in-group memories, loyalties, and consciousness of kind" (See and Wilson 1992, 224)—are fundamental to community-building and place-making in Little Saigon and Fields Corner.[10] However, ethnicity-as-assimilation not only offers a partial frame, it is a factually inaccurate one.[11]

In Zhou and Bankston's study of the adaptation of Vietnamese American children in Louisiana, the authors focus on the internal characteristics of the Vietnamese community in Versailles, a neighborhood of New Orleans. They find that "an ethnic identity based on social relations with other Vietnamese serves as a springboard for upward mobility by means of education" (1998, 235). In their conclusions, they theorize that for young Vietnamese Americans, ethnicity "provides an alternative to the oppositional culture of low-income neighborhoods" (236). The authors do not examine ethnicity in the surrounding black or white communities, nor do they offer a theory or definition of race. They remark only that intertwined with class inequality, racism stands as an obstacle to educational success.[12] Unfortunately, this conclusion reinforces the prevailing ideas about a deficit of culture qua ethnicity among blacks on the one hand, and an absence of investment in racial privilege on the part of whites on the other.

The ethnicity framework is also prevalent, and misleading, in other contexts. Vietnamese Americans in Boston are often compared to the Irish or Italian immigrants of the early twentieth century. In certain limited ways, the comparison holds: both Vietnamese and Irish generally arrived penniless, were unaccustomed to Anglo-Protestant culture, and huddled together in neighborhood enclaves in a time-limited effort to protect and support themselves. After several generations, the Irish joined the "mainstream," read: white, middle-class, suburban America. But the comparison between post-1975 refugees and immigrants from Viet Nam and Boston's classic European immigrants removes from view several important facts. First, the rise into the middle class of the early European immigrants depended partly, of course, on hard work and individual effort. But what turned individual effort into a solid income that could support families was the availability of well-paying, unionized manufacturing jobs, which were quickly disappearing by the time Vietnamese refugees arrived in the late 1970s.[13]

Second, refugees enter U.S. society under much different circumstances and expectations than immigrants. Often, refugees are described as "forced" as opposed to "voluntary" migrants, but the idea of free choice overlooks the fact that the available options have been created by structures and patterns that are outside of most people's control. Still, immigrants are more likely to be people with some means to move, while refugees must move regardless of their means. Furthermore, as people fleeing political persecution, refugees deal with an added dimension of social and psychological fear and trauma.[14]

Third, the Irish and Italians came to America as Europeans who were eventually extended the privileges of whiteness. The long and difficult historical process by which they became white reveals that "race" is in fact produced and constructed as certain groups gain access to the cash value of white identity at the expense of those designated as not white.[15] In contrast, the "Orientalization" of the Vietnamese—beginning with the production and construction of Viet Nam as a site of racial Otherness for the West—set them up centuries ago for a different racial path they would eventually follow as refugees in post–civil rights America. The ethnicity framework gives rise to a mirage of commonality between Europeans and Asians in America that does not apprehend the significance of whiteness as an invisible and entrenched racial category, a category that organizes U.S. social life even today.[16]

All this is not to say that the larger panethnic construct of "Asian America" offers an easy or automatic solution to racism or Orientalism. In certain contexts, the label Asian American is much less meaningful than other possible labels, such as that of "political refugee," which would group Vietnamese together with Cubans, Haitians, and Soviet Jews. Worse, one could argue that any gestures toward Asian America generate "racial thinking," complete with its own problematic notions of fixed and essentialized Asian qualities (Gilroy 2000). Linda Vo and Rick Bonus (2002) write eloquently on the many forces and factors that constantly diversify and reshape Asian America, emphasizing that Asian American community narratives are often rife with their own inequitable and incommensurate categories. As Diep Khac Tran, a queer Vietnamese American writer and owner of the Good Girl Dinette (offering Vietnamese and American comfort food) in Los Angeles, put it to me many years ago, "It seems as if we [as Asian American activists] are conjuring up the idea of racial unity," with the unfortunate result that we deny the complexity of our intragroup experiences.

Indeed, Asian American panethnicity is a purposeful strategy for empowerment, but one that is extremely complicated to carry out given today's demographic realities (Espiritu 1992). A central point of this chapter is that in Orange County and Boston, Vietnamese Americans frame themselves as "Asian American" not because there is any sort of natural, biological, or inevitable connection with other Asian ethnic groups, but because doing so is a way to access resources, power, and visibility in a specific spatial and historical context. To overlook the operation of racial categories would be to miss a core theme of Vietnamese American community-building and place-making.

The title of this chapter—"Q: Nationality? A: Asian."—comes from a statement made by one of my contacts in Fields Corner. After each interview in Boston and Orange County, I asked each person to note their ethnicity and nationality, along with seven other items, on a one-page questionnaire. I purposefully did not define "nationality" or any other terms so that I might tap into some of the definitions that prevail within the community. The most frequent answers were Vietnamese (for ethnicity) and American (for nationality), the response I expected given the common-sense definitions of ethnicity as heritage and nationality as legal citizenship. I did not interview any mixed-race Vietnamese. But one respondent wrote "Asian" for nationality. This response, as a statistical outlier, obviously does not represent a norm. Yet the equation of "nationality" with "Asian" serves as a provocative entry point for a discussion of race as a socially constructed category that informs, facilitates, and circumscribes Vietnamese American community-building and place-making. It should go without saying that her answer seems like nonsense since there is no nation called "Asia." As she put her answer on the sheet I had given her, she explained to me: "I can't put 'American' because I don't have blonde hair or blue eyes." Other researchers have found similar statements by young Vietnamese Americans, but they frame those as conflicts not of nation and race but of "culture" and "identity." For example, Freeman quotes a first-wave undergraduate student who writes: "If one were to ask a Vietnamese in Vietnam if I were Vietnamese, he or she would undoubtedly say no. . . . If one were to ask a Caucasian in the United States if I were American, the answer would still be no" (1995, 112). Zhou and Bankston quote a high school student who tells them: "Looking cool doesn't make you an American. A typical American is blonde, blue-eyed, white, and beautiful. I can never be an American" (1998, 162). Her boyfriend reinforces this: "She's right. An American is *white*" (my italics). By framing these statements in terms of conflicts that are internal to the Vietnamese American community, the larger implications for the racialization of U.S. national identity—and for the normalization of whiteness in U.S. society as a whole—are essentially dismissed.

The notion that someone's "nationality" can be traced to a place called "Asia," and furthermore that if a person calls oneself "Asian" they cannot be American because they lack the required Nordic or Teutonic features, are ideas that reveal much about nationhood and race in Vietnamese America and in the United States more generally. Unlike their white or black counterparts who also have migrant pasts, Asian Americans are often treated as "perpetual foreigners" despite a well-documented history of contribution and connection to the United States. My fieldwork uncovered many other instances in which the concepts "race" and "nation" were conflated, and in which the categories "Asian" and "American" were pitted against each other, making "Asian American" seem an impossible oxymoron.

I found the field was replete with racial issues even when I did not specifically ask about race or racism. Race means many things to Vietnamese American community leaders. Race can just mean skin color, and often race is simply a matter of white—or not white. Color is usually linked in a specific way to nationhood and citizenship. When Vietnamese American leaders refer to "Americans," they usually mean white Americans rather than Asian Americans, African Americans, or Latinos. However, context is everything. When the leaders were differentiating themselves from me, sometimes they called me "American," a gesture to my cultural identity rather than my color. Race can also refer to panethnicity, the idea that immigrants from Asia constitute a unified group, Asian Americans. Race can be an intensification of ethnic difference, as in the controversy over the term "Asian" versus "Chinese." More often, race is interpreted as an ugly term that signals conflict, while ethnicity is a gesture to consensus and harmony.

"Vietnam": An Era, a War, a Country

In the U.S. public imagination, "Vietnam" is, first and foremost, a war—not a country.[17] Vietnam is very much in the forefront of our minds today as a gesture to a war without end. In her innovative analysis of Maya Lin's Vietnam Veterans Memorial in Washington D.C., Marita Sturken (1997) observes that the dominant collective memory of the U.S. War in Viet Nam excludes any references to Vietnamese people. This point serves as an important theme for Vietnamese American community-building and place-making in chapter 4. Vietnam is a gesture also to an era in which dominant categories of nationhood, race, gender, and citizenship were fundamentally shaken, and in which grassroots movements all over the world redefined social and political norms (Buzzanco 1999).

Replete with alibis for prolonged intervention, the Vietnam War racialized the Vietnamese people as "gooks" living in "Indian country" (Shalom 1993). The racial thinking that helped policy makers to justify the war had a lasting personal impact on the Asian American soldiers who were mistaken for the enemy or required to serve as target practice for their platoons because of their physical features (Kiang 1991; Yip 1995). As Asian American civilians increasingly saw themselves in the faces of "the enemy," awareness of their own racial commonalities grew, fueling social movements and panethnic solidarity (Espiritu 1992; Omatsu 1994). Meanwhile, hundreds of African Americans joined the antiwar movement under the slogan "The Viet Cong Never Called Us Nigger." This statement was made famous by the champion boxer Muhammad Ali. Thus, some African Americans delivered their own searing commentary on the relationship between racism at home and U.S. imperialism abroad (Young 1991).

At the chaotic close of the war, over one hundred thousand allied Vietnamese—military and government officials, people employed by U.S. corporations, and their families—fled Vietnam, fearing death under communism. About half of those were escorted out of the country by the U.S. government. In the following years, the Ford administration cast Vietnamese refugees in the same light as Hungarians and Cubans—"people who voted with their feet against communism and came to America in search of freedom and democracy"—an image that meshed cold war ideology with the dominant narrative of immigrant assimilation. Yet the American public was not so quick to switch gears from hating the Vietnamese enough to wage a brutal war against them to suddenly loving and embracing them as future U.S. citizens. Resettlement policy purposefully attempted to disperse the refugees in order to avoid exacerbating widespread nativism and racism at a time of high national unemployment and limited social services, thus lessening the impact of absorbing so many Vietnamese very quickly into U.S. society (Loescher and Scanlan 1986, 112–15).

The "calculated kindness" underlying refugee resettlement policy evidently has served the cold-war aspirations of the ruling class—to "rescue" U.S. allies in Vietnam from communism and to showcase Vietnamese success in America as "a triumph for democracy"—but on the ground level of U.S. society, many Vietnamese Americans are still subject to prejudice and racial lumping. In Orange County and Boston, the impulse to "stay Vietnamese" is fueled in part by a perception that America is a racist society and that Vietnamese immigrants and refugees, no matter how suburbanized or successful, will never fully exercise the privileges of whiteness.[18] Their efforts to reassemble in specific sites such as Little Saigon and Fields Corner signal a concerted effort to resist both racism and the pressures to abandon their identities by articulating and preserving a social and spatial attachment to Vietnameseness.

The "racial faultlines" in Orange County and Boston have their own deep and complex origins, and thus pose distinct challenges and opportunities for Vietnamese American community-building and place-making.[19] Orange County's racial demographics have changed significantly in recent decades, as chapter 1 mentions, but the dominant culture of the place has been slow to reflect those changes. Once the quintessential suburb for the white working class, popular accounts of Orange County such as the TV series *The O.C.* bring to mind spacious oceanfront villas belonging to the superadvantaged and alienated megarich.

Similarly, the image that Orange County—its politicians, developers, and boosters—strives to promote is exclusive, rich, coastal, and often, lily-white. Boston's racial demographics, too, have shifted dramatically since the 1980s. But while Orange County specializes in a glitzy and glamorous style of racial and cultural homogeneity, Boston's recent past is filled with gritty and violent demonstrations against court-ordered busing, student protests against the Vietnam War, and the upheaval and displacement of poor communities due to urban renewal, which affected native-born minorities and European immigrants. Nowadays, Boston's politicians, developers, and boosters celebrate their multiculturalism, touting especially the newer immigrant communities as a sign of the city's cultural sophistication and tolerance of diversity.

Vietnamese American place-making in Orange County and Boston comprise racial projects in at least two ways. On the one hand, their place-making staves off white racism by providing a racial safety zone. There, racial lumping and xenophobia are marginal rather than dominant practices. On the other hand, their place-making provides an alternative cultural and political space for Vietnamese Americans in which the resources and experiences of a panethnic Asian American community may be incorporated in particular ways into Vietnamese-specific community-building and place-making. Little Saigon differs from Fields Corner not only in scope and intensity relative to each other, but also in Little Saigon's notable capacity to define the meaning and significance of the larger category of Asian American panethnicity. For example, Vietnamese Americans in Little Saigon are influential in the public school system and in citywide politics in both Westminster and Garden Grove. They also have a strong say in the content and uses of the Southeast Asian Archive and the Asian American studies program at the University of California, Irvine. In part, Little Saigon's influence over Asian America is a feature of relative population size, but other factors include the influence of preexisting Asian American panethnic networks and organizations and the absence of a competing place called Chinatown.

Orange County: "Because the Cover Is Vietnamese"

Existing narratives of Vietnamese American community growth note that among the difficulties of adjustment to contemporary Western society, new Vietnamese arrivals sometimes face prejudice and racial hatred.[20] But very few researchers expound upon Vietnamese Americans' encounters with racism or analyze the larger implications of racial exclusion, xenophobia and cultural discrimination, or threatened and actual violence on Vietnamese community-building. I concur with the Asian American scholars who observe that the Asian American experience with race and racism is diverse, complex, and covert (Vo and Bonus 2002). I had not intended to investigate whether or not racism was an issue for Vietnamese Americans in either Orange County or Boston. But in 1996, a young Vietnamese American man was brutally murdered in broad daylight in Tustin, an affluent white city in the southern portion of Orange County. His death became a landmark event in Asian American history and left deep—and often unacknowledged—wounds on the communities I studied.

On the morning of January 29, 1996, a janitor making the rounds discovered the body of a young Asian male on the tennis courts of Tustin High School. He had been stabbed multiple times, his throat was slashed from side to side, and his head had been stomped on. He was later identified as Thien Minh Ly, a former student at Tustin High School, and a recent graduate from UCLA and Georgetown University (Fusion Pictures 1998).

The murder of twenty-four-year-old Thien Minh Ly was the second blatant incident of racial violence directed against Asian Americans since

Vincent Chin was killed by disgruntled autoworkers in Detroit in 1982.[21] Thien's primary assailant, Gunnar Lindberg, was convicted of a hate crime by Orange County's district attorney and sentenced to death under California's capital punishment law. A month after the murder, Lindberg inadvertently gave himself away by writing a letter to a friend in a New Mexico prison that described his act in cold and clinical terms. Based on the letter and also on white supremacist paraphernalia found in their homes, Lindberg and his accomplice, Dominic Christopher, were arrested. Excerpts of the letter were published in several newspapers including the *Los Angeles Times* and the *Tustin Weekly*. Significantly, both papers were reluctant to view the murder as a "hate crime," casting it instead as a robbery. The *Tustin Weekly* also omitted key phrases from Lindberg's text, such as "I killed a JAP," presumably hoping to avoid exacerbating racial tensions (Pham 1996).

I am not interested in engaging the controversy over whether specific acts of murder should or should not be labeled "hate crimes." According to federal law, a hate crime must first be a crime and then have an added component of "bias." The most common biases are race, sexual orientation, and religion. Hate crimes require enhanced sentencing. Each state and municipality has its own laws about hate crimes. Despite the media's initial instincts to downplay the racist motivation in Thien's death, the district attorney designated it a hate crime. Asian American community leaders publicized the incident as an example of racial hatred. From at least three perspectives—that of the district attorney, of the Asian American community, and of the killer himself—Thien died because of his ascribed racial identity.

The killing is an extreme instance of "racial lumping," the act of ignorantly lumping together all Asian ethnic groups. In theory, racial lumping leads to "protective pan-ethnicity" (Espiritu 1992, 7). In fact, racial lumping can lead to a protective panethnic political agenda as well as an imaginative panethnic cultural discourse. Within a couple of years after Thien's murder, I attended a performance of *My Country*, a play written by the Los Angeles–based playwright Chay Yew and performed by Cornerstone Theater, a theater troupe that specializes in community-based productions. Staged in an elementary school in Los Angeles's Chinatown, the show gave a playwright's version of Asian American history. In one stirring and somewhat bizarre scene, Vincent Chin's mother, Lily Chin, conversed face-to-face with Gunnar Lindberg, Thien Minh Ly's white supremacist assailant. Until she died in 2002, "Mrs. Chin" was well known in Asian America for her unswerving determination to obtain "justice for Vincent." Her efforts were in vain, since Vincent's killers were not sentenced to prison and never paid one cent of their puny $3,000 fine. I found the scene remarkable for its simple juxtaposition of two well-known events, which suggests to me that Asian American panethnicity can do more than hammer home a political orthodoxy about racism, but can also generate a panoply of new cultural ideas for Asian Americans.

In 1997, I attended three events at the University of California, Los Angeles that were organized by Vietnamese American students: Vietnamese Culture Night (VCN), a screening of the documentary film *Letters to Thien,* and a candle-light vigil. UCLA is among the nation's leading centers for Asian American student organizing and faculty research. Consequently, staging an event at UCLA gives it a certain status within Asian America. I do not know if Vietnamese American students at UC Irvine, the campus that is closer socially and geographically to Little Saigon, held similar events in Thien's honor.

The tenor of VCN was generally light, although a large exhibit about Thien in the lobby of the auditorium cast a somber note over the evening. Several weeks later, about three hundred people attended the film screening. After the film, around fifty people joined in a small candlelight vigil near Royce Hall. Thien's younger brother and sister spoke sadly, briefly, and with great purpose, as if the death of their brother had propelled them into a personal mission for the Vietnamese American community. The gathering closed with a tender song, "Va Toi Cung Yeu Em" (And I Also Love You).

At VCN, I commented to one of the people I was with, a Vietnamese American man and recent graduate of UC Irvine, that only a few of my contacts in Little Saigon had anything to say about Thien, even when I asked their opinion directly. "Were they older?" my friend asked. His explanation was that the older generation refrains from discussing topics like Thien's murder in order not to fan the flames of conflict with mainstream society. They feel that if the younger generation gets too angry, they will take to the streets and make things even worse for the whole community. According to this train of thought, the younger generation is more politically engaged than the older generation because the older generation is more compliant and more fearful of confrontation. Asian American politics are gaining scholarly attention, and the changing attitudes toward political engagement across immigrant generations are of particular interest. My fieldwork suggests that differences in attitudes across the various waves of immigration and age groups can be explained largely in terms of the availability of community resources and perceived opportunities for change. Two leaders from the older generation spoke frankly with me about racism.

Whereas their young counterparts at VCN are engaged at least in a marginal way with Asian American networks and organizations at UCLA, these older leaders are perhaps too deeply enmeshed in Little Saigon to develop connections to a larger panethnic social movement. Consequently, their thoughts on racism are framed in terms of personal survival and professional competence.

Mrs. Lan Le was in her fifties when I spoke to her in 1996. In Viet Nam, Mrs. Lan taught at a music conservatory. Forced to leave Viet Nam in 1978 because of her husband's ties to the military, she ended up in Orange County as a key figure in the preservation and promotion of traditional Vietnamese music. During the day, she earned a paycheck as a family counselor, teaching parents to talk about sex with their kids. In a matter-of-fact voice that brought to mind Dr. Ruth, the famous TV sex therapist, Mrs. Lan made sure to tell me, "Not just Vietnamese have this problem. All parents don't know about talking about sex." She shared with me the many insights into the assimilation process she gained through her day job, especially the conflicts between American and Vietnamese culture.

> LAN LE: When the children forgot the tradition, they will Americanize.
> *What does that mean, for you?*
> LAN LE: They will not have any connection with the culture. They will become disobedient. Maybe they have a conflict between parents and children. Our job is to make the family be happy together. We teach them become capable parenting.
> *For example? They have to live at home. . . .*
> LAN LE: Like, to give order. Beat them. Yell at them. Instead of explain what's wrong or right. But most of the parent give order. Kids today, if they know you give them order, they don't do it. I teach them how to make kids cooperate.
> *That seems like an American approach.*
> LAN LE: Yeah, but you know, no choice! The kids is growing here. They have to go to America. But they still keep their tradition, respect the parents, support the grandparents, eat their own food. Make them more noticeable. They know two cultures, they speak two languages. And they be proud!

One of Mrs. Lan's music students is a relative of Thien, so I asked for comments about Thien's death.

> LAN LE: Why you want to talk about that?
> *Because some people think he was killed because he was a student leader. But other people think it was just a random thing.*

LAN LE: Random thing?

Yeah, it didn't have to do with his being Vietnamese. They think he's just Asian, they don't care whether he's Vietnamese or not. What do you think about that?

LAN LE: It's not mean that he Vietnamese he's been beaten. But because he is not the white, that's all. That night, you know the one who beat him up, meets someone Hispanic or Chinese, whatever, they beat him up. Because not the white.

According to Mrs. Lan, Thien died because he was not white. He might have been killed if he had been "Hispanic" or Chinese; his Vietnamese identity was not the motivating factor. In this context, "Hispanic" is a deeply racialized term although according to the official U.S. census, people of Hispanic or Latino ancestry can be of any race. Mrs. Lan's argument that if Thien had been white, he would not have been a target for white supremacists provides an important, and often overlooked, insight into racism and the unmarked privileges of whiteness. Peggy McIntosh (2002) asserts that white people keep all sorts of tools, passports, credit cards, codes, and keys in an "invisible knapsack" that protect them from dangerous incidents such as that faced by Thien Minh Ly.[22]

Framing Thien's murder in terms of the unseen advantages of whiteness rather than simply in terms of the victimization of Vietnamese puts the racialization of Asian ethnic groups into a broader context that potentially takes into consideration the historical construction of whiteness as an assumed aspect of U.S. national identity. Like many Americans, Mrs. Lan equates nationality and race, and emphasizes that the "cover," meaning physical appearance, is more important than "what's inside," because even complete assimilation cannot change that cover. In the end, Mrs. Lan invokes God, perhaps because she feels racism is an inescapable aspect of life in America.

Do you feel you have to identify as Asian American, because that's how you get seen?

LAN LE: Asian American is still Asian! Do you believe me that? I told my brother, he said, I am American. I said, No! You 100% Vietnamese! Who tell you, you are American. Just you tell you.

Why do you say that?

LAN LE: The cover . . . because they don't see the inside. The cover is Vietnamese. No matter what inside you're American. That's why Thien Minh Ly been killed. If the outside been white, I really don't know the truth. Why he killed. Because the letter, you know, he said he just killed an Asian.

I think he called him a Jap, too.

LAN LE: Any Asian, any colored people. Just keep the simple life. Always pray to God. Live near God. Let God protect you. Do something for the people. That's all.

For a variety of reasons, Mrs. Lan might be more sensitive to prejudice than other Vietnamese Americans. But even some of the most thick-skinned leaders I met feel that they are not immune from racial categorization. Mr. Alex Tran, like many of the people I interviewed, is often featured in the English-language media as the personification of the immigrant success story. In preparing to meet Mr. Alex, I read several of those interviews and tried to develop questions that would elicit more than a "canned" response. At one point in our conversation, the topic naturally turned to racism.

ALEX TRAN: It is very much more difficult to do business when you are a minority in this country.

Because of racism? Or something else?

ALEX TRAN: Yes. Racism.

Has that affected you?

ALEX TRAN: Uh . . . for me, if you asked whether it's really affected me, yes.

Huh. That's hard to believe because you are so successful.

ALEX TRAN: It just makes you have to work harder. . . .

To prove yourself?

ALEX TRAN: . . . waste a lot more time.

Waste time doing what?

ALEX TRAN: Beating their brains out.

You have a way with words. Can you give me an example so that it's not only an image. I can't imagine you having to approach a corporation who is forward-thinking and then having to, you know, beat their brains out around racism.

ALEX TRAN: There are more bureaucracy and more red tape toward minority to government than it is to an Anglo.

You've seen that? Or you feel that?

ALEX TRAN: Oh, I've seen it.

So, maybe working Asia is just easier?

ALEX TRAN: Yeah, I would say so.

Mr. Alex's pugilistic attitude suggests that racial categories are a real obstacle even among elites, and that economic success has not made him "white." As far as I know, the racialized dimension of Mr. Alex's rags-to-riches story is hardly ever told, either because he does not talk about it, or because journalists leave out those comments. He himself freely admits that Asians indulge in intragroup hostilities that approximate racism in the United States. As he puts it, "it is different in Asia."

As an ethnic Chinese Vietnamese, Mr. Alex has been the object of racial thinking within Little Saigon, which I will describe later in this chapter and again in a different context in chapter 5. Entrepreneurialism among ethnic Chinese has led to heated debates about the cultural identity of Vietnamese American places, and specifically whether the use of the term "Asian" refers to "Chinese" rather than to all Asian cultures, which would of course include Vietnamese. The racial categorization of Vietnamese Americans as "Asian" makes the controversial presence of ethnic Chinese within the Vietnamese American community a puzzling sociological issue. How do the two ethnic groups coexist in one place? What kinds of boundaries—social, spatial, historic, symbolic—keep the two groups separate and distinct? Under what conditions do their cultural differences create competition for scarce resources, and when do panethnic similarities overshadow those differences? The answers lie in the specific, local contexts in which Vietnamese Americans create the organizations, networks, resources, and symbols that comprise their communities; these contexts will unfold as subsequent chapters explore other dimensions of community-building and place-making.

Boston: "Together in Our Differences"

In Boston, Vietnamese American community leaders express their awareness of race primarily in terms of panethnic solidarity, that is, in a high degree of involvement in Asian American networks and institutions. My Boston interviews do not contain references to Thien Minh Ly since most of them were conducted prior to the incident. After Thien was killed, however, two Asian American organizations in Boston wrote about his death in their newsletters: the Asian American Resource Workshop (AARW) and the Coalition for Asian Pacific American Youth (CAPAY). In CAPAY's publication, a Vietnamese American high school student named Duong Phan cites the role of the Vietnamese Community of Orange County (VNCOC) in forming a national Thien Minh Ly Ad Hoc Committee. Phan comments on the hidden issue of race:

> As a nation, we convince ourselves that race is no longer an issue. In actuality it is always there only swept under the carpet until one day an incident like this happens. Even then we try to come up with other reasons for the murder besides the obvious one. Why do we do this? The word "race" haunts us from our past. The United States does not want a big commotion about race, a question presumably solved years ago. . . . Foreigners believe us to be the country that holds a welcome mat and carries a friendly smile for all. Once people get inside the country, they will confront the issues. (1996, 4)

This statement articulates an emerging racial consciousness that is rife with interesting contradictions. Addressing Boston's Asian American youth, Phan refers to a nation that is trying to forget about race by sweeping the issue under the carpet. Phan thinks that the murder of Thien Minh Ly obviously points to racism. Phan says race "haunts us from our past," but if this is a gesture to the period of genocide, slavery, and pre–civil rights struggles, Vietnamese were not yet a part of this national past. Thien's death has made the Vietnamese community "distraught," but the United States "does not want a big commotion about race." How can Vietnamese join the national present? Just being "inside the country" is not enough to make Vietnamese into Americans. They need to "confront the issues" and to actively create a space from which the Vietnamese experience of racism may be incorporated into the national identity, a process this book refers to as Vietnamese American community-building and place-making.

The notion that race is an issue that most people try to avoid is echoed by one of the younger leaders who works with Viet-AID, a community development corporation based in Fields Corner. Over the years that I conducted the Boston interviews, Mr. Anh Thach moved around from various social service organizations and university-based programs, including the Vietnamese American Civic Association (the mutual assistance agency), before he became a part of Viet-AID. As far as I know, he is the only leader who has studied formally the issue of community and community development. With regard to the multiethnic, multiracial composition of Fields Corner as a neighborhood, he said that race is an "ugly" term that refers to hostile relationships between various racial groups. "But if we talk about ethnicity, like talking about the Irish and the Vietnamese or Puerto Ricans, it means we want to all get along." By referring to the assimilation framework as "color blind," race-cognizant scholarship makes a similar statement: ethnicity allows people to gloss over systemic patterns of racism and white privilege, while race forces those issues out into the open.[23]

None of Boston's key Asian American networks or organizations is located in Fields Corner, although once the center was built at 42 Charles Street, apparently many Asian American events that might have otherwise occurred in Chinatown have been held there instead. In Boston's Asian American context, Fields Corner remains a site specifically associated with Vietnamese, while Chinatown or the University of Massachusetts, Boston have been sites for panethnic Asian American organizations including the AARW, CAPAY, the Institute for Asian American Studies, and the Center for Immigrant and Refugee Community Leadership and Empowerment (CIRCLE).

Mr. Hoa Nguyen has been a member of several Asian American and Vietnamese American organizations. One year, a local foundation featured him in their quarterly report where he related his personal experience of being racially taunted on the streets of Boston. "Go home, Japanese. Go home where you belong!" Mr. Hoa and several other leaders told me about an event that catalyzed a sense of community in victimhood—later transformed to action and pride—among Vietnamese Americans in 1992. At the annual Dorchester Day parade, city councilor Albert "Dapper" O'Neill was caught on a home video recorder looking at the Vietnamese storefronts on Dorchester Avenue. "It looks like Little Saigon. It makes you sick." Then he added, "I'll be by here this afternoon to drop off the welfare checks." Many in Boston refer to this incident as a "wake-up call for Vietnamese."

By becoming vocal members of panethnic Asian American networks, Boston's Vietnamese Americans are better able to respond to the hostility and disdain that they suspect many non-Vietnamese feel. But in order to join Asian America, Vietnamese Americans must articulate their Vietnamese roots, making connections to Viet Nam—real, imagined, past, present, or future—just as their counterparts in Orange County would. Since the opportunities for strengthening Vietnamese American community in Boston depend on participation in and contribution to Asian American networks and organizations, Vietnamese American leaders must simultaneously reinforce their ethnic and panethnic affiliations.

Binh Ngo, now retired from his position as professor at a prestigious university in Boston, studied in the United States in the late 1960s and has lived in Boston for nearly thirty years. Although he is very knowledgeable about Vietnamese American issues and maintains an extensive personal archive of clippings, documents, mailing lists, and publications about Vietnamese in America, his interests have more to do with U.S. foreign policy than with Vietnamese community-building "on U.S. soil." Professor Binh is a U.S. citizen but a Vietnamese nationalist with an unwavering devotion to rebuilding a bridge to Viet Nam. To this, many of his exiled compatriots are adamantly opposed despite their claims to nationalism.

Professor Binh calls his approach to U.S.–Viet Nam relations a "peaceful" one. He sees three other approaches in the community: hard-liners (people who refuse to deal with Viet Nam at all), terrorists (extremists who advocate military action against Viet Nam), and those in disarray (resulting in the inability of warring factions to settle on a more reasonable middle-of-the-road approach). In Orange County, leaders who adopt Professor Binh's peaceful struggle approach in public are usually ostracized from Little Saigon or labeled as communist sympathizers. In Boston, Professor Binh finds more room for discussion, not because the community is necessarily more open, but because it is less closely regulated. These controversies matter for racialization because Vietnamese American leaders must develop some inroads to Asian American activities. But as Professor Binh puts it, "To be Asian, we must be Vietnamese." And to be Vietnamese, leaders must express some relationship to the homeland—a dilemma that I explore in another way in chapter 3.

Boston's Vietnamese American leaders make themselves comfortable in a variety of community settings, contextualizing their personal experiences of exclusion or discrimination in terms that extend beyond ethnicity or nationality. For example, Patty Vo associates herself with the Republican Party and with organizations directed toward the needs of refugees and immigrants, Vietnamese and otherwise. She is often featured in the local English-language press as a representative of the Vietnamese American community. She has traveled to Viet Nam, most recently for family reasons, and like other first-wave refugees her animosity toward Viet Nam does not preclude such trips. Her family background, her education at private U.S. universities, her personal charm and poise, and the access to elite circles of power in the city that all of this brings set her apart from most Vietnamese in Boston. Nevertheless, her political, economic, and cultural assimilation does not prevent her from describing herself as a "colored" person who sometimes shares a marginalized status with blacks and Hispanics in Boston, or a professional Asian American who must advocate for other Asian Americans who are less privileged than herself.

As a Vietnamese American leader, Ms. Vo finds it necessary to speak for or join various groups throughout the city, not just Vietnamese in Fields Corner. When I interviewed her in 1997, she described some of the exclusive behaviors that in a negative way reinforce her identity as an Asian American woman.

> PATTY VO: I am personally, I try to blend into the Republican women's group. You know how uneasy that is. I was introduced by an older member of the committee. It's a nonprofit group, very informal. They have their own network. I came to the meeting. I felt excluded. I thought maybe because I'm new and because they already know each other for years and here comes a stranger who expects us to be friendly or inclusive. So I invited myself in by doing that. It wasn't like they all try to reach out to me. At least this woman try to connect me, so that's an open door already. But on the other hand, the

friendliness, the welcoming from the other members, I haven't seen. Instead of getting mad, I feel . . . well, I'm stranger, what do I expect? Well, I expect that at least they are more cordial to me.

You mean on a personal level?

PATTY VO: Yeah, like "Hi, ___, thanks for joining us." Maybe they think you're a stranger. Maybe they think . . . I don't know . . . you're Asian? I don't know.

Were you the only Asian in the room?

PATTY VO: Oh, of course.

Was it all white?

PATTY VO: Of course.

Because it seems like there could be other Asians.

PATTY VO: No Asians. If there are Asians I would feel a little more . . . there was one black, another Hispanic. And the rest were all white. They're all older, so I'm younger. Maybe it has something to do with that.

Ms. Vo could probably have achieved a successful career without taking on the mantle of representing the Vietnamese American community. But in her capacity as a community spokesperson, she is continually reminded why, as an Asian American woman, she is "not in the house" with whites. Over the years, she has become invested in building a community that can speak for the range of constituencies to which she belongs.

PATTY VO: [Racism] has nothing to do with Republican or non-Republican. It has to do with the big picture, Asians are invisible. That there are stereotypes out there. In my job, we have gone through diversity leadership training. Each member write down our stereotypes about others, be it white, black, Hispanic, Asian, Indian and gender issues, male, female. Basically that. We jot down our thoughts about others. A lot of the non-Asians put down the stereotypes of the Asians that I mentioned to you. Math-inclined, passive, passive-aggressive. . . .

Is this a stereotype that they have even though they know people don't fit into it? Or is this really what they think?

PATTY VO: That's how they think about Asians. Yeah, take it or leave it. You can't change that reality. That's why you're not in the house with them. They don't want to be inclusive, because of those barriers that stop them from blending in with you. Let me tell you when it comes to promote an Asian to be manager, you have to think twice because of those stereotypes that one has on you. Even a couple of people [at my work] say, I have not seen Asian poor. There are lot Asian professionals, but I haven't seen poor. They're hardworking professionals. Yeah, that's another thing. It's good attribute, but at the same time it kills you, too. Oh, they're hard workers. Yeah, you feel good when you hear that. They're studious. Great. But you know what? They don't need help. It's the blacks who need help, it's the Hispanics. [The Asians] are fine. They're self-reliant, they don't need money. So when it comes to funding, you don't have a piece of the pie, as simple as that. When it comes to promotion, they're not at the table.

Even though it seems like you don't receive that treatment.

PATTY VO: I have opportunity because I work with people who understand the scenario and who want to change that. But I still have to prove myself, harder than my counterparts. OK. I'm being perceived as hard worker and that's why they gave me the opportunities.

Ms. Vo's experience of the cultural barriers she faces as a Vietnamese American professional in Boston reveals something about the white and Republican circles she travels in and also illustrates some of the contradictions in the racialization process that face post-1965 Asian America generally. In a memoir called *The Accidental Asian*, Eric Liu (1998) tells a personal tale that similarly revolves around the issues of professionalization and marginalization. But where Liu is comfortable enough thinking of his Chinese identity as something he can leave behind as he enters the world of white-collar and white men, Ms. Vo is almost too Vietnamese to let go of her roots. Staying Vietnamese in Boston's elite non-Vietnamese worlds forces Ms. Vo to deal with the "glass ceiling"—along with its associated racial stereotypes—that other Asian Americans in Boston also face.

Translating race to place in Boston means making Fields Corner a site of Vietnamese American community that is integrated into the city's Asian American networks and overall agenda. Historically, Fields Corner has been a tolerant neighborhood, according to two outside experts I met who are both native Bostonians. As one of them bluntly states: "The racists moved out in the 1950s [with block busting], and the tolerant residents stayed until they died there. The Vietnamese are replacing that generation." As racial minorities, Vietnamese Americans have been "tolerance-seekers" who look for places they can live and work without fear of racial prejudice or violence.

When Fields Corner emerged in the mid-1980s as a Vietnamese town, it became Boston's other Asian place. As places that include, welcome, or in some way represent Asian America, Fields Corner and Chinatown are the city's principal contenders. Back in 1975, Chinatown was the only Asian American place. Lincoln Le told me that when he arrived as part of the first wave, he was alone. The Boston phone book led him to new friends in Chinatown, single Vietnamese men who helped him find work and a place to live. Tom Chung (1995) describes Chinatown as an "Asian ethnic crossing" through which new Asian immigrants and refugees pass. Although some end up staying in Chinatown, most move on to "one-step up" communities such as Fields Corner or to wealthy suburbs such as Lexington.

Within Fields Corner, there is a certain lack of appreciation for Chinatown and for the particular model of economic growth that it represents. One businessperson told me that opening a storefront in Fields Corner means "you really feel Vietnamese." Another leader told me that Chinatown is not a model for development for Vietnamese Americans "because the Chinese always controlled business in Viet Nam." In fact, Fields Corner cannot become a Chinatown for reasons that are more structural and external than Vietnamese prejudices toward Chinese. Chapter 4 explores in more depth the creation of Fields Corner as a site of marketplace multiculturalism for whom a full-blown ethnic economy is not a feasible path of growth.

Viet-AID's initiative to design and construct an actual building that would physically house Vietnamese American community organizations in Fields Corner came out of a vision for community growth that fits with Boston's emphasis on neighborhoods as community. In this, Boston's Vietnamese American leaders make place in a different way than their counterparts in Orange County. Mr. Anh Thach explained why Viet-AID took up a neighborhood focus.

> *When you talk about developing a Vietnamese model, can you say in a sentence what's unique about the Vietnamese?*
>
> ANH THACH: No, what is not unique about the Vietnamese but I guess, the location is unique. So what you see is, unlike Chinatown or Orange County where you have a concentration of Vietnamese, then you can organize the Vietnamese community. And then you can talk exclusively on the Vietnamese community. But here we are dispersed. We are always a minority in the proper communities. So your organizing model has to be different. What is happening, what is important in the Vietnamese community can also be very important to the brother community. Take Fields Corner for example. Yeah, the Vietnamese community, the residents have their own needs. But also a lot of their needs are the needs of the regular residents or merchants. Fields Corner business district, street cleaning, parking, infrastructure, those are the needs of everyone. Those are the common issues. You have to be to organize based on these characteristics, these factors. How can you on the one hand organize the community, but on the other hand work in collaboration with the brother community?

The center opened in 2002, stamping Fields Corner much more visibly as a Vietnamese American place. Now the contradictions between Viet-AID's neighborhood focus and its dedication to Vietnamese Americans through-out the city of Boston have intensified somewhat, with Viet-AID staff who live in Fields Corner being particularly sensitive to the divergence between "neighborhood" (meaning all residents in Fields Corner) and "community" (meaning only Vietnamese) growth.

Conclusion

The assimilation framework that is usually applied to the Vietnamese American experience prevents an examination of the multitude of ways that Vietnamese American place-making and community-building confront race, racism, and the racialization process. From the racist portrayal of Vietnamese and all Asian people during the U.S. War in Viet Nam to the brutal murder-by-daylight of Thien Minh Ly in 1996, Vietnamese Americans have been subject to a racial lumping that demands recognition. This is not to revictimize a group already stigmatized by the stereotypes associated with refugees, but to acknowledge the complex operation of Orientalism and white supremacy as integral pieces of contemporary U.S. culture and politics. Taking a race-cognizant position vis-à-vis the Vietnamese American experience counters the prevailing dogma of "color blindness" and strives to position Vietnamese Americans in the larger historical context of U.S. racial categories.[24]

Because, as Mrs. Lan said regarding the motive behind Thien's killing, "the cover" is not white, Vietnamese like other Asian Americans cannot escape being grouped together according to racist and Orientalist categories. That does not mean that the creation of panethnic Asian alliances is either desirable or easy. In Little Saigon, the term "Asian" is viewed with suspicion by those who see ethnic Chinese as a cultural threat to an authentic Vietnamese identity. "Asian" in that context means Chinese, but the same term is read by outsiders as a neutral panethnic designation.

As in U.S. political discourse generally, the word race is an "ugly" term in Boston and refers to conflict, whereas the term "ethnicity" refers to neighborhoods and communities in which people from different back-grounds work together and get along. Viet-AID's efforts to fortify Fields Corner as a Vietnamese American place emphasize getting along with the "brother" communities represented by the racial and cultural diversity in the neighborhood.

Does Vietnamese American place-making provide a shield against racism? In part, yes. But the creation of Vietnamese American places also codifies in spatial terms the very same complex social processes of racialization that community-building already confronts. Vietnamese American place-making provides a racial safety zone, but it also marks the regional landscape in ways that make possible other forms of categorization that depend on race. The next two chapters elaborate upon the production and construction of memory, and on the packaging and selling of Vietnamese American identity, both of which inform and overlap with the racialization process.

Chapter 3   Like a Dream I Can Never Forget: Remembering and Commemorating the Past

STAYING VIETNAMESE requires a strategic and purposeful encounter not only with race and racialization, but also with the past. In many important ways, Vietnamese American community-building and place-making looks backward in time in order to confront racism in the present, to recuperate a sliver of Vietnamese nationalism, and to orient the next generations toward an Americanized future.[1] By giving the past—in the form of personal and collective memories and histories—a privileged place in this chapter, I do not mean to reanimate the stereotype of the sad, aging Vietnamese refugee who is psychologically and emotionally trapped in the pre-1975 era. Nor do I intend to evaluate anyone's accuracy or truthfulness in apprehending the past. Instead, I endeavor to give the production and construction of social memory and history a salient position in the conversation about Vietnamese American community-building and place-making.

Paying attention to memory and history in Vietnamese America is a project made necessary by the enormous and complex distortions of two "master narratives": American exceptionalism and immigrant assimilation. Because of the force of these master narratives in mainstream U.S. society, Vietnamese Americans face a specific and thorny kind of social and cultural marginalization. According to the narrative of American exceptionalism, the United States has never been an imperial or colonial empire but has always strived to spread freedom and democracy across the globe.[2] Thus, the U.S. mission in Viet Nam was not to suppress third-world nationalism but only to save the Vietnamese from communism.[3] When that mission failed, the U.S. government ostensibly did the next best thing by rescuing its allies and Americanizing them. The assimilation narrative takes exceptionalism as given and focuses on the mechanisms and pace of incorporation into mainstream U.S. society of the immigrants and refugees who presumably have escaped, or have been saved from, tyrannical regimes abroad.[4]

Vietnamese Americans are often applauded for their successful assimilation, with middle-class incomes, English-language usage, and suburbanization being major indicators of their success. To the extent that the Vietnamese presence in America is treated as a "substitute victory" for the U.S. defeat in Viet Nam, the applause is even louder for Vietnamese refugees than for other groups.[5]

Referring to an individual Vietnamese refugee's success in America is a way of achieving this substitute victory. In Ronald Reagan's 1985 State of the Union address, he singled out Jean Nguyen, a new graduate from West Point military academy:

> Ten years ago, a young girl left Vietnam with her family—part of the exodus that followed the fall of Saigon. They came to the United States with no possessions and not knowing a word of English. Ten years ago—the younger girl studied hard, learned English, and finished high school in the top of her class, and this May, May 22nd to be exact, is a big date on her calendar, just ten years from the time she left Vietnam she will graduate from the United States Military Academy at West Point. I thought you might like to meet an American hero named Jean Nguyen. . . . anything is possible in America if we have the faith, the will and the heart. (Baldwin 1985)

In saying that memory and history need more attention than they already get with regard to the Vietnamese American experience, I do not mean to ignore the very huge impact of certain public recollections of the U.S. War in Viet Nam on the American psyche.[6] Clearly, Reagan's gesture toward the Vietnamese—the text of which occurred under the heading "Role When Freedom Is Under Siege"—was intended to strike a chord of recognition among the electorate by evoking a commonly held view of the war. But that view is a partial, distorted, and exclusive rendition of history that does much more to shape a U.S. national identity than it does to illuminate the complexity of the Vietnamese American experience. Christian Appy goes so far as to say that the dominant collective memory of the war is "self-absorbed":

> So much postwar concern has been expressed about the recovery of American power and pride, with so little attention given to the wreckage that such imperial arrogance produced in Vietnam. What we really need to recover is a greater understanding of alternative, dissenting memories of the war, and a greater curiosity about Vietnam and the Vietnamese. (1999, B6)

From the exile point of view—a viewpoint specific to the older generation who arrived here as refugees and exemplified in the perspectives and experiences of ex–political detainees—a major goal of staying Vietnamese is to generate and preserve an awareness of Vietnamese history and culture for future generations of U.S.-born Vietnamese Americans. Having been displaced forever from their homeland, this group is particularly driven to assert their hatred and anger toward the Socialist Republic of Viet Nam. Thus their slant on Vietnamese history and culture is always stamped with anticommunism. But staying Vietnamese is also about correcting the distortions of the "arrogant" dominant U.S. perspective on "Vietnam." This is not to suggest that Vietnamese Americans hope to promote what Appy refers to as "alternative, dissenting memories" of the war, or that they have any intention of debunking the master narratives of exceptionalism or assimiliation. Indeed, as this chapter will demonstrate, sometimes Vietnamese American community-building and place-making—tinged by an exilic longing for home—assiduously uphold these narratives. In so doing, Vietnamese American leaders can at least create common ground with the U.S. public even if they do not regain the power or stature they once had in Viet Nam.

The fact remains that the dominant U.S. perspective on "Vietnam" as a war makes the actual history of Viet Nam the country and the experience of the Vietnamese people—on either side of that war—invisible and largely irrelevant to mainstream U.S. society. For that reason, a key dimension of Vietnamese American community-building and place-making involves wrestling with the past to produce and construct memory and history so that Vietnamese people in this country—as refugees, immigrants, and Americans—may be materially and discursively recognized.

Remembering as a Social and Spatial Practice

As Vietnamese American leaders in Boston and Orange County endeavor to turn their respective places into platforms for community, they confront an already existing public discourse—entrenched, solidified, and amplified through cultural and physical space in the form of public art, monuments, organizations, and events—that is dedicated to remembering and reassessing the Vietnam War from a non-Vietnamese vantage point. As a result, these leaders necessarily turn to community-building and place-making as avenues to assert and promote a distinctly "Vietnamese" take on that war, and on Vietnamese and U.S. history in general. Their hope is to create and bolster an exile identity for subsequent generations to embrace. This chapter focuses on the strategic memory projects that are designed in part to accompany, to challenge, and sometimes to replace the dominant collective discourse on the war. At the same time, these projects guide community-building and place-making within the Vietnamese American community.

The traces of memory that matter the most for this book are not so much the personal recollections of single individuals as they are the public, spatial manifestations of a collective consciousness about the past, or "social norms of remembrance" (Zerubavel 2003, 5). Strategic memory projects elaborate upon those normalized memories in a specific fashion. As carefully designed plans for thinking about the past, they select, preserve, or generate anew memories with an eye toward their potential uses in the present. Over time, strategic memory projects assist in orienting successive generations toward cultural practices that serve the multiple, simultaneous, and occasionally contradictory goals of staying Vietnamese.

Framing Vietnamese American community-building and place-making in terms of strategic memory projects brings to the foreground a voluminous discussion among scholars about the impact of the past on the construction of group identity in the present. Three aspects of that discussion are most relevant here: the "constructedness" and contested nature of memory; the Vietnam War as a "tangled memory" representing a dominant view of the past (Sturken 1997); and the spatial and platial dimensions of memory. More than anything else, this chapter emphasizes that staying Vietnamese requires establishing roots in the form of an actively remembered, though vigorously debated, past.

Constructed Memories

Memory is a practice, not a thing. In making this assertion, I draw upon a notion of "social memory" (Olick and Robbins 1998) that emphasizes the larger context in which we remember. We think of the past not as isolated hermits but as social, and socialized, people. Zerubavel refers to this process as "mnemonic socialization" (2003, 5), whereby as children and later as adults we follow rules about what to remember—and what to forget—in the context of our families, schools, neighborhoods, and nations. Those rules also tell us to relegate certain periods of time to "prehistory," that is, to a time no one needs to remember or, to put it more harshly, a time we must erase. These mnemonic guidelines reinforce the boundaries of community and nation by attaching a historical timeline to our sense of "self" and "other."

Part and parcel of this concept of memory as a social exercise is the distinction between official, government-sponsored accounts of the past—what we usually are given as history—and unofficial, local, or vernacular accounts, which I call personal memory. According to U.S. history, the War in Viet Nam ended in 1975 as government troops withdrew from Saigon. But according to the personal memories of veterans on both sides, of their families, of a people living on a land torn apart by napalm and Agent Orange, and of those seeking refuge in places such as Little Saigon and Fields Corner, the war still rages into the present. Social memory lies somewhere in the gray zone between official and personal accounts of the past.

I purposefully overlook the extent to which anyone remembers the past truthfully. The task of re-creating what happened before now is naturally laden with problems of selectivity, change, and "missing data."[7] I focus instead on the debate and discussion around the images and narratives that animate and reinforce social memory, regardless of whether or not anyone can prove their accuracy. My research shows that the struggle to piece together a coherent sense of the past through strategic memory projects is an essential element of Vietnamese American community-building and place-making.[8]

Social memories are inevitably caught up in relations of power and powerlessness. This means that who remembers what is not only an interactive event, but also one shaped and influenced by larger patterns of inequality in society. As a result of these patterns, some groups in the community have more access to the production of social memory than others. How can access to memory production—a concept that has no readily discernible boundaries—be restricted? Is it possible to cordon off a section of time and prevent people from going there, even inside their own heads? This chapter says yes, because strategic memory projects require and expend social and spatial resources and investments. Therefore, some restrictions are possible and even necessary, and some groups do exercise control over the practice of memory—or at least seek to do so.

Treating memory, and more specifically strategic memory projects, as tools deployed by Vietnamese American leaders to shape the contours of community and place makes a significant departure from an assimilationist approach to the immigrant experience. Indeed, when the assimilation narrative is in full throttle, immigrants arrive on U.S. shores soaked in memory: their family names, sense of self, and relationship to community all refer to the past. To be "reborn" as Americans, they must dry themselves off, releasing those memories and the cultures of their homeland. In the same step, they embrace modernity, individualism, and progress. To the extent that memory-making involves a trip into the past, memories and modernity do not mix.

This is not to say that researchers who are influenced by an assimilation model do not recognize the impact of memories—especially bad memories of the flight from communism—on Vietnamese American communities. For example, James Freeman (1989) puts into print the thoughts and feelings of Vietnamese refugees who settled into communities in central California in the 1980s. During that period, the prevalence of anti-Asian hate crimes rose; many of those acts targeted recent immigrants and refugees from Southeast Asia suspected of stealing jobs and lowering wages. Showing Vietnamese as humans immobilized by a complex grief was one way to intervene into the dehumanizing stereotypes and popular misconceptions that surrounded them. But this portrayal, though sympathetic, leaves intact the idea that over time, success in America requires abandoning the cultures and histories that once defined their communities.

In a context where Vietnamese are pitted against other racial minorities, the past can become part of a narrative of cultural values that are ostensibly superior to those of native-born minorities, particularly blacks. David Palumbo-Liu (1999) elaborates upon the intricate logistical maneuvers by which the idea of Asian Americans as a "model minority" reinvigorates American exceptionalism. References to "tradition," especially Confucian traditions that demand obedience to authority and individual sacrifice for the collective good, end up meshing conveniently with a broader politicized discourse about Asian Americans as upstanding citizens who succeed in mainstream society without government assistance. Shielded from view are the many ways that Vietnamese and other Asian immigrants have drastically changed their mysterious traditions in order to survive in their new U.S. settings. For example, Nazli Kibria (1993) strikes a blow against the notion that Vietnamese survive and succeed in America because they hang on to tradition. Instead, she demonstrates that Vietnamese families made important changes in gender roles and expectations that allowed them to accommodate, among other things, the demands of the local labor market.

The production and construction of memory for Vietnamese Americans is therefore much more complicated than just remembering for themselves what happened in Viet Nam before 1975. Strategic memory projects involve capturing or creating certain discourses about the past, and integrating them into community-building and place-making efforts. Rather than being stuck on the past, then, Vietnamese Americans are employing memory practices in particular ways so as to reinforce strategically their own rules about who belongs within the boundaries of community and place.

Tangled Memories of "Vietnam"

Memories of the Vietnam War are so deeply inscribed on the U.S. national consciousness that the word "Vietnam" hardly refers to the country at all or to its people, but to the war, to its immediate aftermath, and to a much longer period of postwar history that "transformed American life" and with which most people have yet to "come to terms" (Allen and Long 1991; Buzzanco 1999). Represented and reenacted in films, fiction, memoirs, photographs, political speeches, commemorative events, monuments, and memorials, U.S. memories of the Vietnam War have become an essential part of the nation's cultural and political terrain.

To speak of a "dominant" memory of the Vietnam War is to acknowledge the glaring absence of Vietnamese people from the U.S. recollection of the past—whether as military allies, Viet Cong, communists, war victims, refugees, or the inhabitants of Viet Nam. Marita Sturken writes:

> [T]he narrative of the Vietnam War as told in the United States foregrounds the painful experience of the American Vietnam veteran in such a way that the Vietnamese people, both civilians and veterans, are forgotten. (1997, 8)

This view, of course, puts American—not Vietnamese—veterans at the center of the story. Observing this is not to minimize the deep contradictions and heated conflicts that have always surrounded the public discourse on the war. Indeed, the most striking feature of this discourse is its divisiveness. For many non-Vietnamese Americans, "Vietnam" refers simply to a "difficult past" (Wagner-Pacifici and Schwartz 1991) or to a "tangled memory" (Sturken 1997). But in certain undeniable ways, this dominant memory is achieved with a carefully measured dose of forgetting—at the expense of Vietnamese people.[9]

The American War is, of course, a central part of recent Vietnamese American memories. Speaking only in very broad historical and sociological terms—and thus overlooking for the moment many important exceptions and caveats, which I will address shortly—the American War provides the singular explanation for the post-1975 appearance of Vietnamese as refugees on U.S. soil. As a former colonel for the Army of the Republic of South Viet Nam (ARVN) living in Orange County told me, "The reasons we are here are obvious." After more than a decade of covert and overt intervention by the United States in Vietnam's civil war, the triumph of Vietnamese communism forced the U.S. government to withdraw its troops and offer a permanent safe haven to its South Vietnamese allies. In the absence of a prior U.S. presence in Viet Nam, it would be difficult to imagine hundreds of thousands of Vietnamese leaving their homeland to come to the United States simply to relocate to a California suburb. And yet this is the implication of examining Vietnamese American "assimilation" outside of the context of U.S. foreign policy.

Because the war is still alive in the minds of many Vietnamese Americans, especially those forcibly detained for an average of eight to fourteen years in communist Viet Nam, it is hard to say that the war is over. For ex–political detainees, more so than for other waves of refugees or immigrants, the effects of the war linger in real, tangible ways. Indeed, the past, like a nightmare, endlessly haunts.[10] One Vietnamese veteran who spent several years in a political detention camp after the war, told me that he would like not to think about the past, but it is "like a dream" he cannot forget. It is not only about losing one's homeland and being forced into exile, although that is of course a huge part of the dream. The dream is a nightmare because the status—as powerful men rewarded with lavish benefits—that they enjoyed in South Viet Nam is now meaningless in the United States. Worse, some U.S. veterans look down on their South Vietnamese counterparts as "losers." Even on a good day in the United States, these men are constantly mindful that they are not part of the dominant society. Their dream torments and has no satisfactory resolution in the present.

Gina Masequesmay (1991) was perhaps the first researcher to label Orange County's Vietnamese American community as a "community of memory." In time-warped spaces like these, certain "dominant" Vietnamese American memories fester, like the seething hatred of Ho Chi Minh. But listen more carefully and the process of mnemonic socialization turns out to have more than just one, anticommunist note. In recent years, more people are making themselves heard, making the construction of social memory an even more challenging job. Instead of fading away as the generations pass, memories have become a more prominent feature of Vietnamese American community-building and place-making.

Spatializing Memories

Memory is not only a social issue, but also a spatial one. Of the many fascinating aspects of spatialization, I am most interested in the attachment of memory to particular places at various levels of geographical scale. By giving social memories their "platial" form, Vietnamese American community leaders enable the many goals of place-making to come to fruition.

The spatialization of memory advances the territorialization, regulation, and symbolization of place. Chapter 1 elaborates on these three dimensions of place-making. Specific social events become linked to particular places: for example, every year on April 30, a caravan of former ARVN visits every Vietnam War monument in the city of Boston to commemorate the fall of Saigon to communism. Symbolization works hand in hand with territorialization to add symbol and metaphor to each site on the community's map. Through symbolization, these sites become part of the community's cultural economy. Standing in front of a cold and lifeless monument dedicated to U.S. veterans, Vietnamese veterans imbue the statue with new life and alternative meanings. For the boundaries of place to remain intact, they must be controlled and monitored.

Regulation is a way to supervise what happens where—and prevents the wrong things or people from occupying the wrong places. During the height of the antiwar movement, the U.S. State Department threatened to deport Vietnamese students for participating in antiwar protests. Later, U.S. refugee policy, in an act of "calculated kindness" opened the nation's doors to Vietnamese refugees, but not to people fleeing other repressive regimes. On a smaller scale but with great fervor, Vietnamese American leaders make their own regulations, deciding what kinds of memories the community ought to be celebrating—and which should be forgotten or dismissed. For example, in Little Saigons across the nation, saluting the "heritage" flag (read: the yellow- and red-striped symbol of South Viet Nam) and singing the South Vietnamese anthem are considered standard protocol at public events.

Strategic memory projects by Vietnamese Americans confront the prespatialized dominant collective memories of "Vietnam," that is, of the Vietnam War. These were cast in stone—literally and figuratively—just as Vietnamese American communities were starting to form. In general the preservation of war memories is a task ridden with contradictions, and this was no less true for "Vietnam." Diane Barthel (1996) notes that the traditional goal of war preservation has been to glorify the human sacrifices made on behalf of the nation-state. Exhibits that feature the wonders of military technology, crisp and ornate uniforms, or gleaming rifles are geared toward accomplishing this goal. However, war museum curators may have other goals in mind: to comment on the social causes and consequences of war, to provide a mild sense of the actual war experience, to create an entertaining exhibit about the past, or to invite new interpretations of history. These goals require different kinds of public displays. Regardless of the intentions or expertise of a preservationist, no single exhibit or monument can accurately reflect the complexity and significance of war.

The Dorchester War Memorial, located off Morrissey Boulevard in Boston, lists the names of all the Dorchester residents who lost their lives in the U.S. War in Viet Nam. None of those dead are Vietnamese. This man was part of a moving caravan of Vietnamese veterans commemorating the Fall of Saigon on April 30, 1996.

In the case of the Vietnam War, the contradictions between glorifying war versus commemorating sacrifice—and between making a clear statement about war versus inviting new interpretations of war—were greatly heightened. Controversy engulfed the creation of the national Vietnam Veterans Memorial. When Maya Lin won the competition to design the memorial in 1981, her youth, her gender, and even her race came into question. Disgruntled veterans, led by Texas billionaire Ross Perot, complained that Lin's "black gash" dishonored the memory of their comrades and looked for ways to disregard Lin's artistic judgments. Lin defended her vision, asserting that she meant to document the war, not to editorialize on it.[11] The memorial was unveiled in 1982.

Ten years later, *LIFE* magazine sent a team of reporters and photographers to cover a typical day in the life of the Memorial. Journalist David Duncan wrote:

> The Wall is a sad and intimate place. . . . This is the power of this long black Wall: to tell stories; to elicit pain and grief; to offer a chance to remember and, hopefully, to heal. But remembering does not come easily to Americans. Maybe this is why the Wall is particularly painful for us, because it stands for something we want to forget. (Meyer 1993, 10)

Jan C. Scruggs describes "veterans who are still gathering courage for a pilgrimage to their Mecca—the Wall" (Meyer 1993, 5).

In tangible and observable ways, the prior spatialization of the dominant memory of "Vietnam" has set the terms according to which Vietnamese Americans articulate and express their thoughts about the past to the public today. Within these parameters, Vietnamese American leaders interpret the past so that their communities may be included and recognized as "good citizens" in the present moment. Their memory projects demand hard work precisely because many different kinds of memory compete for attention, not all of which play up the good-citizen idea. In saying all of this, I must emphasize that there is no such thing as a single, unanimous Vietnamese American memory of the past. Indeed, strategic memory projects achieve a certain disciplining of memory-making such that specific visions of the past lend recognizable texture and shape to Vietnamese American communities and places.

Boston: Confronting Local Memories

A strange sight lies in plain view of Boston's Morrissey Boulevard. Emblazoned on one of the Keystone (formerly Boston) gas tanks in Dorchester

Bay is a brilliant rainbow splash; in its blue stripe resides a silhouette of Ho Chi Minh.[12] In 1971, the city commissioned Corita Kent, a pacifist nun, to design the seventy-three-square-foot mural, the largest copyrighted work in the world. Kent died in 1986. When she was alive she denied painting Ho Chi Minh in the blue stripe, but the idea of her inserting his image as a secret gesture of support for Viet Nam's national liberation and a sign of sympathy with the ongoing peace movement is highly plausible. Many Bostonians know about the rainbow's hidden Ho; one local writer even refers to the rainbow as a "blue sphinx" that guards the city's famous anti-war and anti-imperialist tradition (Carroll 2004). Gene Vaillancourt, a veteran who did two tours of duty in Viet Nam, says he does a one-fingered salute whenever he passes the gas tank. As he told the *Boston Globe*, "It's just a ritual, like going to church and blessing myself" (Kahn 2000).

What makes the silhouette one of Boston's "most curious ironies" (Bombardieri 1999) is that Vietnamese American residents of Fields Corner, a village not far from Morrissey Boulevard, can see the tank from their neighborhood. The silhouette itself is not visible from that location, but the pain inflicted is no less severe. According to their most outspoken leaders, Ho is as reviled as Hitler: "You cannot bring Hitler into the Jewish community and see how they respond."[13] Leaders organized protests against the image when the mural was moved to a second gas tank in the early 1990s, and again when the tanks were painted with a new logo in 2000. Yet the image has not been altered and remains a curious—and from the perspective of some Vietnamese refugees, abhorrent—feature of Boston's urban landscape.

The absence of historical references to Vietnamese people in Boston has occurred amidst a plethora of references to the Vietnam War.[14] Three Boston neighborhoods (South Boston, Fenway Park, and Dorchester) commemorate the war with monuments to Bostonians who died in Viet Nam. Dorchester, the neighborhood that now contains the bulk of the city's Vietnamese American population, lost many of its working-class men in the war.[15] Dedicated on Veterans Day in 1983, sixty-two "hero squares" went up along the intersections of Dorchester Avenue, recognizing each of them. In 1986, the Dorchester veterans' association cast the same names in stone in the Dorchester Vietnam Veterans Memorial. The ironic juxtaposition of hero squares along a street now lined with Vietnamese-owned shops and restaurants is not lost on Boston's Vietnamese American leaders. As one Vietnamese veteran I interviewed told a local newspaper, "It is something that meshes together. When we came here, we tried to do something for our new country, and something to honor [those Americans who served in Vietnam]. We'd like to find what we can do to honor our own people."

In 1982, a group of U.S. veterans of the Vietnam War, many of them poets and writers, founded the William Joiner Center for the Study of War and Social Consequences at the University of Massachusetts, Boston. One of the Joiner Center's primary goals has been to promote creative writing, scholarship, and teaching about the Vietnam War, a purpose that has given the center a national reputation.[16] Six years before relations between Viet Nam and the United States were normalized, the Joiner Center brought scholars, writers, and poets from Viet Nam to the United States and vice versa as a way of creating positive relationships between American and Vietnamese people. With the help of scholars nationally recognized for their expertise in the Vietnam War and East Asian History and a grant from the National Endowment for the Humanities, the Joiner Center is currently developing a Web-based curriculum on the Vietnam War for high school and college students.

In 2000, the Joiner Center became a Rockefeller Foundation Humanities Fellowship site for the Study of Vietnamese Diaspora. Over the period 2000–2003, the Joiner Center selected twenty-six researchers from Viet Nam, Canada, France, Russia, and the United States to spend time in Boston and to share their work and perspectives with others. These included well-known dissident writers living in Viet Nam as well as distinguished scholars and writers from the Vietnamese exile community. During the spring semester of 2002, I was also awarded this fellowship, which allowed me to complete my research in Fields Corner.

Because of this program, beginning in April 2000 the Joiner Center became the target of a series of lawsuits brought to the Suffolk County Superior Court and the Massachusetts Commission Against Discrimination (MCAD) by Mr. Luyen Huu Nguyen, a political detainee who spent twenty-one years in prison and who was also enrolled as a graduate student in American Studies at the university. Among an array of complaints, Mr. Nguyen charged that in awarding the Rockefeller Foundation Humanities Fellowships to two particularly outspoken writers from Viet Nam, the Joiner Center engaged in discrimination based on age, race, color, and national origin. In 2001, Mr. Nguyen and eleven other named plaintiffs filed a class-action employment discrimination suit. In 2001, the MCAD ruled that Nguyen had failed to state a viable case of discrimination. In 2003, the court denied the issue was appropriate for a class-action motion.

Across Vietnamese America via the Internet, radio, and print media,

Mr. Nguyen's charges fueled widespread hostility toward the Joiner Center and discredited their efforts to work with writers and scholars from Viet Nam. The suspicion is that these writers and scholars will rewrite the history of the refugee from the perspective of the Socialist Republic of Viet Nam. Among some of the Vietnamese Americans I spoke to in Boston, not only the scholars invited by the Joiner Center but also anyone associated with any department or program at the University of Massachusetts became a possible communist sympathizer. As I discuss in the Appendix, my own position as a neutral—meaning anticommunist—researcher in Fields Corner was somewhat jeopardized by the fact that I held a Rockefeller Fellowship at the Joiner Center. As one of my peers in the program—a Vietnamese American who has conducted research in Viet Nam and then developed close working relationships with people in Fields Corner—put it, "It's a hindrance to be a Rockefeller Fellow."

The position of Boston's most vocal Vietnamese American leaders is that the mission of the Joiner Center entails building positive, ongoing relationships between writers, scholars, and intellectuals in the United States and in Viet Nam, a move that does not respect the perspectives of the refugee community. This is not to say that as individuals, these same leaders are not traveling back and forth to Viet Nam; indeed, at least two who have themselves returned to Viet Nam many times for business or family also shared with me harsh criticisms of the Joiner Center's Diaspora program. Perhaps in their minds, having individual ties to Viet Nam is different from promoting understanding and exchange between writers in the two countries. It might also be possible that as representatives of Vietnamese America, these leaders attack the Joiner Center in order to publicly reassert and refurbish their anticommunist, anti–Viet Nam stance, a stance that might seem weaker because of the relative ease with which they personally communicate with and travel to Viet Nam.

Memory projects in Vietnamese America are not about establishing ties to Viet Nam today but about reenacting certain aspects of the world of pre-1975 Viet Nam. This memory-making is not just for old people; indeed, the purpose of strategic memory projects is to make this pre-1975 world real for future generations. In March 2002, I attended a fund-raising event, "Unsung Warriors: Celebrating Vietnamese Women's Experiences," for the community center project of Viet-AID. By featuring women as unsung warriors, the title of the event carried a message that could be embraced by Boston's mainstream feminists. Other aspects of the event, including the fashion show/auction of *ao dai*, made complex, not-so-feminist statements about the role of women in Vietnamese America. Many younger Vietnamese American men and women were involved in planning and running the show, and several of the relatively older people I have interviewed over the years—including a person from Orange County—attended or played major roles in it.

Although the event took on a theme that was friendly to contemporary U.S. feminism, the evening began with the audience saluting two flags, the "heritage" flag of South Viet Nam and the U.S. flag, and singing both national anthems. When I asked my companion/key contact why everyone including young people just did that, she responded, "We do that so the elders won't be angry at us." She also told me that there is a reign of fear within the community and that to be seen or heard not participating in the salute or the anthem is to risk social ostracization and even physical violence such as broken windows or slashed tires at home. Her remarks suggest that strategic memory projects do not include all Vietnamese American perspectives. Despite internal differences, these projects remain an essential component of community-building and place-making in Boston.

In other venues, memory-making is more of an explicit and public activity. On April 30, 1996 I joined a traveling caravan of Vietnamese veterans and Vietnamese American community leaders that stopped at the Dorchester memorial and the war memorials in Fenway Park, city hall, and the state house. At each stop, the veterans held a short ceremony consisting of flag raising and brief speeches in Vietnamese and English. There were few onlookers. Fliers were distributed that read:

> April means spring in America. It is the time when the beauty of life and hope is rejuvenated by signs of leaves and blossoms. However, to most Vietnamese people living in the United States, April has another meaning. It is referred to, or known as, the Black Month of April.
>
> On the 30th of April, 1975, North Vietnamese Communists took over South Vietnam by force. Within a few weeks, South Vietnam was turned into a living hell. . . . April is and will be a Black Month for us until the situation in Vietnam improves. . . . Last but not least, American people need to be extremely cautious and persistent in pursuing the POW-MIA issues. . . . We urge you to join us by writing to your Representatives and Senators addressing concerns for human rights and POW-MIA. . . . TOGETHER WE WILL MAKE A DIFFERENCE.

From the refugee perspective, the end of the war, the normalization of U.S. trade relations with Viet Nam, bureaucracy and corruption under communism, and the POW-MIA issue are one long chain of interrelated issues. By bringing up the POWs in public events, Vietnamese Americans seek common cause with the families of U.S. veterans who adhere to the idea that Viet Nam still harbors prisoners of war—or who feel disrespected in a general way by the U.S. public.

The POW issue has long been inscribed on Boston's urban landscape. If you pass by the Fields Corner police station today, you will see the Stars and Stripes accompanied by the POW-MIA flag. In 1984, then-Governor Michael Dukakis required every police and fire station in the state of Massachusetts to display the POW-MIA flag. The POW-MIA flag is not accompanied by the yellow- and red-striped flag of South Viet Nam. In the early 1990s, the Vietnamese mutual assistance agency located in Fields Corner proposed flying a flag of South Viet Nam along with two flags already flying at the Fields Corner police station. But the Dorchester Allied Veterans, who built the Dorchester War Memorial, disagreed. In their view, the Army of the Republic of South Viet Nam lost the war despite U.S. support. Why should they acknowledge the losers? For Boston's Vietnamese refugees, reaching common ground with Americans on the basis of war memories is sometimes an elusive goal. The absence of the flag of South Viet Nam throughout Fields Corner—except in front of the new community center on Charles Street—indicates a notable difference in Vietnamese American clout compared to Little Saigon.

Orange County: Disciplining Memory

As in Boston, Vietnamese Americans in Orange County are also concerned to respond to the dominant collective views of the war. Oai Ta, nearly sixty when I met him in early 1997, had just been elected president of a community organization in Orange County's Little Saigon when I interviewed him. In Viet Nam, Mr. Oai taught agricultural engineering but since his degree did not transfer to an equivalent position when he arrived in the United States, Mr. Oai repaired farm machinery. Eventually his family moved to the suburbs of Orange County. When I asked Mr. Oai if he has a paid job here in Orange County, he responded, "I don't have another job than leader of the Vietnamese community."

Mr. Oai told me that Americans are obsessed with having lost the war. In his view, building the Vietnamese American community means dealing with this "Vietnam syndrome." Below is an excerpt from my conversation with him.

> OAI TA: The Vietnam syndrome with the veterans, with the American people losing the son, the people in Viet Nam, the husband . . . OK, suppose you living here. You have a son die in Viet Nam. What do you think now?

I don't like Viet Nam.

OAI TA: Yeah. But why, how explain for them why their son have to leave here, fight in Viet Nam and die? So we have to do so many thing make the American people thinking good about the nation, the free Viet Nam, not the communist Viet Nam.

How do you do that?

OAI TA: Talk together, meet together, helping together, spending time in every time we can see them, talk to them. So, not only build up the life, also do something to explain for the American people we have the same feeling like them. We losing. They are lose, we lose too.

Staging events and designing monuments that commemorate the war from a refugee-as-heroic ally perspective are memory projects that challenge the impulse of U.S. veterans to look down upon South Vietnamese veterans as "losers." Unlike in Boston, Orange County's Vietnamese American leaders are able to take on this challenge not only because their population is large and relatively affluent, but also because they articulate their goals in a way that meshes closely with the region's politically conservative and individualist culture.

The Westminster War Memorial depicts the U.S. War in Viet Nam as a joint venture between Americans and Vietnamese. The monument's proximity to city hall in Westminster reflects the growing impact of Little Saigon's business and community leadership on local, county, and regional affairs.

On the eve of April 28, 2003—commemorating the fall of Saigon to communism twenty-eight years ago—thousands of Vietnamese veterans gathered amidst the rumble of three Marine helicopters to dedicate a new Vietnam War Memorial in the city of Westminster, home of Little Saigon. The memorial features a three-ton, fifteen-foot bronze statue depicting two male soldiers—a tall, white, American and a smaller Vietnamese—holding rifles and standing side by side.[17] Seven months prior in the posh city of Laguna Beach, I unexpectedly ran into the artist, Tuan Nguyen, and the statue. Tuan had just finished giving a talk about the memorial at an exclusive art gallery and was escorting the statue to Little Saigon. However, the statue remained draped in canvas until community leaders and city councilors resolved disputes about funding and whether the sculpture should even depict the two soldiers together (Tran 2003).

Shortly after Maya Lin's Vietnam Veterans Memorial was unveiled in 1982 in Washington D.C., two other monuments were displayed nearby. One consists of three larger-than-life soldiers standing together on the battlefield. The other represents some of the women who served in the war. Both of these monuments provide a more traditional alternative to the Wall. By listing the names of the dead in chronological order, the Wall invites visitors to reflect abstractly on the past—in return, the black stone acts like a mirror, reflecting the faces of its visitors—but makes little substantial commentary on the war. In contrast, the traditional monuments present a more clearly patriotic view.

Similarly, the monument recently dedicated in Little Saigon interprets the war strategically so as to support hegemonic narratives of sacrifice in the name of freedom and democracy in America and abroad. While the monument was still in the planning stages, Westminster's Vietnamese American city councilor at the time went so far as to refer to the sculpture as the "West Coast Statue of Liberty" (T. Nguyen 1995). Flanked by the U.S. and South Vietnamese flags, a fountain, and an eternal flame, the sculpture is now the centerpiece of the new 1.4-acre Sid Goldstein Freedom Park on All American Way, just a stone's throw from city hall.

The Westminster monument's design was carefully planned to deal with the omission of Vietnamese from the dominant collective memory. In 1996, leaders told me that they envisioned a monument that would show "GI Joe shaking hands with a Vietnamese soldier," an image obviously calculated not only to counter the exclusion of Vietnamese from the dominant collective memory of the war but also to address the nativist hostility of white residents of Westminster and other nearby cities. The idea of a partnership with Vietnamese Americans has not always been an attractive concept for Westminster's longtime residents, but since Little Saigon has become a major source of economic development in central Orange County, some feelings have changed, at least in public. While the actual sculpture does not depict handshaking, the sculpture has provided ample opportunities for Westminster city officials to ingratiate themselves to the Vietnamese American community. City Councilor Frank Fry is now sometimes cited as the person who generated the idea for the monument. "It is important for the people not to forget that the Americans and the Vietnamese fought side by side together—and died together," he told the press at the dedication of the monument.

But in 1989, an openly xenophobic Fry served a previous term on city council, rejecting Vietnamese American requests for a parade permit: "If you want to be South Vietnamese, go back to South Vietnam." At the time, Fry was also a member of the American Legion 555 of Midway City, a group that opposed the statue: "Who needs another statue? We want nothing to do with it. We think it's a waste of time" (Tsang 1996). Fry's 180° turn reveals the growing power of Orange County's Vietnamese American leadership to redefine dominant perspectives of Vietnam and the Vietnam War.

As in Boston, where memory-making helps to discipline dissent within the Vietnamese American community, so too in Orange County, gestures toward Viet Nam's past and present are closely monitored. For several weeks before and after the Lunar New Year in 1999, thousands of protestors converged in the parking lot of a minimall along Bolsa Avenue in Little Saigon. With anger raised to a fever pitch by a poster of Ho Chi Minh and a flag of Viet Nam displayed inside a shop named Hi-Tek Video, the protestors destroyed an effigy of Ho, waved the flags of South Viet Nam and the United States, and denounced communism in banners, speeches, and performances. At one point, the actions of the protestors were seen as menacing enough to require four hundred police officers called in from several Orange County cities, fully equipped with pepper spray, batons, and other riot gear. As if to illustrate the significance of memory to community, the shop owner's act became the focal point of one of the longest, most massive, and violent demonstrations of collective rage in the Vietnamese American community.

The Hi-Tek incident itself raised many important issues about the memory projects that shape Vietnamese American places such as Little Saigon. The shop owner, Tran Van Truong, claimed he chose January 15, Martin Luther King Day, as the date to exhibit the poster and flag because he wanted to exercise his "freedom of speech." In the days and weeks that followed, infuriated refugees—many of whom spent years in Vietnamese re-education camps before escaping to the United States—made loud and clear in banners and rallies their opinion that "freedom of speech is not free." The lawyers for Mr. Tran's landlord, whose lease included a stipulation about violating the peace, declared that his act was akin to yelling "Fire!" in a crowded movie theater. This argument implied that Little Saigon operates by rules of speech that are different than in other places, presumably because images of Ho Chi Minh or other references to communist Viet Nam incite intense feelings in places where Vietnamese refugees have settled.

The Hi-Tek incident provided an opportunity for Vietnamese refugees to put forth a specific memory project on the Vietnam War designed to explain to other Americans why they should also denounce Ho Chi Minh and communism in Vietnam. I visited the protest site during the daytime shortly after the height of the demonstrations. One of the most interesting exhibits I saw consisted of a bulletin board presenting dozens of images of young, clean-cut, white men, obviously homemade reproductions of photographs from an American high school yearbook in the late 1960s or early 1970s. Above the photographs appeared a statement I now paraphrase from memory: "Ho Chi Minh Killed 58,000 U.S. Lives." This exhibit, like many of the public statements issued to the media during the protests, intended not only to rewrite history from a Vietnamese refugee perspective but to do so in such a manner as to find common ground with Americans who are presumably equally upset about the U.S. defeat in Vietnam. Among those other Americans who called for an end to the carpetbombing of the north and the withdrawal of U.S. troops from the south, this refugee perspective might not inspire solidarity.

The Second Generation: "I Lost the War Not Once, But Twice"

The strategic memory projects that I describe here are primarily the activity of first-generation Vietnamese refugees. This is not to ignore the active participation of younger Vietnamese Americans, especially those born here, on the production and construction of memories. Indeed, rather than being free of memories of Viet Nam, the U.S.-born children of refugees and immigrants are in a sense doubly burdened by them, although their personal investment specifically in wartime memories may be nil. To qualify in their family's eyes as "true" Vietnamese, they have to attach themselves somehow to a particular history of Viet Nam, which includes the refugee perspective on the war. They must try to see the war from the perspective of their elders. At the same time, as "good" Americans, they must come to grips with a dominant collective memory of the war that, though conflicted, ultimately excludes them. Consequently, the memory projects of the second generation are rife with their own unique contradictions. In the years that I pursued my interviews, second-generation leaders—current university and college students and recent graduates—had a limited say when it came to the place-making activities of their community in part because of a gerontocratic culture that privileges the opinions of elders over young people. Understandably, traumatic personal and family experiences make open conversation between the generations about topics such as the war difficult and unpleasant. Yet in recent years, younger leaders have made their own complex views about the past and its relation to the present known over the Internet and in various media. For example, a group of Vietnamese American teachers and scholars in Orange County have compiled an interdisciplinary curriculum and resource guide for high school students called *Vietnamese Americans: Lessons in American History.*

Theories of immigrant assimilation posit a loss of cultural memory over time. But many second-generation Vietnamese Americans—pushed from the outside by a society that treats them as fallout from the war and as racialized Others—are grappling actively and collectively with the past as a way to locate themselves in the present. Phuong Lam, a recent graduate when I spoke with her in 1997, devoted her political energies in two directions: toward a "progressive alliance" between Asians and Latinos in Orange County, and toward a more solid sense of "Vietnameseness" among her cohort. As a student at the University of California, Irvine, she had organized a series of discussions about images of Vietnamese in films about the war in an effort to answer the question, "What does the war mean to *us?*" This is an excerpt from my interview with her.

> Because I know, growing up, that's the last thing I want to watch. Because there's just something totally wrong to me about those movies, the way it is portrayed, the way Americans always came out as the hero, and the communists are always the bad guys. But then all the communists were Asian, and they all look like me! . . . They deserve to be, get blown up. But here, you grow up here, you face that kind of racism and you kind of look at it and think: but they don't have people on our side. They don't have *us*. Those who are not communist. Those who are fighting alongside with the Americans. You know, they're not there.

Looking at one's self through the eyes of others—a practice that W. E. B. DuBois termed "double consciousness" (1994, 2)—is a painful and conflicted process that I have found characterizes the experience of young racial minorities in my college classroom. For some Vietnamese Americans, looking for images that reinforce their sense of who they are is a particularly burdensome task that involves reopening the dialogue about the war. Whereas the Vietnam Veterans Memorial leaves out the story of America's Vietnamese allies, in Phuong Lam's eyes films about the war leave them out again in order to turn U.S. "losers" into "victors." Phuong Lam continues:

> basically we thought: This is the way American saw the world. And they've been spending the last twenty years trying to redeem themselves. Making themselves feel better. We didn't really lose the war. Because it was the American morality, morals. They made us lose the war. So in these movies, they were able to win. They won the war. But at the expense of us!

Phuong Lam and her peers explored and rejected the dominant collective memory as a way to find their own identities. In late 2004, an event known as the VAX controversy illustrated that for young Vietnamese Americans, the only way to express a Vietnamese identity is to accept the parameters set up by the older generation's strategic memory projects. VAX, or Vietnamese American Experience, was an MTV-style show produced briefly in Orange County's Little Saigon and oriented toward young Vietnamese Americans around the nation. Each episode featured fast-paced, sound-bite interviews with famous athletes and celebrities (not necessarily Vietnamese) or whirlwind trips to places of interest to a young audience. In the last episode of 2004, the show exhibited a clip from *Saigon, USA*, a documentary film about Orange County's Vietnamese American community (Jang and Winn 2003). The segment VAX featured included images from the Hi-Tek protest of 1999. The idea behind the show, according to writer Joseph Trinh, was not to editorialize about the protest but just to let young Vietnamese Americans know about the film as a resource for their own information.[18] Almost immediately, Little Saigon TV was apparently bombarded with complaints by older viewers offended by the video clip, which reignited their Hi-Tek furor. To quell their anger, and to allow the show's writers and producers to explain their actions, VAX held an intergenerational community forum in November 2004. After the forum, VAX stayed permanently off the air.

In a rich and fascinating analysis of the Hi-Tek incident and the VAX controversy, Cam Nhung Vu and Thuy Vo Dang (2005) observe that while the English-language media tend to caricature Vietnamese refugees as passive war victims, these events show the older generation as active agents of "anticommunism" as a cultural practice, or what I refer to as strategic memory projects. Significantly, they point out that in both events anticommunism was much more than a political ideology and operated instead as an intervening practice that concomitantly disciplined the community—and silenced dissent. Vu and Dang recognize that the views and actions of the VAX writers and producers were not intended as "dissent." During the VAX forum, the younger generation revealed a certain lack of awareness about the importance of the cultural practice of anticommunism by failing to salute the heritage flag and the U.S. flag or to sing the national anthems, or to realize that the elders needed and wanted to do so. One of the young people associated with VAX showed up to the forum dressed in full camouflage, a thoughtless fashion statement that probably had more to do with the U.S. war in Iraq than with the one in Viet Nam. The elders interpreted this fashion faux pas as a disrespectful gesture. Finally, the forum organizers conducted the meeting in English and had made no arrangements for translation, so that elders who were more comfortable speaking Vietnamese understandably felt uneasy participating in the discussion.

While the VAX controversy revealed a naïveté on the part of Orange County's young Vietnamese Americans, the elders appeared consistent in their investment in a strategic memory project that shapes the cultural and political identity of Little Saigon and of Vietnamese America generally. Instead of articulating a dissenting view of the Hi-Tek protest or of anticommunism as a cultural practice, the VAX writers and producers demonstrated a lack of awareness of the depth and complexity of the issues they were airing on the show. For this reason, what appears as a generational divide along political lines is perhaps less an indication of actual conflict and more of a show of a lack of substantive and thoughtful dialogue between the young and the old within Vietnamese America. The generation gap is made more complex by the social disenfranchisement of the elder refugees. It is one thing that young people are not able to approach their own parents or elder relatives to engage in complex discussion; it is another thing that because the Vietnamese American experience is a marginalized one, there are few other venues in which young Vietnamese Americans would be able to explore and learn about the many possible interpretations of history and memory in their community.

In Fall 2003, Vietnamese American scholars connected through an Internet-based Listserv took up the issue of the South Vietnamese "heritage" flag. Across the nation, Vietnamese Americans are reclaiming this flag as an icon of anticommunism and also as a representation of their community and history. This particular discussion was sparked by a debate over the display of the red flag of the Socialist Republic of Viet Nam at a graduation ceremony at California State University, Fullerton. Some Vietnamese American students and their parents confronted the university administration insisting that only the yellow heritage flag be flown because, according to them, that flag represents not only the Vietnamese American community but also freedom, democracy, and independence from communism and totalitarianism. The university chose to compromise by flying both flags.

Viet Thanh Nguyen, a professor of English and American Studies and Ethnicity at the University of Southern California, wrote an editorial expressing his own personal stance on the flag that was circulated through the Listserv and also published in the *Orange County Register*.[19] In it he writes,

> Because of the war in Viet Nam, my parents were separated from their families for forty years. . . . This story is not unusual at all in the Vietnamese American community. Everyone can speak of families dissolved, homes stolen, and relatives tortured, killed, and imprisoned. The ones who speak out most on these wounds are the ones who blame the Communist regime of Viet Nam for the war's tragedies. Who can fault them for nursing these wounds, which are not yet, for them, scars? Periodically these festering wounds bleed again in the Vietnamese American community, when its most passionate members see the specter of Communism arising in the United States and lead others in vigorous, spectacular protests. *What the Vietnamese American community wants to do with these protests is to remind themselves, and other Americans too, not to forget the old South Viet Nam that they know and love.* (V. Nguyen 2003, italics added)

Recognizing that the Hi-Tek protest, for example, came out of a desire "not to forget" reinforces the notion that strategic memory projects are an essential piece of Vietnamese American community-building and place-making. Professor Nguyen proceeds then to refer to the flag debate at Cal State Fullerton, pointing out that neither South Viet Nam nor the Vietnamese American community itself practices the democracy and freedom they want to punish Viet Nam for not practicing. He continues:

> Anyone in the Vietnamese American community who speaks out in favor of reconciling with Viet Nam or criticizing the South Vietnamese regime has risked vicious protest and even violence. Meanwhile, younger Vietnamese

Americans often feel reluctant to voice contrary opinions on these issues because they don't want to offend their parents or their elders. Because of political pressure and filial piety, there has been no true freedom of speech in the Vietnamese American community.

Professor Nguyen's editorial was remarkable for its frank criticism of the community and spurred a fascinating conversation among Vietnamese American studies scholars and Vietnamese American community leaders. One of the comments I found particularly relevant to the notion of strategic memory projects was a suggestion made by a graduate student that all of the fervor around the flag and anticommunism would fade if we just wait long enough for all the Vietnamese American elders to pass away. While this horribly ageist suggestion likely comes out of frustration over censorship by elders and could be taken as practical advice about how to deal with intergenerational conflict—"just be patient and it will all blow over"—there is also the implication that memory making is only an old people's problem. This, of course, brings us back to the caricature of the aging refugee as passively traumatized and obsessed with the past, soon to be replaced by the modern, Americanized, second-generation Vietnamese. At least one scholar pointed this connection out, emphasizing once again that history and memory are social processes that involve the entire community, not just the elders.

Weeks after Professor Nguyen published his editorial on the flag debate at Cal State Fullerton, he found himself writing another editorial about "Communist Free Zones" in Garden Grove and Westminster. On May 11, 2004, Garden Grove passed a measure that requires the federal government to provide the city a fourteen-day advance warning if Vietnamese government or trade officials are planning to visit the city. This is supposed to give city police time to prepare for the massive protests that would undoubtedly erupt if the visits took place. More importantly, the measures would make the federal government accountable for at least some of the expenses incurred by heightened security due to a protest. Westminster passed a similar measure shortly after. Both measures were passed in response to the Hi-Tek incident of 1999 and go a great distance toward territorializing, regulating, and symbolizing place. Now, not only is Little Saigon a thriving tourist/business district with which the cities of Westminster and Garden Grove hope to be equated, but it is also off-limits for anyone bearing an official association with the Socialist Republic of Viet Nam.

In Boston, too, second-generation Vietnamese Americans are doubly burdened by war memories. One important difference from Orange County, however, is that young Vietnamese Americans in Boston are more likely to develop a forum for their perspective in Asian American panethnic settings or in primarily white settings than in places devoted to Vietnamese Americans only. In a *Boston Globe* column featuring writers in their twenties, Quong Bao described his desire to understand the war, which an uncle calls "the American war." He then took a course at the University of Massachusetts, Amherst, called "Vietnam: Literature & Film." Five other Vietnamese Americans also enrolled in the course. He wrote:

> I didn't know what position to take in the course. As a Vietnamese person, I wanted to mourn the loss of more than 2 million Vietnamese lives; as an American, I pondered the way the United States had debased itself in the killing. *I felt as if I had lost the war not once, but twice.* (Bao 1997, italics added)

Boston's second-generation Vietnamese American leaders conduct their strategic memory projects in a context that simultaneously demands Asian Americanization *and* staying Vietnamese—and all of this while paying respects to the view of the older generation. U.S. born and educated, Ngoc Nga Nguyen is very knowledgeable about the new community center in Fields Corner. Her parents escaped communism in Viet Nam twice, first in 1954 then again in 1975. Her family has been subject to many acts of harassment even though her father is "very anticommunist" because of their Northern Vietnamese accent. She is older than most U.S.-born Vietnamese Americans.

I interviewed Ms. Nguyen multiple times over the years of this project. She explained that the older generation is not really thinking about making a place in America as much as they are hoping to recover their lost homeland of Viet Nam. "Sometimes," she noted, "people are frozen in time."

> For the older generation it's about a future they don't accept. For the older generation it's not about building a life here. It's about how can we topple the government in Viet Nam and return to our rightful place.

Importantly, Ms. Nguyen sees the war not simply as a memory that defines the older generation but as an experience that sets Vietnamese refugees as *an entire community apart* from other Asian Americans. Her comments reflect a sense of belonging to two worlds—Viet Nam and Vietnamese America—and to neither, and of a responsibility for the communities to which she is not always sure she belongs.

NGOC NGA NGUYEN: The refugee agenda has a lot more to do with the polit-ical connection to their country. With human rights. The refugee community is pushing for the U.S. to pressure Vietnam on human rights conditions. . . .
   I see.
   NGOC NGA NGUYEN: The Asian American agenda pushes for Asians in this country to have access and to become full American, but does not look at Asians in a global context. What about Asians in Asia?
   So war is only seen in national terms, even though everyone dies in the war?
   NGOC NGA NGUYEN: Yeah. The Asian American agenda separates Asian Americans from Asia. Makes a different class of Americans, and Americans as imperialists. Asian Americans are fighting for their right to be American, but what does it mean to be American? Do you want all that it means, because that means becoming imperialist.

Elsewhere in the interview, Ms. Nguyen argued that "the Asian Ameri-can community claims legitimacy because of the new refugee population," for example by building scholarship funds based on the needs of refugee kids but then channeling the funds to the children of professors who are not refugees. I cite her not to evaluate this idea but to air the more important point that the Vietnamese American refugee experience entails a history and an implicit agenda that is sometimes out of synch with the impulse of the larger Asian American population to establish itself as separate and distinct from any place in Asia. For second-generation leaders like Ms. Nguyen, becoming Asian American and retaining a sense of Vietnamese-ness are difficult tasks to accomplish simultaneously because the structure and symbols associated with national, cultural, or racial identities demand contradictory interpretations of the past.

Conclusion

Observing the importance of the past to people across American cities and towns, Robert Bellah et al. noted that "Where history and hope are forgotten and community means only the gathering of the similar, community degen-erates into lifestyle enclave" (1996, 33). But Bellah and his colleagues made this remark in light of the culture of individualism, not in the context of immigration. The idea that Vietnamese Americans—as refugees, immi-grants, and also as citizens—might also demand a serious encounter with "history and hope" tends to be obscured by the master narrative of Ameri-can exceptionalism, which assumes that immigrants, especially non-Anglo-Protestants, are only hindered by an attachment to their past. Assimilation furthers the expectation that to be successful, these immigrants need to conform to the values and attitudes of the white mainstream, a group that has no need for a collective sense of history.[20]

Vietnamese American strategic memory projects are redolent with both history and hope. The strategies involved in remembering and commemorating the past for Vietnamese Americans are partially dictated by the already existing dominant collective memories of "Vietnam," a term that signals an era, an epoch, and of course the war, but not a people or a nation. Against a glaring absence of commentary on the experience of Vietnamese people during or after the war, Vietnamese Americans put forth their own social memories as a way to assert their presence in this country.

The production and construction of memory is also a way to shape the identity of Vietnamese American community by creating mnemonic guidelines that organize the internal community memory-making process. One of the most important rules is that gestures to the "homeland" must refer to pre-1975 Viet Nam, not to the current Vietnamese nation, society, or government. In this way, the exile perspective defines and dominates the path that Vietnamese American memory-making must take.

To the extent that these strategic memory projects take spatial form, they are an essential component of Vietnamese American place-making, which territorializes, regulates, and symbolizes place. Displaying flags, putting up monuments, and staging protests are activities that help to extract structure out of the physical landscape, monitor who belongs, and attach symbolic weight to place. Part of the strategy of memory-making is the creation of community and nation at higher and higher levels of scale. Adopting the flag of South Viet Nam as the Vietnamese American "heritage" flag is powerful precisely because it invokes both a place and a time that are larger than, and therefore beyond, the local moment. Designing a war monument as a West Coast version of the Statue of Liberty and then placing that monument next to city hall in a park called Freedom on a street called All American Way represents an intentional jumping of scale from the local Vietnamese American community to the United States as a global standard for democracy. Making this jump comprises another strategy to counter the critical omission of Vietnamese experiences and perspectives from the dominant collective memory of the war.

The social and spatial contexts in which Vietnamese Americans are pushed to develop strategic memory projects are strikingly different in Boston and Orange County. Each region has its own way of understanding and interpreting the past: one region is laden with history; the other is apparently devoid of historical references. The dominant collective memory of the war thus presents itself differently in each region. For example, several Boston neighborhoods contain commemorative war monuments. Fields Corner, Boston's Vietnamese village, is the site of sixty-two "hero squares." Each square is dedicated to a Dorchester resident who died in the war; for obvious historical reasons, none of these was Vietnamese. Until the Vietnamese American community emerged, Orange County had no comparable public references to the Vietnam War.

In Boston, a city replete with history, cramped physical space discourages the expression of new memories by Vietnamese Americans. In addition, Boston's liberal, antiwar tradition—a tradition backed by solid organizational resources—does not mix with the hard-line anticommunism that fuels the extreme right wing of the Vietnamese exile community. Consequently, Vietnamese American community-building and place-making cannot revolve around memory as much as it must deal with other themes, such as multiculturalism. In Orange County, a region bereft of an official history, Vietnamese Americans enjoy much more leeway to tell about the past as they know it. Their story reinforces southern California's famous disdain for government and embrace of individuality. Better yet, the revenues brought in by the Little Saigon business district make it increasingly desirable for city government to open up to the demands and perspectives of the Vietnamese American leadership.

In their impact on place and place-making, Orange County's Vietnamese American strategic memory projects are often more effective and definitive for other communities than those of Boston's. But that is not to ignore the very important questions, conflicts, and discussions that these projects are also raising. The VAX controversy indicates an interest among the younger generation to touch base with their roots, even if their efforts to do so are clumsy, superficial, and even unintentionally offensive. If the strategic memory projects of the exile generation only discipline and dictate but do not engage real conversation, younger people will have great difficulty exploring for themselves what it means to stay Vietnamese. Professor Nguyen's editorials suggest that these conversations might be happening with greater frequency and with more positive results for the community overall.

Whereas Vietnamese American community leaders in Orange County put forth their memory projects in such a way as to uphold and boldly reinforce the region's conservative and individualist political culture, their counterparts in Boston are at a clear disadvantage. Finding common ground with Boston's residents, particularly Vietnam veterans, is a challenge because the city already has expressed its often conflicted opinions about the war in the form of monuments, public art, and an organization devoted to forging relationships between people in the United States and Viet Nam. Rather than copy Little Saigon by creating a Vietnamese American monument to the war—a move that would probably incite much opposition from the rest of the city—Boston's Vietnamese American leaders have chosen instead to embed their memories in other kinds of community-building projects, such as forging a multicultural neighborhood in Fields Corner. The size of the Vietnamese American population and their geographic concentration are important factors in explaining the differences between the scope and character of Vietnamese American memory projects in Orange County and Boston. But a fuller view must take into account the composition of that population as well as the local contexts in which Vietnamese America is produced and constructed.

Chapter 4   **What's Good for Business Is Good for the Community: Packaging and Selling Vietnamese America**

MARKETPLACE MULTICULTURALISM consists of a discourse and a set of policies and practices that link the global capitalist economy to the sociospatial terrain out of which Vietnamese America emerges. Imposed from "above" civil society, marketplace multiculturalism may be understood as a state-sponsored directive whose intention is to manage, control, and take advantage of recent transformations in global capitalism, including refugee migration due to war and the expansion of international markets.[1] Across the uneven spaces of development that result from the capitalist production of space in the United States, marketplace multiculturalism installs pockets of "difference" to attract tourism, to boost real estate values, and to enhance the overall distinctiveness of a metropolitan region.[2] Often, marketplace multiculturalism entwines itself with ongoing racial and strategic memory projects to produce specific and localized forms of community and place.

To be sure, U.S. multiculturalism has been a project not only of the state but also of popular social movements for racial democracy organized "from below," as Avery Gordon and Christopher Newfield (1996) note. Multiculturalism as a more broadly defined social and political discourse has the potential to challenge the racial status quo, for example, by encouraging cultural diversity in public schools.[3] However, marketplace multiculturalism is a much narrower undertaking with much more limited effects on the prevailing structures of power. Indeed, marketplace multiculturalism probably adds to the variety of cultures present in a metropolis more than it challenges the rank or privileges associated with dominant forms of culture. To the degree that marketplace multiculturalism presents alternatives to an increasingly homogeneous globalized experience at the level of local spaces, Néstor García Canclini (1995) points out that a certain "hybridization" results, juxtaposing elite, popular, industrial, and indigenous cultural forms. In Vietnamese American communities and places, hybridization manifests in the sociospatial juxtaposition of Vietnamese and Chinese language and culture, along with U.S. references to "Vietnam" in the form of memories of the war and familiar stereotypes of Asia. Once, I saw a disabled U.S. veteran begging for money on the sidewalk outside a shop in Little Saigon. His appearance struck me as a sad and fascinating example of the cyclical motion of people, history, and culture in a Vietnamese American–centered multicultural marketplace.

Ultimately, the main prerogative of marketplace multiculturalism—to make a profit off of cultural diversity—has a mixed impact on the growth and character of Vietnamese American place-making. Ethnic Chinese have a corner on business activities in the Vietnamese American community, as they did in South Viet Nam during the French colonial period all the way up to the present. In Viet Nam today, the ethnic Chinese of Cho Lon (Sai Gon's "twin city") and of Quang Ninh province in the north embody what Aihwa Ong (1999) would term "nomadic subjects" whose loyalties have historically been split between China and Vietnam. Now ethnic Chinese are considered by the government of Viet Nam to be "undisputed citizens."[4] Yet the presence and role of ethnic Chinese in driving the ethnic economy creates an interesting problem for the cultural identity of Vietnamese American places.

The racialized ethnic minority groups who are understood by dominant U.S. society to represent cultural "difference" to a certain degree also buy into the content and goals of marketplace multiculturalism. On a good day, these groups articulate their own perspectives and develop their own practices regarding diversity in reaction to the hegemonic discourses and practices of marketplace multiculturalism. In Vietnamese America, small business owners, elected officials, community advocates, social service providers, and even university students all endeavor to position themselves and their constituencies uniquely within or against mainstream definitions of nation, race, ethnicity, and community. Their responses are integral to community-building and place-making because the dominant narratives of the state and market do not speak to, distort, or simply disregard the full complexity of the Vietnamese American experience.

In Orange County and Boston, Vietnamese American community-building and place-making accommodates—and sometimes challenges—marketplace multiculturalism. By doing what they need to do to generate and preserve Vietnamese-specific networks and associations, to resist marginalization, and to hang on to a sense of the past, Vietnamese Americans have carved out economic, political, and cultural niches for themselves, claiming spaces and identities that in earlier periods might have been off-limits to them as foreigners, refugees, or racialized minorities. Their collective efforts to survive and prosper have helped to revitalize and rejuvenate depressed and blighted areas, providing the local state with economic and cultural levers for growth and new ways to sell place and culture.

Marketplace Multiculturalism: Linking Global to Local

Marketplace multiculturalism refers to the local state's agenda to incorporate Vietnamese Americans and other groups as laborers, small business owners, homeowners, and taxpayers who can stimulate the economy and collaborate with the region's "place entrepreneurs" (Logan and Molotch 1987, 29). The term refers also to attempts by the local state to promote Vietnamese American places as sites of multicultural consumption in the form of urban or regional tourism, enhancing what Sharon Zukin (1993) calls the "cultural economy" of the city. In the Vietnamese American context, culture goes hand in hand with history. But marketplace multiculturalism has little use for history, and therefore the dominant collective memories of the Vietnam War need to be managed or erased so that the undesirable aspects of history—U.S. intervention and defeat, the tragic loss of lives on all sides of the war, the trauma of Vietnamese refugee resettlement in drastically unfamiliar and often hostile places—may be removed from public view. The war is not just a memory; above all else, the war is a landmark in the history of U.S. involvement, neocolonialism, and imperialism in Viet Nam, and a gesture toward the specific policies of intervention and withdrawal that created a Vietnamese refugee population to begin with.[5] Marketplace multiculturalism offers a number of ways for Orange County and Boston to incorporate Vietnamese as Americans, to detach culture from history, and to turn culture into profit.

Marketplace multiculturalism puts serious demands on the community-building and place-making agenda that Vietnamese Americans already face. Vietnamese Americans strive to legitimize their presence in the eyes of local residents and government officials who previously demonstrated xenophobia, racism, or simply disdain against them by making gestures to U.S. society as a land of diverse and multicultural immigrants, and to themselves as hardworking and heroic allies during the U.S. War in Viet Nam. For ex–political detainees, memories of the war are particularly painful. Thus, the need to solicit recognition for their sacrifices—and to protest anything related to communism in Viet Nam—is often their highest priority for community-building and place-making. Only a few of the leaders I spoke with come from this group, but frequently first-wave refugees took up these "exilic" views as their own. As a result of their influence, the local state often frames Vietnamese American ethnic entrepreneurship as a model for local growth and as an ideological statement about a freedom-loving people who rely on their own individual resources to pull themselves up by their bootstraps.

In this statement, of course, the role of the U.S. imperialist nation-state in creating the refugee situation in the first place, and then later in providing safe haven to Vietnamese refugees as a "showcase for democracy," falls conveniently out of the picture. Also not visible is the specific role of ethnic Chinese in generating and supporting the Vietnamese American economy, a role that sometimes causes conflict around the authentic identity of Vietnamese American places. Nor does this statement acknowledge the relative ease with which first-wave refugees and ethnic Chinese businesspeople in particular travel back to Viet Nam to renew family ties or establish overseas relationships, a phenomenon facilitated by the normalization of trade and diplomatic relations between the United States and Viet Nam in the mid-1990s. In Vietnamese America's public discourse, travel to Viet Nam has been treated as taboo and even a sign of softness toward communism. For the growth of business in Little Saigon to appear beneficial to the broadest possible constituencies, marketplace multiculturalism needs to smooth over—or simply erase—these complex historical and political realities. Vietnamese American community-building and place-making temporarily caters to state-sponsored marketplace multiculturalism by separating "business" from "politics," leaving the job of small business ownership to ethnic Chinese. Yet in the end the task of packaging and selling Vietnamese American culture cannot avoid completely the many contradictory requirements of the local state and the community itself.

The title of this chapter comes from an interview in 1997 with Nhat Le, then a representative of the Vietnamese Chamber of Commerce in Orange County (which has since amended its name to the Vietnamese American Chamber of Commerce and has gone through several changes in directorship). Mr. Nhat was a U.S. citizen devoted to the business community in Little Saigon, although he also made clear to me his sentimental attachments to Viet Nam: "No matter how long I stay here, I'm still, my heart is still in the Old Country." Harboring a personal nostalgia for the Viet Nam of his past, however, did not prevent Mr. Nhat from understanding the current-day uses of Little Saigon. As a businessperson, he emphasized the necessity of attracting non-Vietnamese customers. For him and for the chamber, the growth of Little Saigon as a business district was and is central to place-making and community-building. As he put it, "What's good for business is good for the community."

Staying Vietnamese in the context of marketplace multiculturalism is a project that is full of opportunities for new forms of community and identity, but a project that is also bound for complex and perhaps irresolvable distortions. At the outset, staying Vietnamese involves a distortion of culture because values, attitudes, and practices in Viet Nam are constantly changing, while Vietnamese in exile in the United States seek to reproduce a culture they remember from before they left their homeland, a culture that therefore ends up frozen, permanently stuck in time. But there are many other reasons to expect that staying Vietnamese according to the prerogatives of marketplace multiculturalism will produce inauthentic versions of Vietnameseness and will also exacerbate divisions—of class, culture, and ideological orientation—within the Vietnamese American community. To the extent that marketplace multiculturalism means serving a non-Vietnamese clientele, Vietnamese Americans must transform their communities and places into things—resources, objects, or symbols—that can be packaged and consumed by non-Vietnamese in the capitalist marketplace. Because one important measure of its success is salability, marketplace multiculturalism is not necessarily concerned about an accurate representation of the Vietnamese or Vietnamese American experience. What matters most is whether someone is willing and able to pay for and consume multiculturalism or cultural "difference" in the form of a resource, such as a ready labor pool or a real estate investment; identity in the form of cuisine, music, novelty items, or clothing; or an experience, such as a tour of exotic Little Saigon. Looking for marketplace multiculturalism to produce an authentic rendition of culture is almost sure to disappoint. When Stanley Karnow, the prize-winning journalist of the Vietnam War, visited Little Saigon in 1992, he declared the place to be merely a "facsimile" of the Saigon he once knew.[6]

Marketplace multiculturalism also serves as one context in which Vietnamese Americans cater to their own community. But just when it would seem that the production and construction of Vietnamese America would be most "pure"—when the ethnic economy serves its so-called coethnics—some of the most interesting and troubling divisions within the Vietnamese American community reveal themselves. Stephen Steinberg (1981) points out that throughout U.S. history, the people who live on the economic margins are the ones who preserve ethnicity for their more affluent counterparts.

The poor are trapped in one culturally identifiable place, while the rich are free to move about and circulate with others in a mainstream universe. Put in a different way, Peter Kwong (1996) notes the contrasting situations of New York Chinatown's poorest residents/workers, whom he labels the "Downtown Chinese," and the well-to-do owners and managers of China-town's real estate and industries who live in outer-ring suburbs, and whom he labels the "Uptown Chinese." The Downtown Chinese are sometimes undocumented and often unfamiliar with the language and customs of mainstream U.S. society. They have no choice but to work and live in China-town. The Uptown Chinese benefit from the disadvantages of their Down-town brethren, hiring them at near-slave wages, denying them proper benefits, and firing them at will. What appears to outsiders to be a protected haven is instead a site of intragroup dependence and exploitation.

Beyond the Ethnic Enclave

Mainstream social science often frames immigrant community-building in terms of "ethnic enclaves" or "ethnic entrepreneurship." By framing Viet-namese American community-building and place-making instead in terms of the state-sponsored discourse of marketplace multiculturalism I hope to highlight the important connections between and among sociospatial pro-cesses of racialization, memory/history, culture, and the economy. Place, after all, has value in and of itself, not only as real estate but also as cultural anchor and symbol. I intend to point out the important role of the state in shaping culture and identity. I intend also to sidestep some of the more ide-ologically driven aspects of the enclave/entrepreneurship approach, espe-cially the idea that Asian immigrants draw on rich Confucian traditions to pull themselves up by their bootstraps, while culturally deficient U.S.-born blacks and Latinos prefer instead to claim victimhood and demand govern-ment subsidies—or bask in poverty. The divisiveness of this idea is especially obnoxious given the pretense among social scientists and policy makers to be "race-blind."[7]

The enclave/entrepreneurship literature is immense and enormously influential, and I make no claim to summarize it fully here. Nor do I intend to overlook its many positive contributions. By offering a simplified thumb-nail sketch here, I mean to say that framing Vietnamese American commu-nities and places as "enclaves" that facilitate "immigrant entrepreneurship" will produce a well-known set of questions that drive an already well-known conversation. The terms of this conversation need to be expanded by in-cluding the surrounding cultural and political context in which marketplace multiculturalism—along with racialization and strategic memory projects—shape community-building and place-making efforts.

Much ink has been spilled on the precise definition and indicators of an "ethnic enclave." In colloquial usage an "ethnic enclave" is synonymous with an "ethnic neighborhood," suggesting that an enclave is primarily a place where immigrants live and congregate. In social scientific usage, however, ethnic enclaves refer specifically to the upward mobility of immigrants, made possible by a combination of spatial concentration of homes, workplaces/businesses, and social networks. In an economic context in which Asian and Latin American immigrants and their families can no longer depend on the well-paying, unionized jobs in manufacturing industries that supported their Euro-American predecessors, ethnic enclaves offer important material opportunities to immigrants—and a fascinating ideological battleground for social scientists.[8]

Social scientists have framed ethnic enclaves as avenues for immigrant advancement implying—without examining why—throughout the enclave/entrepreneurship literature that native-born minorities lack the cultural values, ties, or trust to build and sustain their own enclave economies.[9] Meanwhile ghettos, barrios, and reservations have been theorized by a few stalwart social scientists as places that subject native-born minorities to the forces of internal colonialism.[10] In those places, racialized minorities enjoy very limited spatial mobility; in addition, their culture is ignored, devalued, and treated as inferior—including their histories, languages, religions, and values. These internal colonies serve the larger mainstream society by providing easy access to cheap labor and natural resources such as real estate, minerals, and oil. Because they are governed either by whites or by minority elites who once interacted with but no longer represent them, the people who live in these places do not exercise true sovereignty over the material or discursive aspects of their community life.

As a theory of racial oppression, internal colonialism is not applied to ethnic enclaves such as Chinatown or Little Saigon. Instead, ethnic enclaves are treated as self-created mechanisms for ethnic community advancement. The narrow focus of the ethnic enclave/entrepreneurship literature puts out of the picture some of the most important similarities between and across racialized ethnic groups and thus overlooks many core aspects of Vietnamese American community-building, including place-making itself. For example, the extent to which the ethnic enclave is "racialized," that is, devalued as a place occupied by racialized others, is not revealed. By refusing to theorize whiteness in relation to place or to the economy, this literature caves into the notion that privileges of the white Americans, including access to jobs and housing, are normal and natural and definitive of U.S. citizenship rather than historical and social constructions. Furthermore, the enclave/entrepreneurship frame posits "ethnic" communities in contradistinction to "racial" groups and gives the ethnic enclave privileged status in explanations for the incorporation of immigrants into mainstream society. By focusing on the characteristics of particular immigrant communities rather than on the broader and deeper structural and historical processes that inform ethnicity, race, social stratification, and citizenship, the ethnic enclave/entrepreneurship literature supports a prevailing notion that immigrants, especially Asian immigrants, are largely self-sufficient. The role of the U.S. nation-state in "making Asian America" by ushering in skilled and professional labor is not a prominent aspect of the ethnic-enclave literature (Hing 1993).

The spatial attachments of Vietnamese Americans are essential to community-building not just because they potentially enable the formation of ethnic economies thus providing income and jobs to otherwise economically disadvantaged refugees, but because they allow Vietnamese American leaders to participate in ongoing activities and discourses that are shaped by marketplace multiculturalism. In certain ways, Vietnamese Americans have no choice but to form ethnic economies so that they can provide jobs, services, and products for themselves. Orange County's Little Saigon and Boston's Fields Corner exemplify the efforts of Vietnamese Americans to integrate themselves into a racialized society by creating a place where non-Vietnamese can shop, eat, and otherwise consume their culture. On the way, Vietnamese Americans also gain recognition as a distinctly "ethnic" community and elaborate upon their own history as the heroic allies of the United States during the War in Viet Nam. The tag "ethnic enclaves" only partially fits the purposes and functions of Little Saigon and Fields Corner.

On the Map with Mickey Mouse: Growth as a Business Issue

Tour Asia in Your Own Backyard

"Tour Asia without the airfare," a reporter broadcasts in a short blurb about Public Places in the *Los Angeles Times*.[11] The blurb focuses specifically on Little Saigon. Take a daytrip in Little Saigon and see the "cultural and commercial capital" for the largest concentration of Vietnamese people outside of Viet Nam, recommends Anh Do, a Vietnamese American newspaper editor, writing for *Westways*, the magazine of the Auto Club of Southern California.[12] In the 1930s the urban theorists of the Chicago School saw Chinatown and Japantown as exotic, Oriental places where Western-ers—even knowledgeable scholars—would be lost. They turned to their Asian American graduate students for help in investigating social life there, and determined with their help that the racial and cultural differences between Orientals and whites would eventually recede with increased con-tact and intermingling between the two groups. Nearly half a century later, the Asian American population has multiplied and diversified, and a grow-ing body of Asian American studies scholarship continuously reconceptu-alizes the very meaning of Asian American community (Vo and Bonus 2002). Yet at the level of urban and regional development—and especially local tourism, a boom industry for many areas—these conceptual nuances matter very little. Little Saigon still occasionally stands for all of Asia, prom-ising an adventuresome retreat for curious travelers who cannot afford the international airfare. Even for the more sophisticated individual who knows the difference between various Asian cultures, the tourist industry hopes to frame Little Saigon as a compelling destination because it is unusual and distinct, not to mention cheap. Little Saigon has to be portrayed as "differ-ent" since tourists cannot be expected to pack their bags for a place with which they are already familiar. In important ways, tourism depends upon and reinforces the idea that Little Saigon is different because it is a place where people are "staying Vietnamese."

Tourism links globalization—with its flows of capital and labor—to local and regional development as a form of consumption. As a strategy for growth, local tourism requires a certain appreciation of and desire for cul-tural diversity, along with an ability to pay for the experience. Our everyday notion of travel and tourism is that we go to new places to see things we have never before seen. But John Urry (1990) argues that tourism in fact consists of a "heuristic circle" in which we go to new places in order to cap-ture live an experience that we have previewed through tourist brochures, postcards, and other travel literature. This secondhand exposure—provided by profit-seeking tourist businesses hoping to lure us in—offers the lens through which we gaze at the "new" places we visit. In a related vein, Catherine Lutz and Jane Collins (1993) observe that middle-class European Americans view the non-Western world with eyes that are heavily influenced by nontourist, semiscientific sources such as *National Geographic* magazine. By looking at *National Geographic*'s iconic photographs of the non-Western world, readers gather information not so much about others but about themselves, as Westerners and as white people.

The *Westways* map of Little Saigon is fascinating because of the subtle manner in which it presents and frames information about the Vietnamese American population in Southern California for the middle-class, non-Vietnamese reader. At the top left corner a paragraph describes the growth of Little Saigon. From a "little enclave" along Bolsa Avenue in the mid-1980s to a business district spanning four cities, now Little Saigon has 3,500 Vietnamese-owned businesses. "On weekends," the paragraph happily boasts, "busloads of tourists come searching for deals and ready to bargain." Many of these tourists are Vietnamese Americans. The map points out eight sites for the day-tripper, including the Asian Garden Mall, three restaurants (two of them with French-influenced menus, and perhaps for that reason less scary for European Americans), a Buddhist temple, and the Vietnam War Memorial. The description of the war monument is nonchalant and bereft of controversy or historical insight: "Two soldiers cast in bronze, an American and a South Vietnamese, represent cooperation between the servicemen who fought side by side in the Vietnam War." The map also recommends the 2005 Tet Festival with an explanation of the holiday reminiscent of the touristic captions accompanying the travel photographs in *National Geographic*: "When the year of the rooster is ushered in on February 10, families gather in their homes. Children are given *li xi,* or lucky money."

In analyzing the *Westways* map, I do not intend to diminish the knowledge of the author or the magazine editors. I do not believe anyone is purposefully exotifying Little Saigon. I merely suggest that marketplace multiculturalism encourages a particular framing of Vietnamese American places, one that entices tourism. This frame requires that Little Saigon appear inviting yet unusual, familiar yet distinct. Certain distortions are necessary. The background roadways, including the Garden Grove and San Diego Freeways, give Little Saigon's spatial coordinates. Ostensibly, people who receive this magazine drive these freeways regularly, but have never ventured to take the exit to Little Saigon. One of the ways the map invites visitors to Little Saigon is by flattening out the huge racial, cultural, and historical boundaries that have set Vietnamese Americans off from the mainstream by suggesting that one merely has to take the Little Saigon exit to see this other world. In a sense, the map erases many of Little Saigon's social coordinates.

The map's references to Asia are tasteful, not overdone—there is no garish bamboo script or references to ancient gongs ringing in the background—but nevertheless the accompanying imagery of an ornate collapsible paper fan, pagoda rooftops, a Buddhaesque statue, and a rooster potentially trigger for many readers a whole chain of related images and memories most likely acquired during visits to another "Asian" place, Chinatown. In this small way, the map invites AAA members to complete their own orientalized hermeneutic circle, this time by visiting a Vietnamese place. The small photograph of the war memorial is the only visual gesture to something Vietnamese. Even so, this gesture references the war, not the country or the people, thus subtly invoking the dominant collective memory of the war.

When the first Vietnamese refugees set up shop along Bolsa Avenue in Westminster in the late 1970s, they were met with a combination of hostility and indifference. But the deepening commitments of the local state and of Vietnamese Americans to promote Little Saigon as a tourist site suggest the emergence of marketplace multiculturalism as a nascent strategy for growth in central Orange County, including Westminster and Garden Grove. On the one hand, they reflect relatively recent efforts by the local state to take advantage of globalization in the form of Vietnamese American commerce and culture. On the other hand, the slogans convey the increasing desire on the part of Vietnamese American business owners to draw a nonethnic clientele. These twin impulses to capitalize on multiculturalism by catering to local tourists affect Orange County's Vietnamese American community-building and place-making in deeply complex and sometimes contradictory ways.

Shop Westminster (Communist Free Zone)

Efforts to revitalize the city of Westminster by celebrating and supporting business growth in Little Saigon have been boldly interlaced with a neoconservative ideological agenda. Michael Omi and Howard Winant describe neoconservatism as a political project based on individualism, market-based opportunity, and the curtailment of excessive state intervention, and as a racial project that refuses the legitimacy of "group rights" (1994, 128). By meshing their community-building and place-making demands carefully and closely with the requirements of Westminster's city officials, Vietnamese Americans have been able to advance their own business and political projects. In a climate that does not acknowledge the racialization of Vietnamese Americans, marketplace multiculturalism demands that Vietnamese American leaders promote a post–cold war culture of anticommunism and obtain positive recognition for their role as U.S. allies during the War in Viet Nam.

Marketplace multiculturalism took hold of the city of Westminster most definitively in the 1990s. In 1992, the city created a steering committee to address long-term planning. According to city manager Don Anderson, the idea of the "Bolsa Corridor Specific Plan" was to bring more tourism into Westminster by improving parking, auto and pedestrian traffic flow, and the aesthetic appearance of Little Saigon (Norman 1992). The Specific Plan was never adopted; instead, the city's General Plan incorporates some guidelines for future commercial and residential development. The General Plan contains a simple statement with regard to development in Little Saigon: "Little Saigon is the only recognized CPA [community plan area] at this time. Westminster desires to establish a regional tourist destination commercial, social, and institutional attraction *[sic]* based on an Asian ethnic theme in this area."

Turning an "Asian ethnic theme" into a tourist attraction should not strike anyone as an unusual idea since hovering over Orange County is the aura of Walt Disney. Sharon Zukin (1993) has argued more broadly that the logic of public consumption of ethnic culture across the nation is heavily influenced by the Disney Company. Andrew Ross notes, "'Theming' has been a feature of urban design and planning for some time now; private and public properties alike are being gussied up like Disney sets" (1997, 25). Efforts to convert Little Saigon into an ethnic "variation on a theme park" (Sorkin 1992) are both literal and figurative. Mr. Le Pham, a respected elder and one of the first to set up his newspaper business in Little Saigon, shared with me an idea that Little Saigon could become part of a big tourist triangle in southern California. The following excerpt comes from my first interview with him in 1996.

> LE PHAM: The most important business in Little Saigon in the future should be eating.
> *Eating? You mean like Chinatown?*
> LE PHAM: Yeah, eating. Because the basic tourist concession is a triangle of Disneyland in Anaheim, Knott's Berry Farm, and Little Saigon.
> *Huh.*
> LE PHAM: With, very far away, the Queen Mary in Long Beach.
> *Yes. Uh-hm.*
> LE PHAM: Let me tell you. In the three other place, the eating was very bad. . . . I think in five years, or around 2000, along Bolsa will be a good place for a hundred of eating places. It's look like Waikiki.

Mr. Le's comments suggest that one of the prerogatives of marketplace multiculturalism could be to turn Little Saigon into Orange County's Asian ethnic kitchen. The notion of Bolsa Avenue converting itself into a giant wok for starving tourists may boggle the minds of some readers, but other business leaders seem to think this dream is plausible. The short distance to Disneyland, "only ten minutes by freeway," has been described as one of Little Saigon's "big advantages" (Norman 1992).

Just what would Little Saigon look like if Walt Disney really did take over? In 1997 I interviewed Sam Banks, a non-Vietnamese real estate developer in Little Saigon whose family used to own large tracts of land in Westminster. Above his desk, a watercolor painting depicted his dream. In the center of the painting, a glamorous upscale hotel on Bolsa Avenue served as a convention center for out-of-town business people and wealthy tourists. The city block was sparkling and immaculate. Ethnic shops and restaurants dotted the street. In the picture, the real-life chaos and conflict of Little Saigon was reshaped into a fantasy of marketplace multicultural-ism—and social control. Mr. Banks was frankly pessimistic about the chances of his vision ever coming to fruition. In the years following this interview, I frequently perused publications of the Orange County Tourism Council and the guidebook of the California Cultural Tourism Coalition, *California: Culture's Edge*. The former rarely mentions Little Saigon, and the latter leaves Orange County out all together, possibly as a way to prevent the rest of the world from equating Disneyland with "California culture." The leaders of Little Saigon do not seem to have made much headway on the tourist triangle idea, but perhaps it is still too soon to tell.

By the late 1990s, Little Saigon had become an essential part of West-minster's self-marketing lexicon. In the 1996 Business Directory of the Viet-namese Chamber of Commerce, the Westminster Redevelopment Agency occupied a two-page spread with this announcement:

> Westminster: A great place to shop, live, play, or visit! With all that Orange County has to offer, visitors and residents alike will find Westminster centrally located, with a wide variety of shopping and one of Southern California's more unusual ethnic shopping districts—Little Saigon!

Soon thereafter, Westminster got an external boost from All-State, a private foundation that doles out awards of $10,000 to U.S. cities for whom rapid demographic changes require a revamping of civic infrastructure. In 1997, the All-State Foundation chose Westminster, along with nine other U.S. cities, as its "All-America City Winner." The label "All-America City" has since been plastered throughout the streets of Westminster, even on the doorway of city hall. Strangely, to my knowledge not one such label appeared along Bolsa Avenue or in the midst of Little Saigon. For years, a huge billboard announcing the All-America City award loomed over the Santa Monica freeway. The award is a shining example of marketplace multiculturalism: it both reanimates the notion of America as a haven for immigrants, and advances a well-worn notion of a common national culture based on individualism and free enterprise. The *All-America City Yearbook*, published by the National Civic League that year, provided this narration of the challenges and opportunities facing Westminster:

> With the fall of Saigon in 1975, Westminster, California drew a remarkable influx of Vietnamese refugees fleeing the chaos of the Vietnam War. They settled in the city, began to adjust with remarkable speed, and soon developed a five-mile corridor of enterprises now known as "Little Saigon" that attracts not only Southeast Asian shoppers but tourists as well. . . . The sudden influx of newcomers strained city services, streets, and schools. . . . There was a clear need for an intensive campaign to address and resolve the community's ethnic struggles. Hard work and the cooperation of thousands of residents has helped this unique city write a fascinating new chapter in the story of America as a nation of diversity.

In celebrating this "new chapter" in America's history, the All-State Foundation accomplished a delicate task of smoothing over the controversial and traumatic history of the war. Just as the *Westways* map describes the Westminster War Memorial with aplomb, so this statement treats the war simply as another date in America's long history of multiculturalism. Treating American history this way removes from view the intense, often life-and-death struggles between and among groups wielding hugely different amounts of institutional, structural, and representational power. Referring to the community's struggles in "ethnic" terms also prevents any discussion of the racialization of Vietnamese Americans, or of the constructions of and possessive investments in whiteness throughout Orange County's postsuburban landscape. Simultaneously, by focusing on the strain created by the unexpected arrival of thousands of Vietnamese refugees in 1975, rather than on the much deeper and longer problems caused by uneven capitalist growth across the central, coastal, and southern regions of Orange County, the diversity narrative makes city hall into a moral hero in a familiar immigrant success story.

At certain times, marketplace multiculturalism requires an even more pronounced political collaboration on the part of both city hall and Vietnamese American leaders, whether in business or community issues. The

Westminster Redevelopment Agency's strategy to entice people to "shop Westminster" and the All-America City award suggest that the city must attend equally to "doing right" by the Vietnamese American community and to making money off of them. The city certainly does not want to lose money because of anything that happens in Little Saigon.

Thus, in 2004, the Vietnamese American city councilors of Westminster and Garden Grove proposed and then passed resolutions that were commonly understood to establish Little Saigon as a "Communist Free Zone." The resolutions ban communists from Little Saigon by declaration and demand. First, they declare that they do not "condone, welcome, or sanction stops, drive-bys, or visits" by "representatives or officials from the Socialist Republic of Vietnam." Westminster adds that they do not welcome "commercial or trade delegations" from Viet Nam either. Second, they resolve to obtain ten to fourteen days' prior warning from the U.S. State Department of any such travel plans on the part of Vietnamese officials. Finally, the cities resolve not to repeat "the mass demonstrations of 1999" and the "*unprecedented financial burdens*" (my emphasis) they incurred. Westminster specifies that it paid $750,000 to the Westminster Police Department and neighboring police forces because of the Hi-Tek incident. Garden Grove states simply that it spent "an inordinate amount of public safety funds" to maintain "peace and order in Little Saigon" at that time. Basically, the resolutions mesh together the political sympathies of Vietnamese Americans with the budget fears of everyone else. Both cities hope to avoid overspending public funds on conflicts that are internal to the Vietnamese American community.[13]

Thus, a close reading of the so-called Communist Free Zone resolutions suggests that for Westminster and Garden Grove the budgetary implications of managing political conflict in Little Saigon were at least as frightening as the conflicts themselves. Certainly, neither city intends to find itself in the red ever again because of a poorly handled protest against communism. In addition, the sheer size of the Vietnamese American population in Westminster and Garden Grove, and their growing economic and political clout—both have elected Vietnamese Americans onto their city councils or their school boards—make it financially advisable for both cities to take seriously the cultural and political claims of the Vietnamese Americans in their midst.

Controversy over a Too-Chinese Bridge

When it comes to issues that do not play directly into the local state's development or ideological agenda, the dilemmas posed to Vietnamese Americans by marketplace multiculturalism may not receive the same kind of attention from city hall. The 1996 controversy over Harmony Bridge, described in detail in the Introduction, revealed the divergent implications of marketplace multiculturalism for the local state, and for Vietnamese American business and community leaders. While city hall lauded the project for its potential to boost tourism and to showcase "freedom" in Little Saigon, Vietnamese Americans fought bitterly about whether or not the project would turn Little Saigon into an "Asian Town." In the end the Harmony Bridge was never built, but the controversy that ensued has complicated subsequent efforts to develop Little Saigon.

> Whoever is the author of the bridge . . . is the one to control the politics of Little Saigon.—Frank Jao, bridge developer
> It's the uniqueness that attracts tourists to come, not diversity, [which] is boring.—Mai Cong, community leader
> [The bridge] would have helped promote Little Saigon as a tourist destination and as the cultural and economic capital of the Vietnamese free world.—Charles Smith, former Mayor of Westminster[14]

The "collapse" of Harmony Bridge illustrates the tensions between and among the potential uses of culture and ethnicity in Little Saigon, and the tendency of marketplace multiculturalism to exacerbate those tensions. On one side, Orange County's premier developer, the Chinese-Vietnamese rags-to-riches entrepreneur Frank Jao, thought that building a minimall on a footbridge would be good for his business—and therefore, good for the Vietnamese American community. In Jao's eyes, using Chinese architectural references only would have enhanced the bridge's aesthetic appeal to tourists. On the other side, Jao's detractors saw in his scheme a hidden plot to transform Little Saigon into a Chinatown, thinly disguised under the label "Asian Village."

Blissfully unmoved by the controversy over whether or not Jao's project was too Chinese and therefore an illegitimate addition to Little Saigon, Westminster's city officials simply returned to the trusty theme of the free-market economy and anticommunism. Referring to Little Saigon as "the cultural and economic capital of the Vietnamese free world," Charles Smith confirmed that the political-economic and the symbolic/cultural dimensions of globalization are indeed intertwined, and that the rise of Little Saigon fuels both the city's economic growth and its neoconservative ideological agenda.

Meanwhile, the English-language press treated the Harmony Bridge conflict with a condescension that sometimes bordered on racism, especially when they focused on the petty skirmishes between the eccentric personalities of Frank Jao and Mai Cong. The idea that Vietnamese are prone to bickering was one of the justifications for increasing U.S. military involvement during the war: the Vietnamese, the hawks told the U.S. public, are not capable of governing themselves. At other times, reporters were more attuned to the deep historical roots of this conflict, resulting from centuries of Chinese colonialism in Viet Nam, or to the obvious loss of revenue to Westminster's singular business district.

For young Vietnamese Americans, the Harmony Bridge controversy provoked a discussion of Vietnamese identity that often took an indignant tone. For instance, Malia Cong, then an undergraduate at the University of California, Irvine, observed the New Saigon Mall, then a recent development of Frank Jao (this mall was razed to the ground and replaced by a housing development in later years), with discernible outrage.

> Inside the Mall is a culturally self-contradictory environment. . . . The exterior resembles Chinese architecture, the statues are only of Chinese figures and some signs in the mall read "Chinese clothing sold here." Though some of the foods sold are Vietnamese, a significant portion is American style food like peanut butter cookies or hybrids like "Saigon burger," a previously-never-seen-before invention. . . . claims of Vietnamese character do not coincide with its actual architecture and activity. Architecturally, New Saigon Mall may be a beautiful swan amid the ugly ducklings of some of Little Saigon's other shopping centers. . . . But while beauty can be created, authenticity cannot. (1997, 5)

This student writer's observation that Jao's New Saigon Mall is "culturally self-contradictory" rests on an idealistic notion that culture and identity in Little Saigon can and should be purely Vietnamese. Instead, presumably because Jao is a Chinese entrepreneur and is therefore insensitive to issues of authentic identity, the mall is also shamelessly Chinese. Then, as if to add insult to injury, the mall also contains "American" and other "hybrid" influences, therefore worsening the impurities not just of this mall, but of the entire business district.

Perhaps this undergraduate student has since developed new views about identity and authenticity in Little Saigon. But in an article analyzing the "sense of community" produced by commercial establishments along Bolsa Avenue, two more advanced scholars treat the social identity of Little Saigon in a similar way as if it were linked naturally and inevitably to commerce, ignoring altogether the major role of ethnic Chinese in business and thus making no comment on the Chinese-Vietnamese divide (McLaughlin and Jesilow 1998). The article also fails to contextualize the impact of Little Saigon in revitalizing an otherwise depressed region, reinforcing instead the image of entrepreneurial Vietnamese pulling themselves up by their bootstraps. They argue that the promotion of tourism in Little Saigon will ruin its distinctiveness and essentially sell out the culture.

Yet what all these writers miss is that the drive of marketplace multiculturalism is precisely to merge local and global influences so as to enhance urban growth and enliven the region's cultural and symbolic landscape. Staying Vietnamese depends on the extent to which Vietnamese American business and community leaders can ride the marketplace multiculturalism bandwagon and obtain something for themselves and their constituencies—despite the many cleavages in the community that marketplace multiculturalism opens up. There is no way to preserve the true identity of Little Saigon. This is not to dismiss the troubling implications of market-driven development for Little Saigon's place identity, or for the residents' feeling of belonging to the place. Sentimental and symbolic attachments to place are important, especially for young Vietnamese Americans who are looking for their roots in local settings.

As if to soothe a sore spot, the *Nguoi Viet Yearbook* for 2005 included an essay titled "Mot Cong Dong, Hai Anh Huong/One Community, Two Cultures." This essay celebrates and affirms the contributions of ethnic Chinese to the growth of Little Saigon. Anti-Chinese sentiment among Vietnamese is real and has historical roots in Viet Nam. The inclusion of this essay alongside an unusual discussion of current scholarship on Vietnamese Americans suggests an important effort by *Nguoi Viet* editors to widen the perspectives of its readers.

"We Are Still Struggling With What Is Community": Growth as a Neighborhood Issue

Reviving Dorchester

Far away on the nation's other coast, marketplace multiculturalism has posed a different set of challenges and opportunities to Boston's Vietnamese American community. Aside from its much smaller population size—Suffolk County had 10,818 Vietnamese in 2000, compared to 135,548 in Orange County—Boston's Vietnamese American community is also geographically dispersed into several nonadjacent neighborhoods and without a strong, self-sustaining ethnic economy. Where the *Nguoi Viet Yearbook*

2005 contained thousands of listings in more than seven hundred pages, the last Boston Vietnamese American business directory that I know of was published in 1996 and contained about one hundred listings in some eighty pages. Little Saigon's massive business district spans five square miles, where the Vietnamese-owned shops in Fields Corner continue for about five blocks along Dorchester Avenue.

To top off Boston's greatest disadvantage regarding the growth of a distinct and separate Vietnamese American economic enclave, the already existing neighborhood of Chinatown has been rejuvenated by Vietnamese entrepreneurship, some of it Chinese Vietnamese. In the 1980s, a few restaurants and shops moved back and forth between Fields Corner and Chinatown, but in the end, Fields Corner's zoning laws will not abide the full range of industries—for example, noodle or textile/garment factories—that are the mainstay of Chinatown. A key figure in the neighborhood told me of a plan to build a noodle factory in Fields Corner. The idea, put forward by an alliance of Chinatown moguls and white developers from Dorchester, never got off the ground because, in his words, "the diversity of Fields Corner keeps it from being an exploitative economy base on low-wage jobs à la Chinatown." My point is not to affirm or question the portrayal of Chinatown as a trap for ethnic labor, but rather to offer a glimpse of the way things are done differently in Boston. Where Orange County's Vietnamese American leadership debates the authenticity of Little Saigon, Boston's Vietnamese American leaders forthrightly eschew Chinatown as a model of development. For a number of reasons having nothing to do with the history of Chinese colonialism in Viet Nam, making a Vietnamese version of Chinatown in Fields Corner never has been, and never will be, an option.

Thus, instead of assembling a huge business district à la Little Saigon, Vietnamese American community-building and place-making in Boston consists mainly in highlighting the physical presence of Vietnamese Americans in the Fields Corner area of Dorchester and in helping to revitalize the area through the creation of jobs and affordable housing. This is not to downplay the important role of ethnic entrepreneurship in giving Fields Corner a Vietnamese reputation. But whereas small business ownership drives marketplace multiculturalism in Little Saigon, in Fields Corner marketplace multiculturalism is driven by a mix of neighborhood development strategies—including but not limited to business development—along with carefully fashioned and, relative to Orange County, subdued references to Vietnamese culture, politics, and history.

Dorchester has a fascinating history of immigration and development, from 1630, as a series of villages to a distinct town which was incorporated into the City of Boston in 1870. It also has an exciting future, as diverse ethnic groups continue to make their homes here. Succeeding groups have created local institutions and made contributions to the life of the neighborhood which are shown here. We hope this map will be an inspiration for more and new chapters to be recorded about different aspects of Dorchester's villages.—Dorchester booster map, June 1996

Just as the All-State Foundation helped the city of Westminster to frame the arrival of Vietnamese in terms of a new chapter in America's history of diversity, so for Dorchester's boosters the revitalization of Fields Corner by Vietnamese American entrepreneurs extends a centuries-old tale of immigration and assimilation. Storefronts inherited from Jewish, Greek, Irish, and finally Vietnamese owners tell a familiar story of ethnic "invasion and succession" (Park, Burgess, and McKenzie 1968, 51). In the past decade, Vietnamese American entrepreneurship has had a dramatic effect on neighborhood life, facilitating a unique juxtaposition of cultural elements such as Vietnamese doctor's offices and nail salons, Irish pubs, and a fried chicken franchise along "Dot (Dorchester) Ave." Inside the shops, it is not unusual to see interactions between Vietnamese shopkeepers and, for example, Haitian or Cape Verdean youth. Such multicultural exchanges are a celebrated feature of Boston's contemporary urban scene, but they are certainly not left to happenstance. Marketplace multiculturalism means that Boston's city managers, planners, and developers keep a close eye on the potential sources for new growth and do what they can to steer, control, and promote them.

Yen T. Vo is a former political detainee who is well respected by many elders in the community. Active in his church parish, he is also the owner of a bottle redemption center. The case of Mr. Yen and his small business is one example of the local state channeling the revitalizing impact of Vietnamese American small businesses to meet the interests of the neighborhood at large. In Mr. Yen's case, the channeling occurred at his expense. Mr. Yen told me that the city's Public Facilities Department (PFD) recruited him and his bottle return center to a Dorchester neighborhood adjacent to Fields Corner in 1991. (In 1997, the PFD was renamed the Department of Neighborhood Development, or DND.) Mr. Yen had just closed his three-year-old gift shop in Fields Corner because the work was too hard on his wife, and he was looking for another business opportunity. Mr. Yen said he was assured by the PFD that they would take care of all the necessary paperwork. At the time of this interview in 1995, Mr. Yen had just been told that his operating license was in question. Rising displays of xenophobia in the neighborhood were making his store's location even more of a problem. During the summer of 1994, someone spray painted the message "Vietcong Go Home" on his storefront windows.

Mr. Yen's operating license was under question because his landlord neglected to file a variance permit to inform the city of a change in tenant. It is not clear whether the PFD was then selectively enforcing a little-known rule, or if somehow the rule was genuinely overlooked. Mr. Yen told me that a PFD official had driven him around nearby residential areas to encourage him to choose a new site. This is puzzling, since zoning laws require that redemption centers be located in industrial areas.

A key figure in the development of the Fields Corner neighborhood believes that Mr. Yen was recruited specifically in order to revitalize the adjacent blighted area. As the value of the surrounding real estate increased, that mission was accomplished. I was not able to secure an interview with the PFD. Years later, I found Mr. Yen had moved his bottle redemption center a few miles down Washington Street in Codman Square, an area with its own distinct non-Vietnamese identity. This new location suggests that Mr. Yen's identity as Vietnamese, the emerging identity of Fields Corner as Boston's Vietnamese neighborhood, and the role of Vietnamese entrepreneurs in reviving Boston's depressed areas were not necessarily linked. In other words, at least at that point in time, the local state saw the potential of steering Vietnamese ethnic entrepreneurship to different points around the city, even outside of Fields Corner.

One of the accomplishments of Vietnamese American place-making in subsequent years has been to attach to Fields Corner an identity so strongly Vietnamese that the place becomes nearly synonymous with the Vietnamese American community. In part this is a requirement of marketplace multiculturalism in Boston. Once an industrial city, neighborhood boundaries historically contained ethnic populations: the North End/Little Italy, the South End/Southie, and Chinatown are examples of this old-fashioned overlap between neighborhood and ethnic territories. As Boston developer Alex Kreiger et al. write,

> Boston remains a city of strongly defined neighborhoods. Mostly it benefits from this. Sometimes it suffers from an attendant tribalism. In Boston the dialectical relationship between neighborhood lines and the wariness of one neighborhood toward an adjoining one seems part of the physical fabric itself. (2001, 154)

The fact that Boston's Vietnamese American residents are scattered across several, nonadjacent neighborhoods may be considered a political and cultural hindrance, because one way that Bostonians orient themselves—and confer power and resources to new arrivals—is to refer to neighborhoods as communities.

The New Bostonians

Boston's multicultural agenda has different demands and consequently different effects on Vietnamese American community-building and place-making than Orange County's does. Without the human, financial, or geographic resources needed for a full-blown shopping/tourist zone à la Orange County's Little Saigon, Vietnamese American leaders have turned for their community-growth strategy to neighborhood development in Fields Corner, a multicultural, multiracial area of Dorchester. Meanwhile, the Vietnamese American community is Boston-wide, not confined to one neighborhood. They also take great pains to distinguish Fields Corner from Chinatown, Boston's other Asian American place.

In 1994, Viet-AID, a Vietnamese American community development corporation, took over as the main engine for Vietnamese American place-making in Fields Corner and one of the key Vietnamese forces behind Boston's marketplace multiculturalism. Their stamping Fields Corner as a Vietnamese village—most visibly in 2002 by constructing a new two-story community center there—propelled the Vietnamese American community into a stronger phase of clout and recognition in the city. Boston's Vietnamese American place-making is happening in an active arena that is crowded with many other stakeholders: the federal, state, and local government; the private sector, including foundations and corporations; and neighborhood organizations and initiatives such as the Fields Corner CDC, the Fields Corner Civic Association, and the Fields Corner Main Streets Program.[15] With an annual budget of approximately $200,000 and a staff of ten, Viet-AID is a small but mighty advocate for Vietnamese American community growth.

Viet-AID's approach to community growth represents an important and critical shift from the post-1975 era of mutual assistance agencies, social service providers, and "volags" (voluntary agencies) that in turn subsisted on federal- and state-level funding for refugee resettlement. As that funding dwindled, the Massachusetts Office of Refugees and Immigrants pushed the Vietnamese community to form a community development corporation (CDC) and to think in terms of economic development, which requires a geographic rather than ethnic base for community. CDCs are quasi-public/private organizations developed nationwide in the 1960s and 1970s that seek to address housing construction and management, social and educational programs, and business development assistance and lending. To my knowledge, there is no CDC in Little Saigon, and perhaps no such inclination to create a CDC in the whole of Orange County. The Massachusetts Association of CDCs, of which both Viet-AID and Fields Corner CDC are members, states as part of its mission for 2004–2008:

> We support and advance the affordable housing, economic development, and community-building strategies of our members. We work to build the power of low and moderate income people to achieve greater economic, social and racial justice.[16]

Every CDC is free to define its own mission and values. For example, Viet-AID's mission is "to build a strong Vietnamese American community in Boston," a statement that specifies a citywide Vietnamese focus rather than a neighborhood one. Just a few blocks away, the much older Fields Corner CDC is obviously a neighborhood organization. Their executive director, Jane Matheson, follows private-sector practices—and proudly votes Republican, a rarity in the CDC world. Matheson believes that accepting public money means "the tail wags the dog," and that Fields Corner must define its own needs.[17] Although occasionally friction presides, the distinct perspectives and commitments of these two organizations sometimes overlap, with productive results for the neighborhood. Certainly neither organization can afford to ignore the other one for very long, and both must attend to the voices and needs of local residents, even those who are not Vietnamese American.

By straddling two frameworks—one defined by being Vietnamese, and the other defined by neighborhood development—Viet-AID occupies a potentially difficult and sometimes openly conflicted position regarding which definition of "community" they actually serve. This is a dilemma not of their own choosing. Throughout the many years I interviewed the dedicated and thoughtful people behind Viet-AID, this difficult question about community always has persisted and remained unresolved. In recent years, the question apparently became a central point of discussion. In 1997, I met with Mr. Hoa Nguyen for the third time. By then, he was familiar with my research, and sometimes asked me for answers I was hoping he would give me.

Is Fields Corner still growing?

HOA NGUYEN: In terms of businesses it's still growing. A new video store, a new jewelry store. It's just incredible. Recently a building that was vacant is full, they mow down stuff, rehab it. . . . Fields Corner is really coming alive. At the same time, residents, Fields Corner citizens, are preventing development. They just afraid, they want to keep it like a little urban, a little suburban. . . . Viet-AID is just about to get sixteen thousand feet of land for the community center on Charles Street . . . the Fields Corner CDC likes the idea of the center but wants to prevent more garage, bars. But development that is healthy they will support.

How does the development help the community? Not everyone lives in Fields Corner.

HOA NGUYEN: Right now we still have a good number who lives in Fields Corner. . . . Vietnamese are buying houses. Early waves in late 1970s, early 1980s have no desire to stay in Dorchester area. But late waves, late 80s, early 90s, they really want to buy houses in the Fields Corner area. I don't know why. That population will continue to stay. The poor and elderly always stay, there's no way that they can go.

They're trapped?

HOA NGUYEN: In a way, yes. As long as we retain the businesses, we'll still have the population to come back to the area to utilize the center, the businesses, there will be a sense of Vietnamese community there. We also try to get into affordable housing for the elderly.

What about Vietnamese in other areas?

HOA NGUYEN: There still some, but not much organizing for them. . . . I have a thought. Have you been able to define what is community?

[laughing] *That's why I'm talking to you.*

Later on in the interview, Mr. Nguyen told me with reference to Vietnamese Americans in Boston that "We are still struggling with what is community, how do we define community." In chapter 1, Mr. Nguyen explained what he describes as the "exile concept of community," that is, that the older exiled generation looks at community-building as the opportunity to establish a place of their own in lieu of their lost homeland of Viet Nam. In the absence of a business/tourist district that could serve some of these exile functions, Boston's Vietnamese Americans had to come up with an alternative plan. Viet-AID led in the conceptualization and, later, the construction of an actual two-story edifice now referred to as the Vietnamese American Community Center, or just "the Center." As a symbol of Vietnamese American community, the Center accomplishes the very important task of marking Fields Corner as a Vietnamese American neighborhood.

In truth, Fields Corner is home to Vietnamese and to a range of other racialized ethnic groups, including third- or fourth-generation Irish Americans and newer immigrant arrivals from Mexico and other Central American countries, Haiti, and Cape Verde.[18] In this sense, Fields Corner is the spatial locus for Vietnamese Americans, but this symbolization is accomplished against some resistance, both by longtime residents, who might resist any kind of change, and by newer immigrant groups who resent the Vietnamese American rise to power and recognition.

Yet within Viet-AID, a divide between staff, nearly half of whom live in Fields Corner, and board members, most or all of whom do not, means that the strain between Vietnamese and Latinos or Cape Verdeans is not perceived as significant by everyone in the organization. In 2005, a board member of the Viet-AID told me that a staff member took a survey of the neighborhood and actually documented this resentment, which should press the organization to become aware of two questions: Should Viet-AID become multiethnic? If not, how should Viet-AID engage with the neighborhood and speak on its behalf? These questions are made more urgent by the ongoing revamp and restoration of the Fields Corner subway station, which could become a "destination point" in the city if the entire neighborhood were organized to campaign for it. In addition, unlike Chinatown whose population has been and may continue to be replenished by immigration, Fields Corner will not be receiving new flows of Vietnamese refugees or immigrants. Thus, for Viet-AID to keep its geographic base strong, becoming a multiethnic CDC seems an inevitable option, but one with difficult implications for its original mission to build a strong Vietnamese American community in Boston.

Historically, as scholar and community organizer Marie Kennedy recently reminded me, Boston has been a "city of turf." Memories of racism, particularly during the days of restrictive covenants and court-ordered busing, meant there were places that, if you were black, you avoided because that turf belonged to whites (King 1981). In that context, the struggles of poor, minority neighborhoods such as Roxbury could be seen as struggles for community empowerment *and* neighborhood empowerment: the processes of internal colonialism forced an extremely close overlap between racial and spatial boundaries. For that reason, Marie Kennedy and her late colleague Mauricio Gastón took pains to distinguish between Roxbury's "community"—its working-class minority residents—and its neighborhood: the land, the buildings, and the location. "As a neighborhood," they wrote, "Roxbury is a commodity," underscoring the greater value given to real estate rather than to people (Gastón and Kennedy 1987, 181). Ultimately, Roxbury's demise as a community was the result of displacement and gentrification, the flip side of downtown's revival.

Fields Corner, too, was an area neglected in those heady days of urban renewal. In the following three decades, however, the resuscitation of Fields Corner depended upon the search by Vietnamese and other immigrants for cheap rents and access to public transportation, and upon the willingness of older residents to accommodate and abide by their new neighbors. Still, conflict brewed. Journalist Lowell Weiss described Fields Corner as an "inner-city melting pot . . . on the verge of boiling over" (1994, 36). The Fields Corner CDC and Viet-AID have expended great resources in addressing racial tensions, cleaning up the streets, clamping down on crime, and creating affordable housing. In time, Boston's marketplace multiculturalism may succeed in turning Fields Corner, as both a neighborhood *and* a community, into a saleable commodity: the diversity of the population, packaged properly as part of the continuing saga of Dorchester's immigrant villages, could become part of the lure. Meanwhile, for the poor and elderly who are more or less trapped in place, not only in Fields Corner but in every neighborhood of nearly every city, marketplace multiculturalism may have a less salutary impact, at least in the short run.

Never a Chinatown

In Orange County's Little Saigon, the contribution of ethnic Chinese to the Vietnamese American ethnic economy is massive and undeniable. Because the visible presence of ethnic Chinese contradicts the notion of an ethnic community bounded by a unified national culture and history—a notion that would at least in theory support the project of staying Vietnamese in America—the Chinese influences in Little Saigon have been the topic of heated controversy. The argument over Harmony Bridge brought that debate out to the public and dampened the enthusiasm of some Chinese Vietnamese entrepreneurs to go out on a limb for the Vietnamese American community. Yet Little Saigon, like other Asian enclaves in the United States, continues to attract overseas Chinese as potential investors.

Vietnamese Americans who have positioned themselves as leaders in the Fields Corner area of Boston refer disparagingly to Little Saigon as "another Chinatown," which they say they do not want to emulate. As an Asian American ethnic place, Chinatown is a competitor for resources, including ethnic entrepreneurship. Most of the Vietnamese businesses in Chinatown are owned by ethnic Chinese who capture a bigger customer base there than they would in Fields Corner. But as middle- and upper-class professional Asian Americans head out to outer-ring suburbs, the most lucrative Asian ethnic markets are moving to places that suburbanites can easily access on the way into or out of the city. Recently, a Chinese-Vietnamese mega-grocery called Super88 opened in the South Bay Mall off the 93 expressway.

Ethnic Chinese in Little Saigon play leadership roles as real estate developers and business owners. But my Boston interviewees believe that ethnic Chinese do not play an important role in the leadership of Fields Corner or of Boston's Vietnamese American community in general. As Tuyet Huynh so clearly put it to me in an e-mail communication in 1999, ethnic Chinese "have terrible reputations for community participation or community giving. . . . The Chinese give to Chinese causes or to Chinatown, the Vietnamese give to Vietnamese causes, and the ethnic Chinese from Viet Nam give to neither."

This is not to say that Boston's Vietnamese Americans do not understand the importance of ethnic entrepreneurship as an alternative path into the job market; one of Viet-AID's goals is to stimulate and support small business growth in Fields Corner. However, without the real estate opportunities or the coethnic customer base, Fields Corner does not have the option of developing itself into a full-blown enclave economy in the image of Little Saigon. Therefore, Viet-AID's strategy must consider other ways to harness ethnicity as a resource and to engage with Boston's marketplace multiculturalism.

Trang Q. Lam owns a drugstore, a mom-and-pop version of CVS or Rite Aid, that is a landmark in Fields Corner because of its prominent marquee and location, on Dorchester Avenue, Fields Corner's Main Street. Mr. Trang will fill your prescriptions and sell you all manner of food and drink: onions, apples, imported noodles, sacks of rice, rice cookers, Vietnamese baked goods, sweets, canned coffee. You can also get a lottery ticket or leave your film to be developed.

Mr. Trang left Viet Nam in 1975 when he was twenty-three years old. He had served in the South Vietnamese Army (ARVN) for four years and had achieved the rank of lieutenant. Via fishing boat, he escaped to the Philippines with his pregnant wife and a dozen other people. After more than one year in the refugee camp, he used his ARVN background to make a connection to Catholic Charities in southern Massachusetts. A former professor of Mr. Trang's encouraged him to come to Boston.

Mr. Trang and his wife moved to Dorchester because of its cheap rents, good schools, and accessibility to public transportation. Although he had a college degree in philosophy from Viet Nam, Mr. Trang returned to college and obtained a bachelor of science degree from the University of Massachusetts, Boston. He also took classes in pharmacy. He became a naturalized citizen in the mid-1980s and shortly afterward opened his business.

Unlike Mr. Le in Little Saigon, Mr. Trang is not ethnic Chinese. Also unlike Mr. Le, Mr. Trang is deeply and openly invested in homeland politics. The shop offers a means of livelihood, and he is a participating member of the Dorchester Board of Trade, but his personal mission is clearly political. At times during the interview, it seemed he had visions of running for public office. He talked like a politician, making big statements about big issues and trying to win my vote. When I asked him why he became a Republican, he told me, "If we want to be active in society, we should be in a group. The GOP has a similar platform to us: democracy, freedom, advancement, opportunity to go to the middle class, help people around the world."

From Mr. Trang's point of view, community-building is for the next generation. The future is complex for his children, though, because they have to learn to be Vietnamese without ever going "back" to Viet Nam. Maintaining cultural and political ties, then, is a parent's responsibility.

> I tell them stories every day. I tell them obey your parents, we will never abandon you. Don't take too much individual freedom. Over here, children forgot parents' rights. In Viet Nam, children are the extension of the parent's life. Parents need to discipline children so there will not be broken homes. The reason we stay here is to invest in the education of our children. We cannot say "Que será, será."

Mr. Trang is probably not the most successful Vietnamese American businessperson in Boston. The most lucrative businesses are located outside of Fields Corner or Chinatown, where they can access a larger and more affluent clientele. However, because Mr. Trang is a vocal member of the Vietnamese community and because his store is a prominent feature of Fields Corner, he plays an important role in the business and political decisions in the neighborhood and the community. In this sense, Mr. Trang is an agent of marketplace multiculturalism who puts forth a particular perspective on history, and whose frequent minispeeches about freedom and democracy make a direct connect between Boston's local Vietnamese American community and the international Vietnamese diaspora.

Selling Vietnamese Identity

In Orange County and Boston, Vietnamese Americans are packaging place and community so as to incorporate themselves into the cultural, symbolic, and financial economy. Producing Vietnameseness for sale and consumption involves naming places such as Little Saigon and Fields Corner as sources of cultural diversity. But to transform Vietnamese culture into a desirable commodity in America—rather than a gesture to a lost war, bad memories, or inassimilable refugees—leaders must attend to the stigma of history and racism that U.S. public discourse attaches to the idea of "Vietnam." Earlier in the book, place-making demanded attention to racialization and memory. In this chapter, place-making attends to the prerogatives of marketplace multiculturalism.

During the past twenty years, neoconservatives have rendered the political agenda of multiculturalism nearly toothless by reducing the civil rights–era objective of racial justice to a much more benign act of putting a few brown faces "at the table"—while whites remain in charge. But within U.S. metropolitan regions, multiculturalism has become a hot ticket to economic growth and development and a necessary feature of tourist and heritage districts often constructed around ethnic enclaves such as Chinatown and Little Saigon. In other words, multiculturalism as it actually exists today in the United States is more of a strategy for selling culture—linking global changes to local development—than a road to political and social justice.[19]

The consequences of this marketplace version of multiculturalism for the economic and political empowerment of racialized ethnic groups such as the Vietnamese Americans are mixed. On the one hand, thriving Vietnamese business districts such as Little Saigon in Orange County are better able to provide jobs, services, resources, and a "sense of home" to a population that is otherwise marginalized from white, middle-class society. On the other hand, the growth of these districts depends upon the reification and commodification of Vietnamese culture, which leads in turn to complex problems of authenticity and misrepresentation.

While these problems are inherent to marketplace multiculturalism, they manifest in unique ways within Vietnamese American communities and places that deserve their own telling. First, Vietnamese American place-making gives significance to Little Saigon and Fields Corner as sites of Vietnamese American commerce and culture despite the fact that in both cases, middle- and upper-class Vietnamese Americans are moving away to more affluent cities and neighborhoods. For example, the median household income for the city of Westminster is $49,450 (Vietnamese population: 27,887), compared to the median household income for Irvine of $72,057 (Vietnamese population: 4,734). Boston has a median household income of $39,629 (Vietnamese population: 11,376), compared to the median household income for Quincy of $47,121 (Vietnamese population: 1,850). The city of Quincy is an up-and-coming destination for middle-class Asian Americans. Trapped in Little Saigon and Fields Corner, the poorest Vietnamese residents nonetheless give credibility to those places as "authentically Vietnamese."

Second, the Vietnamese American economy is owned and run primarily by ethnic Chinese from Viet Nam and fueled with investments by overseas Chinese (Gold 1994). The normalization of trade relations between the United States and Viet Nam in 1994 may have sparked some interest in Little Saigon on the part of businesses in Viet Nam, but in terms of scale of investment, more Vietnamese Americans seem to be finding business opportunities in Viet Nam.[20] Ethnic Chinese were purged from Viet Nam, and many arrived in the United States in the early 1980s under less than favorable circumstances. Now, Orange County's Little Saigon is a thriving business district. Has marketplace multiculturalism allowed these Chinese Vietnamese entrepreneurs in Orange County to transform themselves into an "Uptown" class that preys on the misfortunes of the "Downtown" Vietnamese who are not Chinese? Or are they merely fulfilling the same business function that they still play in Cho Lon, Chinatown in Ho Chi Minh City, and allowing the Vietnamese to run the show in every other way? Marketplace multiculturalism exacerbates these questions in Orange County. These questions, however, do not plague Fields Corner. Ethnic Chinese Vietnamese generally locate their businesses in Boston's Chinatown neighborhood and do not contribute in a significant way to Vietnamese American place-making or community-building.

Third, many Vietnamese American leaders in Little Saigon see a division of labor between those that "do politics"—that is, they attend to internal and external community relations—and those that "do business." This demarcation reflects the cultural boundary between Vietnamese, who presumably take more interest in political/community issues, and the Chinese Vietnamese, who are businesspeople ostensibly not so interested in politics. Certainly among the people I spoke with in Orange County and Boston, those who identified themselves to me as ethnic Chinese were all primarily business owners. In Little Saigon, where business is a defining element of the community, I was not surprised when a spokesperson for the Vietnamese Chamber of Commerce told me that "Whatever is good for business is also good for the community." Yet the Hi-Tek incident of 1999 shows that business and politics, where politics equals anticommunism, are tightly linked in Vietnamese America. Indeed, in Orange County, marketplace multiculturalism encourages Vietnamese American leaders to play up certain aspects of their politics, specifically their anticommunist, anti–Viet Nam sentiments, as a way to solidify their alliances with the local neoconservative establishment.

Framing Vietnamese America in terms of marketplace multiculturalism rather than in the more familiar terms of ethnic entrepreneurship and the ethnic economy allows me to disrupt the easy equation between the advancement of individual businesses with the well-being of the entire community. I do not mean to belittle the significant impact of the ethnic economy on the power and clout of the community, but I do intend to bring into view some of the external factors that shape the directions the Vietnamese American economy must take.

Juxtaposing Orange County and Boston puts in direct relief two contrasting views of community growth, one based on spurring the business district and tourism, the other based on fortifying the neighborhood by spurring affordable housing and jobs. Boston's Vietnamese Americans work within a multicultural discourse that emphasizes neighborhoods, and so their priorities are sometimes conflicted between the spatial area of Fields Corner and the social networks of Vietnamese throughout the city of Boston. This conflict between place and Vietnameseness leaves a central question permanently unresolved for Vietnamese Bostonians: What is community? From what I have observed so far, community is a process and a struggle over resources, including platial identity.

Chapter 5   Implications for Community and Place

MORE THAN THREE DECADES after the "shock of arrival," Vietnamese refugees, immigrants, and their U.S.–born children have transformed themselves from unexpected strangers to familiar, and often celebrated, ethnic minorities.[1] Mainstream social scientists and policy makers have analyzed meticulously the pace and character of Vietnamese assimilation, pointing to their positive inclination to vote, speak English, take up white-collar professions, and move to the suburbs.[2] Looking for the mechanisms by which Vietnamese have been able to advance themselves in the absence of larger structural opportunities, researchers have focused on the significance of "ethnic" community ties, trust, geographic concentration, and in the case of ethnic Chinese entrepreneurs, links to overseas capital.[3] These findings are important because of the possibility that future refugees and immigrants might face similar conditions in U.S. society, and their difficulties might be mitigated by policies and practices that enable a smoother incorporation. At the same time, to the extent that researchers and policy makers frame Vietnamese accomplishments in model-minority terms—erasing U.S. militarism and imperialism and emphasizing Confucian traits of collectivity, perseverance, and sacrifice so that the concurrent claims of structural racism on the part of poor blacks and Latinos may then be downplayed as racially coded "cultural" or "behavioral" deficiencies—then the efforts of Vietnamese to make a home in America have also been twisted to reinforce complicated and racialized narratives about belonging and national identity. It is as if Vietnamese refugees and immigrants inadvertently have become agents of a structural adjustment plan to remake the face and body politic of the United States.

This book emerged out of and in response to my unease with the treatment of Vietnamese Americans in the social scientific literature. I saw how easily Vietnamese Americans were slipped into existing accounts of belonging and nationality without the discussions of ideology or history that are necessary to contextualize that experience. I was confused by the absence of sophisticated theorizing about the racialization of Vietnamese—instead, they are either assumed to be "Oriental" or treated as "junior whites"[4]— and by the inattention to overall spatial issues which, because refugees are displaced by definition, seemed a phenomenal and gaping omission. I suspected that Vietnamese Americans were not oblivious to the dominant collective views of the Vietnam War, and that their efforts to make a life in the United States were circumscribed by these and other prevalent beliefs. I set out, then, to investigate what community and place meant for Vietnamese Americans, outside of what I saw as factually inaccurate narratives of immigration and assimilation.

I took seriously the admonition that Vietnamese refugees were a "deprived and captive" population (Yu and Liu 1986, 499). I did not want to participate in what my students commonly refer to as an "anthropological" problem by creating a situation where as an academic I would lord over refugees who had little choice but to tell me exactly what I wanted to hear. By focusing on community-building and place-making from the point of view of Vietnamese American leaders, I hoped to avoid exploiting subordinate and helpless people. Leaders are people with vested interests, and I acknowledge the limitations of my leader-centric approach. At least by interviewing leaders, I focus on people who intend to—and often do— make an impact on the outside world, rather than reanimating the idea of the refugee *cum* passive victim. By comparing two instances of community and place, I orient the project away from description toward explanation. In this book, I have attempted to explain why Vietnamese American community and place in Boston and Orange County are different, despite similar goals among leaders. These goals include creating networks, businesses, agencies, events, monuments, neighborhoods, and whole places that generate and support Vietnamese culture and identity in the United States.

I reject the notion that community and place are fixed or given. Both community and place are active, contested, and multidimensional categories. I do not intend to glorify or romanticize either one.[5] Community-building and place-making involve debate and struggle. Moreover, the kind of community-building that I emphasize here must involve place not merely as a spatial gesture but as a multidimensional reality involving location, physical form, and narrative or symbolic representation. Certainly some important forms of Vietnamese American community-building do not involve place as I define it here, for example, virtual or aesthetic communities. But I suspect that these placeless forms of community are enriched and fortified by the survival and growth of place-based communities such as Little Saigon and Fields Corner. Platiality makes a real difference to the nature and scope of power and resources that community-building can offer.

My fieldwork emphasizes three themes as driving influences in Vietnamese American community-building and place-making in Boston and Orange County. The first I refer to as "racialization" in order to stress the point that racial categories are socially, historically, and spatially produced, negotiated, and challenged. In part because Vietnamese Americans are racialized minorities, their community-building and place-making efforts cannot accurately be compared directly to or framed as comparable with those of their European forebears. The second revolves around the strategic creation of memories especially regarding the Vietnam War. U.S. society is both obsessed with "Vietnam" and at the same time has no desire to remember that conflict in any of its complexity and tragic scope. Vietnamese Americans cannot help but to traipse carefully around the tormented public memories of the war in order to produce a benevolent and deserving image of themselves in mainstream eyes. The third consists in turning culture into a saleable object. I use the term "marketplace multiculturalism" to describe the impulse of metropolitan regions to take advantage of Vietnamese American places such as Little Saigon. Vietnamese Americans gain nothing, monetarily speaking, by resisting the trend to sell Vietnameseness in the form of cuisine, "Asian culture," or the distinctiveness of place. Indeed, they do well to underscore aspects of their culture and identity that others might recognize as interesting, exotic, and therefore worth an investment of a few dollars or more.

By arguing that place occupies a central role in Vietnamese American community-building, I confront directly the widely accepted notion that assimilated Vietnamese Americans are abandoning place. Residentially, Vietnamese Americans in Boston and Orange County have dispersed to outer-ring suburbs, if they can afford them, and they have concentrated in less expensive core districts if they cannot. Regardless, place-making has heightened the recognizability and distinction of Little Saigon and Fields Corner as Vietnamese American places. Through their place-making endeavors, leaders have harnessed the power of place to define the social boundaries of community: who is and is not "really Vietnamese."

Racializing Vietnamese

When the first refugees arrived from Viet Nam, policy makers dispersed them into all fifty U.S. states in part to speed assimilation but also to lessen the possibility of racial hostility and violence directed against Vietnamese. The creation of Vietnamese American places such as Little Saigon and Fields Corner was often initially described to me as areas where everyone knew they could find fish sauce and other Vietnamese specialty products— an impulse that does not betray any awareness of racism or white privilege. But other things people told me suggest that these places should also be interpreted as racial safety zones or holding areas intended to protect new arrivals until they were able to navigate mainstream society, understand English, and defend themselves against racism and xenophobia. We live in a post–civil rights era that is purportedly race blind, but at the end of the last century the need for these safety zones still had not dissipated. In 1992, Vietnamese Bostonians were forced to recognize the need for solidarity when City Councilor Dapper O'Neill was caught on videotape referring to Vietnamese in Fields Corner as welfare cheats. Four years later the brutal murder of Thien Minh Ly by a white supremacist in Tustin, a predominantly white city of Orange County, reminded Vietnamese Americans throughout the country that despite economic success and model minority stereotyping, anyone who looks Asian is a potential target of racial hatred.

As elsewhere in America, in Vietnamese America the word "race" has ugly connotations. In our public and political discourse we prefer an approach that blames contemporary patterns of inequality on bigotry, ignorance, laziness, and anything else but structurally embedded practices or policies of racism.[6] Most of the leaders I met catered to this color blindness. Yet a few leaders I spoke with frankly commented on the racism they personally face despite their relatively high status in the community. Their voices add depth to the picture of Vietnamese America as a racialized population. On the whole, however, older people were reticent to appear ungrateful to the United States government and consequently declined to frame their community-building work in ugly, racial terms. Younger people were sometimes more forthcoming about the battles they face as Americans who do not have "blonde hair or blue eyes" and who are therefore marginalized from mainstream society. Younger Vietnamese Americans were often more likely to have taken Asian American studies courses at the college or university level in which they acquired an awareness of and a vocabulary for dealing with racism. Their experience as U.S.-raised offspring of Vietnamese might have only highlighted the contradictions of a post–civil rights society in which Asians are sometimes "near white" and other times "near black."[7]

Vietnamese American community-building and place-making comprise racial projects in the sense that they speak, directly and indirectly, to the racialization of Vietnamese in America. This racialization is not uniform or complete: for example, Vietnamese in Orange County have much more power to shape the policies that will affect all Asian Americans in that region, whereas Vietnamese in Boston must follow and work within the panethnic Asian alliances that influence city hall. Platially, Little Saigon dominates the region as an ethnic economy and as a neighborhood that depends on Vietnamese but also incorporates the general population as consumers, residents, investors, workers, or tourists.[8] In contrast, Fields Corner serves as an important platial symbol of Vietnamese American community. Vietnamese in Fields Corner strive, on the one hand, to be recognized apart from Chinatown and, on the other hand, to speak to the needs of a racially and culturally diverse neighborhood. Because Boston is a relatively small city whose neighborhoods have long been equated with ethnic identity, exhibiting a healthy respect for multiculturalism is one of the requirements of good citizenship there.

Vietnamese American community-building and place-making creates a shield against racism and at the same time puts into motion an idea about race that is confusing and contradictory. In the United States, Vietnamese are considered part of the "Asian" race. As far as most non-Asian Americans are concerned, Little Saigon and Fields Corner are "Asian" places. Their Vietnameseness works merely to specify their Asianness. But due to the long and disputed history of ethnic Chinese as citizen-subjects of Viet Nam, the presence of an ethnic Chinese population in Vietnamese America places poses a perplexing issue for the leadership.[9] In Little Saigon, ethnic Chinese play a pivotal role in the Vietnamese economy. By one estimate, up to 60 percent of small businesses in Little Saigon are owned and operated by ethnic Chinese.[10] In contrast, Fields Corner is a Vietnamese American place with a relatively weak ethnic economy; ethnic Chinese have no force in Boston's Vietnamese American community. If ethnic Chinese are so important and influential in the growth and development of Little Saigon, is Little Saigon really Vietnamese? Orange County's Vietnamese American leaders seem to want to split Little Saigon's identity away from its material reality in order to solve their predicament.

As a racial project, Vietnamese American community-building and place-making hovers dangerously close to promoting a sense of Vietnameseness as a pure, ahistorical, and self-contained unit, one that can be exhibited on a shelf next to Americanness (popularly understood to mean blonde hair/blue eyes) and Chineseness (something that is Asian but not Vietnamese).

Thinking of identity in this historically inaccurate way allows people to treat Vietnamese as if they cannot become Americans unless they remove all their old racial and ethnic tags. This idea of Vietnamese identity leads one to decry the ethnic Chinese as an "inauthentic" aspect of Little Saigon. In certain ways, the racialization of the Vietnamese—during the years of the war and then later in the ensuing decades of migration and resettlement—makes this Vietnamese American project compelling and necessary. Vietnamese American community-building and place-making provides an alternative to being isolated and alone, assimilated perhaps, but without any sense of historical or geographic origins. What has happened? The solution to one set of problems has opened the door to another. This is so not only for racialization, but also for history and memory.

A Certain Sense of History

Living in exile halfway across the world from their country of origin, many Vietnamese refugees are understandably homesick. Their longing for *que huong*—a word that loosely translates as "homeland"—is so deep that life in the United States often feels more like a dream, or a nightmare, than a reality. To say, as sociologist Gina Masequesmay does, that Vietnamese America is a "community of memory" is to pinpoint the integral role of memory in the Vietnamese American experience.[11]

Vietnamese American community-building and place-making is in part an effort to recover that sense of history and belonging by establishing social practices and spatial landmarks that remind people of the past. It turns out, however, that memory-making—or what I term "strategic memory projects"—revolves around various individuals' feelings of nostalgia for Viet Nam. More importantly, memory-making comprises a heavily planned and power-ridden activity that challenges the prevailing collective memories of "Vietnam" and simultaneously puts forth a view of the past that Vietnamese Americans dispute only at great risk. The Hi-Tek incident of 1999 involving a poster of Ho Chi Minh, the flag of Socialist Viet Nam, thousands of protestors, and hundreds of police outfitted in riot gear—not to mention a documentary film, *Saigon, USA*, whose exhibition led to another controversy in 2004 over a youth-oriented TV show called *VAX*—illustrates the intensity with which memories are constructed, produced, circulated, and contested in Vietnamese America.

It bears repeating that strategic memory projects in Vietnamese America do not occur in a vacuum. Above all else, Vietnamese Americans confront a prevailing view of "Vietnam" that equates the country with the war and that disregards entirely the nuances and complexities of Vietnamese experiences. This view, one Marita Sturken (1997) calls the dominant collective memory of the war, comprises its own pervasive and strategic memory project. In this memory, the people of Viet Nam—whether as allies or as enemies—are absent, the objects of purposeful amnesia. Christian Appy describes this memory as "self-absorbed" (1999, B6) because it involves only the U.S. side and demonstrates no curiosity or concern about the Vietnamese people. If they want to be seen and acknowledged as anything other than ghosts of war, Vietnamese Americans have no choice but to counter with their own strategic memory narratives. In Boston and in Orange County, these narratives depict the refugee as an honorable and deserving citizen, instead of a loser, a criminal, or a public expense.

Boston's Vietnamese confront a plethora of public references to the Vietnam War that are engraved onto the urban landscape but do not include their views. For instance, one of the city's "most curious ironies" is a public mural in the shape of a gigantic rainbow in which the silhouette of Ho Chi Minh is plainly visible. The artist, a pacifist nun who was commissioned by the city in 1971, reportedly denied the silhouette's presence. The mural has been the object of at least two protests by Vietnamese Americans. Then in 1982, a group of U.S. veterans of the Vietnam War formed the nationally recognized William Joiner Center for the Study of War and Social Consequences at the University of Massachusetts, Boston. The Joiner Center's mission is to promote teaching and creative writing about the Vietnam War, and to facilitate cultural exchange between the United States and Viet Nam as a way to promote healing from the war. Because of its open dealing with writers and poets in Viet Nam, the Joiner Center has been the target of a lawsuit by Vietnamese Americans, and its projects have been widely discredited especially among the local Vietnamese American leadership. Ironically perhaps, my own research in Boston was supported for one semester by a Rockefeller Foundation fellowship hosted by the Joiner Center.

History has mapped yet another irony onto the streets of Boston. The city of Dorchester lost many of its working-class residents during the war (Appy 1993). In 1983, the Veterans' Association of Dorchester created sixty-two "hero's squares" to commemorate each of the lost soldiers. In Boston, an intersection of two or more streets is called a square or a corner. These hero's squares line Dorchester Avenue, the main street that runs through Fields Corner. Boston's Vietnamese are literally surrounded by other people's memories of "Vietnam," and these memories have little or nothing to do with the Vietnamese refugee perspective. There is not much hope for removing or altering those existing memories. Consequently, Vietnamese American community-building and place-making takes a relatively subdued tone when it comes to discussions about the war. Rather than pursue an agenda that prioritizes memory, Boston's Vietnamese concentrate their energies on multiculturalism and neighborhood growth.

In contrast, Orange County's Vietnamese American leadership seems vocal and insistent on strategic memory projects that affect many people. In 2003, on the anniversary of the fall of Sai Gon to the communists, the city of Westminster inaugurated the nation's first Vietnamese American monument to the war. A massive bronze sculpture portraying two soldiers—American and Vietnamese, side by side—is adorned by the flags of the United States and South Viet Nam and a torch lit with an eternal flame. The sculpture is the centerpiece of the Sid Goldstein Freedom Park, a small grassy spot at the end of a street called All American Way. The celebration featured the deafening appearance of three Marine helicopters; thousands of Vietnamese attended, many of them veterans.

The monument concretizes the thoughts and feelings of many of the leaders I spoke with. One person told me, several years before the statue had been cast, that the monument would show GI Joe "shaking hands" with the Vietnamese. I understood that description as a Vietnamese response to the unfriendly nativism of the local residents. At that time, Westminster city hall did not yet demonstrate the full appreciation for the Vietnamese that it performed effusively in the following years. The monument restores a glory and heroism to the Vietnam War that Maya Lin—the creator of the nation's most prominent monument to the war, the Vietnam Veterans Memorial in Washington, D.C.—purposefully refrained from expressing. Significantly, Freedom Park's bronze soldiers are nearly the same size in terms of height and body mass, giving an appearance of equality to American and Vietnamese men that exaggerates both historical and political reality. This aspect counters the dominant collective memory in which Vietnamese are literally and figuratively diminished.

The idea that there is a correct way to remember "Vietnam" the war and Viet Nam the country is frequently reenergized in Orange County. The "heritage" flag (three red stripes on a yellow background for South Viet Nam) is ubiquitous in Little Saigon, but recent debates about the uses of this flag instead of the red flag of the Socialist Republic of Viet Nam at Vietnamese American community events or at other public events where Vietnamese Americans are in attendance—for example, university graduation ceremonies—provide occasions to revisit and reformulate strategic memory projects. Risking his own status in the community, Viet Thanh Nguyen, a professor at the University of Southern California, wrote an editorial about the flag in which he observed that people do not want to forget the old South Viet Nam that they know and love, but that "because of political pressure and filial piety, there has been no true freedom of speech in the Vietnamese American community" (V. Nguyen 2003).

Cam Vu and Thuy Dang (2005) develop this point more fully in their argument that anticommunism in the Vietnamese American community is not only a political stance but more importantly consists of a "disciplinary cultural practice." In other words, strategic memory projects involving protests, monuments, and flags should be understood not so much as acts of wrath and hate that will fade as the old generation passes, but as purposeful efforts to construct and produce memory in such a way as to reinforce the long-term boundaries of the community—social, political, and, I would add, spatial.

Strategic memory projects in Vietnamese America encourage a particular set of ideas about what staying Vietnamese means: saluting the heritage flag and refusing to recognize the Socialist Republic of Viet Nam, among other things. Disobeying the rules embedded in memory projects could make someone an outcast, a person who is not "really Vietnamese."[12] Yet despite the efforts to prescribe strict rules for belonging in community and place, Vietnamese American leaders must also bend to the prerogatives of place-based capitalism—what I term marketplace multiculturalism. This version of multiculturalism promises political clout and material resources to Vietnamese Americans, but also distorts and reduces the complexity of Vietnamese culture and identity.

Culture and Identity For Sale: Buy Vietnamese!

Vietnamese American community-building and place-making makes a substitute home for Vietnamese in Boston and Orange County, and in so doing significantly alters the social and spatial landscape. Orange County is hardly the same now as it was before 1975; although the region's public personality is still lily-white and archconservative, in fact the social life and streetscapes of many Orange County cities—especially Westminster, Garden Grove, Santa Ana, Anaheim, and Fountain Valley—show a distinct Vietnamese flair. On the other side of the nation, Boston's neighborhoods are just as cozy and tribal as they have always been.[13] But since the 1980s, Vietnamese influences have made themselves visible in many nooks and crannies of the city, particularly in Fields Corner. Whether in the form of beef noodle restaurants, nail salons, or celebrations of Tet (the Lunar New Year), Vietnamese American community-building and place-making has made certain aspects of Vietnamese culture integral to U.S. society. The process sometimes generates Vietnameseness anew, with Vietnamese California enforcing a stronger influence than Viet Nam. For many years, Pho Bolsa was a restaurant in Boston's Chinatown named after Bolsa Avenue, the main street of Little Saigon in Orange County. In the United States, Bolsa is probably at least as popular a place name as Pasteur (after Louis Pasteur, a French name frequently seen in Viet Nam).

The name of this Vietnamese noodle shop in Boston's Chinatown references Bolsa Avenue, the main street in Little Saigon, Westminster, California. Where is Vietnamese America's true point of origin—Orange County or Viet Nam? Where do ethnic Chinese-Vietnamese belong in America—Little Saigon or Chinatown?

By and large, the aspects of Vietnamese culture and identity that Boston and Orange County use to promote themselves as "diverse" and "multicultural" regions have been meticulously cleansed of their negative racial and historical connotations. This is not to disregard the efforts of Vietnamese to contextualize their own experiences by engaging in the racial and strategic memory projects I describe above. But the impulse of marketplace multiculturalism is to emphasize culture's *consumable* dimensions. Planners and developers think of metropolitan regions as mega–shopping malls, and ethnic districts like Little Saigon are the equivalent of specialty boutiques. Shoppers and investors need to be enticed by pleasant sights and sounds that encourage them to spend—and do not tax their consciences by reminding them of the war, of U.S. losses, or of structures and systems of racial inequality.

Thus, in order to synchronize themselves with the demands of marketplace multiculturalism, Vietnamese American leaders must downplay or smooth over details of Vietnameseness that otherwise are crucial to community-building and place-making. A monument that carries huge symbolism and political meaning for Vietnamese Americans joins a list of less controversial tourist attractions, along with a French bistro and a Buddhist pagoda. A once tense and depressed neighborhood that has been populated by former political detainees and boat people becomes a shining example of "new immigrants" pulling themselves up by their bootstraps. Non-Vietnamese with money to spare can enjoy and participate in diversity by eating pho or buying Sriracha (Vietnamese hot sauce) at an "ethnic" grocer. This is not to deny that many non-Vietnamese wish for a more meaningful and substantive interaction with Vietnamese Americans. But that type of interaction is simply not the goal of marketplace multiculturalism. This form of multiculturalism is about culture for profit. Culture and identity are inevitably distorted; Vietnamese Americans are not immune to this distortion.

The impulse to equate commerce and culture throbs in Orange County, the home of Disneyland. In Little Saigon, leaders told me about plans to turn the place into the third leg of a tourist triangle with Disneyland and Knotts Berry Farm. In their dreams, Little Saigon would serve as the ethnic kitchen for hungry tourists. Surely, growth for businesses in Little Saigon means catering to non-Vietnamese, or expanding outside of Little Saigon to a more affluent Vietnamese clientele. Could Little Saigon actually pull it off? That depends on whether Vietnamese restaurateurs can close the social and spatial gap between those two tourist traps and their "ethnic" business district.

Forced by survival into community-building and place-making, Vietnamese Americans in Orange County are finally flexing their political influence in city hall and beyond. In 2003, Westminster and Garden Grove set up identical concrete slab markers on the major boulevards welcoming visitors to the Little Saigon business district. The mayor of Westminster, however, stated that Little Saigon belongs to Westminster, not Garden Grove. Meanwhile, the city of Santa Ana promised to arrange for similar markers in the near future. In this sense, business has been good for the Vietnamese American community, because without the massive sales revenues that Little Saigon brings into all these cities, Vietnamese Americans would still be the targets of open racism and undisciplined xenophobia.

The growth of the business district exacerbates an identity crisis for Little Saigon. Marketplace multiculturalism's ultimate prerogative is to treat Little Saigon as a tourist's adventure, "a flight to Asia without the plane fare."[14] Featuring the trials and tribulations of Vietnamese refugees as a group who sought freedom under the Statue of Liberty's gaze paints Little Saigon as ideologically simpatico with Orange County. But this story has no room for the tale of the ethnic Chinese, for whom commerce has been a way of life in Viet Nam since the French colonial period. Moreover, delineating the Chinese and the Vietnamese elements of Little Saigon might entertain a scholar of ethnic history but has no useful purpose as far as increasing revenues goes. As one frustrated anti-Chinese Vietnamese put it, "Diversity is boring." At the end of the day, marketplace multiculturalism could care less about the actual multiculturalism that informs Vietnamese history and identity.

Boston's Vietnamese do not have the same options for economic growth through small business ownership that exist for their counterparts in Orange County. They do not seek those options. Indeed, many leaders here have negative things to say about Little Saigon's model of growth, which they describe as too much like Chinatown. In part, this is because an already existing Chinatown provided a base for the small population of ethnic Chinese who arrived in the late 1970s as refugees from Viet Nam. Ethnic Chinese do not play a noticeable role in any aspect of Boston's Vietnamese American community-building. The now well-established community in Fields Corner sports a tiny ethnic economy that marks the place as Vietnamese. But this mini shopping district cannot generate the jobs and resources needed to support the entire Vietnamese population of the greater Boston area.

Instead, as Boston's Vietnamese Americans find work and small business opportunities throughout the greater metro region, Vietnamese American community leaders discursively frame their needs within the city's narrative of neighborhood as community. According to this frame, the health of each neighborhood district is strongly associated with the well-being of the resident ethnic groups. Viet-AID, a community development corporation that emerged in the 1990s as federal and state funding for refugee resettlement dried up, is the main engine behind Vietnamese community growth in Boston. Viet-AID's mission, to serve Boston's Vietnamese population, exists in some tension with neighborhood development because Vietnamese are in fact dispersed throughout the city. Even in the census tracts most heavily populated with Vietnamese, only 35 percent are Vietnamese, compared to 65 percent in the Orange County city of Westminster. Consequently, Viet-AID is caught in a permanent conundrum: Does the organization serve Vietnamese only? What should they do for the non-Vietnamese residents, who represent the majority in Fields Corner?

The "community question" is so difficult and conflictual for Boston's Vietnamese that it surfaced repeatedly and without resolution throughout all the years of my research. At one point, a Vietnamese American leader who had just received a graduate degree in community development turned to me and asked, "Have you been able to define what is community?" Just when I thought I was going to get answers from him, he reversed the direction and put it on me. The truth is that even though I offer many insights into community in this book, it is not for me to say what community is for Vietnamese Americans. Furthermore, it appears to me that the clout garnered by Vietnamese American place-making represents a kind of wealth that is distributed to most Vietnamese Americans. I describe and analyze the divisions and conflicts I think place-making has wrought. But I cannot offer, and do not pretend to offer, an insider's view.

Even with all its negative implications, marketplace multiculturalism offers to Vietnamese Americans a validation of culture and identity that was not available to poor, minority communities in the time of Boston's urban renewal. From the 1950s to the early 1970s, neighborhoods like Roxbury were valued primarily for their existing infrastructure, the possibilities of future real estate development, and their proximity to downtown. Roxbury's black residents were not celebrated for the "diversity" or "multiculturalism" they brought to the city. They were not praised for overcoming adversity or for pulling themselves up by their bootstraps, even though their survival over decades of social and spatial segregation implies a great amount of personal and collective fortitude.[15] When young black children were bused into white neighborhoods as part of a court-ordered program to integrate Boston's neighborhoods, the price of diversity was clearly not being paid equally by children of all races. The race-based social movements of the 1950s and 1960s—what others call "civil rights" and "black power"— made it possible for nonwhite refugees and immigrants in the 1970s and onward to appeal to mainstream multicultural agendas with less horrible consequences all around.

Today, Vietnamese Americans fit neatly into Dorchester's booster theme of "diverse ethnic groups" who contribute to the vitality of local institutions. By putting up their own two-story community center at a time when new construction was rare in the neighborhood, Vietnamese Americans stamped Fields Corner as a Vietnamese American place. Now they can harness the language of marketplace multiculturalism to their benefit, regardless of the persistent and unanswerable question of community that they may face forever.

How Place Works: A "Platial" Story

Place shapes and influences community. In the very early stages of this project, an established sociologist complained to me that "place cannot do things, people do." This sociologist had a degree in geography but he took what I call an "empty-space" perspective: space contains people but has none of its own effects. Instead, I adopt an active spatial lens that allows me to consider the ways that space actually does affect social life. Of course, I also insist that social relations of power and inequality in turn influence space.

Places affect people, and people also do things to affect place. In earlier chapters, I laid out in some detail the spatial theory that guides this book. To capture the idea that place, not space, does things, I use the word "platial." Careful readers will notice some slippage in my use of this term: the slip is not a miscalculation. Out there in the world, the specific moments in which space mutates into place are hazy and full of perceptual bias. My efforts throughout this book to tell a clearly "platial" story—not merely a spatial one—are constantly deterred by the underuse of spatial theory on the one hand, and the instantaneous appeal of the concept of place on the other.

Most readers will not have heard of "platial," but a group based in Oregon has been using this word since at least 2004, the year they created the cybersite and concept of a free "people's atlas" at www.platial.com. Referring to the service as simply "Platial," cofounder Jason Wilson writes:

> Platial enables anyone to find, create, and use meaningful maps of Places
> that matter to them. Our dream is to connect people, neighborhoods, cities,

and countries through a citizen-driven common context that goes beyond geopolitical boundaries. We are building Platial because we adore Places.[16]

For skeptical readers, "platial" gestures to a concept that does not deserve its own word, at least in English. Indeed, an Australian philosopher and a British geographer took sides on "platial" in a discussion of spatial history in a recent issue of *Philosophy and Geography*. On the con side, "platial" is awkward and should not be used because place connects with too many other terms that have their own, better adjectives such as locale and topography. On the pro side, "platial" is necessary though odd, and the necessity of distinguishing between space/place and spatial/platial is both historical and linguistic.[17]

Place shapes and influences community through specific platial processes: territorializing, regulating, and symbolizing. In other words, the places that Vietnamese Americans make not only navigate the complex themes of racialization, memory, and the commodification of culture, but that navigation occurs in such a way as to extract an identity out of a territory, to impose rules that govern the territory and the people who are attached to it, and to put forth symbols that give meaning to the territory and to its attendant community.

Each in their own way, Little Saigon and Fields Corner territorialize Vietnamese America. They assign platial coordinates to the Vietnamese American community. In Orange County, territorialization has been accomplished rather blatantly by the "Little Saigon Exit" signs off the Garden Grove and San Diego/Santa Monica freeways that went up with some controversy in the early 1980s, then more recently by the city-sponsored concrete slabs that announce the "Little Saigon Business District." In Boston, territorialization is a brand new step. In 2002, Viet-AID identified a lot and various sources of funding for a two-story Vietnamese community center that now marks Fields Corner as Vietnamese. The step is subtle and full of interesting contradictions: the population of Fields Corner is less than one-third Vietnamese; the Center therefore serves a multilingual, multicultural, and multiracial clientele; and to fill the space of the Center, Vietnamese must travel from all over the greater Boston area.

While nineteenth-century immigrants from Europe first settled in ethnic neighborhoods and then dispersed throughout the city and its interstitial suburbs, Boston's Vietnamese Americans have done the reverse. They came to Chinatown, moved to a few different neighborhoods, and later pursued Fields Corner as their platial focus. Some affluent Vietnamese skipped

Fields Corner altogether for the nearby cities of Quincy and Randolph. Stamping Fields Corner as Vietnamese gives the community power and clout in city hall; territorialization is a must for recognition in multicultural Boston.

Little Saigon has far more capacity to regulate Vietnamese American community than Fields Corner due to the size and relative affluence of the population, the economic pull on local government, the power of the Vietnamese vote, and the convenient mesh of ideological commitments. The Hi-Tek incident made clear that certain rules of speech and behavior apply to Little Saigon; borrowing a slogan from right-wing conservatives the protestors declared, "Freedom of speech is not free." The price, of course, is censorship. The Westminster War Memorial is an impressive physical structure that tells a refugee-oriented story about the war. Pushing the cities of Westminster and Garden Grove to declare themselves "Communist Free Zones" in a historical period when in the rest of the nation terrorism has replaced communism as the Number One Enemy is an excellent example of Little Saigon's platial ability to regulate not only the Vietnamese American community, but the local regional community as well.

In contrast, Boston's Vietnamese have very little regulatory power, a situation that is worsened by a surrounding culture that is reputedly "liberal." When a group of twelve Vietnamese brought a suit against the William Joiner Center because of its cultural exchange programs with Viet Nam, the result was merely to tarnish the image of the Joiner Center. National philanthropic support did not stop. Scholars and writers who desire opportunities to conduct research in Viet Nam or about Vietnamese diaspora are still likely to see the Joiner Center as a potential avenue of support. Being wedged into a city crowded with many other people forces the Vietnamese American community in Boston to moderate its demands. This is not to overlook the regulatory impact of the informal punitive measures directed toward people who might be soft on communism that two Vietnamese Bostonians revealed to me. In small, less visible ways, the Vietnamese American community disciplines itself internally.

In many ways, symbolization is a full-time job for Little Saigon and Fields Corner. Their methods for putting forth the symbols that define Vietnamese American community differ somewhat depending on the nature of the symbolic discourse they are attempting to challenge. In Orange County, free enterprise is king. Little Saigon promotes an image of Vietnamese as productive and free-enterprise-loving citizens by celebrating its ethnic economy and the proclivity of Asians to pull themselves up by their bootstraps.

Significantly Bob Dole, Robert Dornan, and recently George W. Bush made Phuoc Loc Tho/Asian Garden Mall in Little Saigon a stop on their campaign trails. This symbolizing work is all the more important given the decades during which Vietnamese were sneered at as losers, welfare cheats, prostitutes, and gangsters.

Fields Corner also strives to symbolize a hardworking Vietnamese community that is deserving of citizenship. To some degree, Bostonians also respond to the idea of Vietnamese as an entrepreneurial group, which gets easily woven into a racialized narrative directed toward blacks and Latinos. Observing that Vietnamese had established their own community center, an educated and well-recognized Chinese American told me that Vietnamese are culturally more inclined to work than are Puerto Ricans or blacks. Clearly, an Asian American consciousness does not necessarily entail an antiracist analysis. Because Fields Corner is much less of a Vietnamese business district than a residential village, Boston's Vietnamese Americans stress their efforts to get along with the "brother communities" and to take care of things in the neighborhood that everyone cares about such as crime, clean and well-lit streets, and parking. Could it be that the fraternal approach helps everyone get past dead-end identity issues and on to the material conditions of a place to which they are all somehow attached and committed?

Place generates and supports community not in the abstract but through the particular mechanisms of territorialization, regulation, and symbolization. Because the type of Vietnamese American community-building that this book examines has to happen somewhere—it cannot happen on the head of a pin—then place-making needs to be understood as an essential and dynamic component of Vietnamese American community life.

Vietnamese American community-building and place-making in Orange County and Boston builds a platial base for Vietnamese identity whose scope and contours reflect the perspectives and investments of many people, particularly the leaders. Whether we are talking about a war monument that concretizes a public memory or a shopping district that integrates Vietnamese American life into the larger symbolic economy of a region, the point is that community and place are sites of struggle and contestation. No one group has a total grip, but surely some groups get more air time than others. Because leaders, even self-proclaimed ones, can have a big effect on the shape and scope of community and place, I have concentrated my efforts on understanding and explaining their views.

Framing Vietnamese America in platial terms allows us to see how identity is constructed and produced at various levels of spatial, not just social, scale. Most sociologists think of ethnic identity as something that happens in networks, but they are less likely to consider the spatial corollary of those networks.

Place-making is an attempt not only for the community to survive; place-making should also be seen as an effort to make the community endure. That is to say that the project of staying Vietnamese is a platial project with a timeline that revolves around the past yet impacts all the future generations. Refugees, who are by definition displaced peoples, work to stay Vietnamese not only for themselves but also for their children and grandchildren; the overall platial plan is to create a home that anchors Vietnamese identity and community in a volatile global context where identities are merging and flowing out of force and necessity.

Place-Making and the Second Generation

In *Growing Up American: How Vietnamese Children Adapt to Life in the United States*, sociologists Min Zhou and Carl Bankston (1998) emphasize the importance of ethnicity in the successful adaptation of Vietnamese American youth. Their findings are useful because they bring to the foreground an essential question for the future of all U.S. youth: What do communities need to give their young people so that they can succeed in school, in work, and more broadly, in life? Their study focused on Vietnamese American high school students in Versailles Village, an area of New Orleans occupied in 1993–95 mostly by Vietnamese refugees, immigrants, and their families. The Vietnamese youth who were most likely to animate the "valedictorian" stereotype were able to take advantage of the resources ethnicity provides— especially supportive relationships with their elders, most of whom were refugees or immigrants. In contrast, those Vietnamese who fell into the "delinquent" stereotype were usually also cut off in some way from those supportive networks; they did not speak Vietnamese well and they were disconnected from their Vietnamese culture and history. This made them open and vulnerable to the negative influences of their mostly worse-off black peers. Thus, the book concludes, ethnicity is a necessary resource for Vietnamese American success.

Zhou and Bankston valorize "success" without taking apart the normalizing dimensions of that term. But even if they did take the time to unpack and interrogate the racist, heteropatriarchal, and consumerist assumptions behind success, the truth would remain that communities with insufficient social and physical infrastuctures are hard put to propel their youth onto any kind of positive path. All communities, not just "ethnic" ones, need to provide resources, structures, and relationships that youth can depend on as they navigate the complex journey into adulthood. In the case of Vietnamese in New Orleans, ethnic ties provided a surrogate means of upward mobility that was not provided to most youth by the local or regional infrastructure.

In the late 1980s and early 1990s, urban youth of color were particular susceptible to unemployment, poverty, and stereotypes; they were seen and treated as "superpredators," or criminals on the loose.[18] Especially in neighborhoods and communities that as a result of neoliberalism's regime of deindustrialization and privatization were stripped of their social and economic infrastructure, youth became ever more helpless and enraged. Many, rejecting the unskillful guidance of their school teachers or other mentors, became ensnared in the criminal justice system. Surely many would have turned to their elders for advice and support—but what advice could those elders give? Most faced similar problems and, worse, were blamed for their own problems. Unfortunately, the step up provided to Vietnamese youth in New Orleans by positive social relations within their ethnic community was available only to them, not to black youth, and could not work as an overall cure to the blight of the area.

The Zhou and Bankston study of how Vietnamese "grow up American" does not insert either a platial or a racial analysis of the experience of youth in New Orleans. The authors do not offer enough critical insight into the idea that immigrants can move up the ladder because of some group traits, values, or internal resources that black people purportedly do not have. Nor do they shed light on the larger social and political decisions that have rendered communities in places like New Orleans to be largely without social or other kinds of capital. Consequently, their book is unequipped to do much more than feed the myth of the model minority.[19] To avoid the same mistake, *Little Saigons* theorizes carefully the platial and racial dimensions of Vietnamese Americans in Orange County and Boston. What, then, are the consequences of this book for subsequent generations?

Vietnamese American place-making gives structure and order to the Vietnamese American community—and to the rest of the region and nation as well. Internally, this structure and order clearly have disciplinary effects. But particularly for the younger, second generations and beyond who are born in the United States, the impact of these places has great potential to shape, influence, and even determine what they understand is either "Vietnamese" or "American." It is not only a matter of what the elders say about Viet Nam's legacy in the context of their own homes or directly to their own children and grandchildren. Now, because Vietnameseness also resides in bigger places, including shopping malls and war monuments, there is a larger, more widely circulating set of messages about how to be a good (or bad) Vietnamese person in America. These messages are replete with complex and contradictory information about race and racism, memory and war, and the whole business of multiculturalism. Nevertheless, by projecting Vietnamese American identity onto the actual landscape of Orange County and Boston, leaders—as place-makers and community-builders—have succeeded in "jumping scale" from the displaced, disoriented, and isolated refugee to a place-centered and group-oriented collectivity that claims to embrace Vietnamese America and reach out toward all Vietnamese outside of Viet Nam.

While place-making aggregates and concretizes identity, no place is permanent or fixed. The job of every generation consists of working out and through the complexities of already existing places. Out of necessity, the younger generations will navigate the locational, physical, and narrative elements of places like Little Saigon and Fields Corner. If they want to be good citizens in any context, they will have to employ strategies that take into account history, racial formations, and the ongoing spatial and social demands of global capitalism. They will have to think platially, despite the overarching disregard for place that is encouraged by corporate transnationalism, technology, and mass consumerism. In the end, they will probably overhaul Vietnamese America.

In theory, Vietnamese Americans could just walk away from place. Under what conditions might later generations simply abandon the places that now constitute and symbolize Vietnamese America? To put it another way, would there ever be a day when Vietnameseness substantively disappears, existing only as an optional label such as "Norwegian" offers to some white people? We cannot know for sure, but the findings I present here suggest that many big things would have to change quite drastically before most Vietnamese Americans could detach themselves totally and completely from places like Little Saigon.

First of all, U.S. racial formations would have to be seriously transformed. Until all Asian Americans can cut off their racial identity tags, Vietnamese will still need theirs. What might happen instead is that people just turn in their old tags for new ones. According to Eduardo Bonilla-Silva (2004), the "Latin Americanization" of U.S. racial categories will propel East Asians (and Filipinos) into some sort of honorary white status, while Vietnamese will join the other Southeast Asian refugees in a collectively occupied category of blackness, to which, I would add, no honors are attached. His claim should be hugely controversial because it is historically misinformed, but it does give rise to some interesting new questions. Will there come a point in U.S. history when economic mobility will somehow trump racial distinction for Asian Americans? If so, then which Asian groups will move up the ladder, and how will they relate to those left behind? Since Vietnamese refugees and immigrants came to the United States in specific and widely divergent waves, it is reasonable to expect that later generations of Vietnamese Americans will continue to reflect internal stratification, and those divisions may play out in racial and platial terms.

For example, it is likely that instead of dropping altogether the idea of Vietnamese American places, some upwardly mobile and entrepreneurial Vietnamese Americans will discover the advantages of hiring other people—poor Vietnamese, Mexicans, or blacks—to do the grunt work required to run the places they will continue to sell as "Vietnamese." In what ways will the relationship between Vietnamese American places and these groups, including ethnic Chinese, blow up into even larger contradictions over the next generation? Who will be considered the "true Vietnamese" in this scenario?

Vietnamese American places not only support and generate Vietnameseness for Vietnamese people, but those places also contribute to the surrounding cultural and symbolic economy of a region. In both Orange County and Boston, platial ethnic identities have eased local blight by revitalizing neighborhoods and improving the value of real estate. They have also added to the multicultural feel of each region, which has tangible, salable consequences. As planners and developers cook up more ways to draw private investors into their regions, ethnic themes add color and variety to their recipes for growth.

But the enduring result of Vietnamese American place-making may not have a strict dollar value. In a few decades, perhaps "Little Saigon"—the words are in quotations as a general reference to all Vietnamese American places—will carve itself out to be more significant as a repository for U.S. collective memories of the war than any other sort of place. The Vietnamese American leaders I met will have had a strong hand in making that happen because of their own impulses toward recognition as the heroic allies of the United States during that war.

Since extant war memories will continue to have platial form, Vietnamese Americans will be forced to confront the lost U.S. war as they search for their Vietnamese identity many generations from today. One potentially long-lasting function of "Little Saigon" will be to operate as a Vietnamese Vietnam War Monument or, put another way, a "Museum of the Dead." I borrow this phrase from a young Vietnamese American woman I interviewed who bemoaned the fact that, in her opinion, many leaders are stuck in a pre-1975 time warp. In making this observation, I do not intend to give a death sentence to Vietnamese American place-making or community-building. Indeed, the whole point of this book is to treat place and community as constitutive of ongoing projects in which multiple parties engage simultaneously and often with partial or mismatching goals and strategies. How place works is a very messy and unpredictable thing.

Platializing Race and Ethnicity

Many social scientists have been conditioned to apply the "master trend" of assimilation to immigrants and refugees and to refer to their situation in terms of ethnicity rather than race, unless they are "dark skinned," in which case blackness is invoked. Ironically, some of these same researchers go to great lengths to define race as a "social construction" and something that is not equivalent to skin color. The big question immigration poses in these circles is whether or not newcomers to the United States will somehow "cross racial lines" rather than help to eradicate them.[20] Strangely, this same literature hardly ever tackles the idea that native-born whites might have arrived at their status by unnatural or undemocratic methods or that they might be playing an active role in sustaining racism now, at the same moment that new immigrants cross the borders.

As sociologists, our relative inattention to and undertheorization of spatial matters makes spatial assimilation our default framework as far as space and place are concerned: we tend to look for neighborhoods that immigrants move into, and then out of, after a generation or so of "hard work" (this usually means small, family-run businesses in which family members are unpaid and do not receive health or any other benefits). We then focus on how fast and by what mechanisms each group gets into and out of its designated spatial container. We do not ask similar questions about black people, and the terms "ethnic enclave" or "ethnic entrepreneur" have not been to my knowledge applied to a post–civil rights black context. Yet as Stephen Steinberg writes, "no less than any other 'hyphenated' Americans, African Americans possess all the essential elements of a viable ethnicity" (1995, 9). This insistent neglect of ethnicity among African Americans might be construed as an intellectual contribution to racism.

Consequently, when most of us put the terms "ethnicity" and "place" together in our heads, what comes first to mind is a residential or shopping district run by Asian or Latino immigrants. This is not to ignore recent scholarship on suburban Chinatowns and Koreatowns (Fong 1993; D. Lee 1995), diasporic Puerto Ricans (Whalen and Vazquez-Hernandez 2005), and urban transnational Mexicans (Jirasek and Tortolero 2001), all of which surely adds more depth and detail to our sense of how immigrants locate themselves vis-à-vis residential and regional boundaries. I wonder if those studies reinforce the idea that "ethnicity" is somehow flexible, mobile, and perhaps in the long run optional, as is the case for many white Europeans.

When "race" and "place" come together, the image that immediately appears is an impoverished black ghetto full of drug addicts and broken windows. Suddenly we confront a blockage. Blackness becomes associated with spatial entrapment—and by implication, then, whiteness continues to enjoy its unexamined link with mobility and freedom. The bottom line of this book is that the interactions of race and place need more explicit and critical theorizing all the way around because race—meaning racial difference and inequality—is not just about black people (and not all black people are drug addicts or criminals), and place—meaning a specific spatial reference point—is not only about commerce or containment.

Multiculturalism and neoliberalism have not erased the categories of race or place in the case of Vietnamese Americans. Indeed, the findings in this book suggest that if we take seriously the need to adopt an active view of space and a critical race framework that theorizes whiteness—that is, if we can platialize race and ethnicity and, vice versa, to racialize place—we might ask new and different questions not just about Vietnamese but about the general incorporation of racial and ethnic minorities into U.S. society.

I should point out that the platial basis of grassroots community organizing among racialized and ethnic minorities has been obvious to many people for decades if not centuries, although I doubt anyone uses my label. Surely the community-control movement of the late 1960s—whose advocates ranged from the National Urban League and the NAACP to the Black Panther Party—took as its starting point the fact that physically and socially segregated urban blacks could and should take control of the practices and institutions that gave collective racial power to whites. Starting with public schools and moving on to small businesses, police stations, and city hall, community-control activists theorized about "internal colonialism" and worked to transform their territorial, social, cultural, and political entrapment.[21]

Political scientist Claire Jean Kim refers to the "differential positioning of Blacks and Asian Americans . . . in the American racial order and their physical juxtaposition in the urban economy" as potential sources of antagonism (2000, 11). The black-Korean conflict in New York—as well as the collective responses to that conflict—reflect broad and entrenched patterns of racial power, she argues, dispensing with the more widely accepted view she terms the "racial scapegoating story." Koreans, unaware of the nuances of U.S. racism, go out and forge their own economic future; blacks, left out of the inevitable process of social change, lash out unfairly at Koreans; meanwhile whites look on aghast at the violence, bystanders to a racialized situation in which they are (thankfully) no longer implicated. While Kim does not engage in spatial or platial theorizing per se, the language she uses gestures to the continuing importance of "position" in defining racial and ethnic relations of power in the post–civil rights era.

Like Kim, I want to consider the operation of Vietnamese American communities and places in the light of a dominant logic. Instead of reducing everything to spatial assimilation and who gets to be white, we need to explode the hegemonic underpinnings of white supremacy and look for its platial ramifications in the settlement and community-building efforts of all groups, including whites. This means exposing the relationships between and among racial categories, including the symbolic and cultural narratives that platialize racial groups. Space and place provide rubrics and frameworks through which we might theorize racial formations wholistically, emphasizing relationality across entire systems rather than obsessing over the anatomy of isolated racial units.

Putting racial formations and platiality together in this twenty-first-century context will help us expand the social scientific repertoire for connecting race and place. If we see place in terms of movement as well as location, we can then analyze broad processes of demarcation, discipline, and control. For example, groups may take on racial features not only when they are trapped but also when they traverse certain platial boundaries and become objects of state surveillance or community control. Vietnamese can hardly escape the gaze of the state or of self-appointed community leaders; tales of their migration are tightly woven into racialized narratives of freedom and self-sufficiency under capitalism.

Platializing race may also allow us to grow connections to practical and applied projects, such as "glocalization." Where thinking platially forces us to recognize the groups who depend on the resources or identities afforded by place, acting glocally encourages people to consider the often overlooked and negative consequences of global capitalist expansion. Hooking "platial" and "glocal" together, and harnessing them both to a race-cognizant or antiracist agenda, has tremendous potential for theory, policy, and activism in a global environment.

Demarcation, Discipline, and Control

In their foundational text on U.S. racial formations, Omi and Winant describe the post–civil rights period as one of "racial hegemony" (1994, 66). This period contrasts to the prior era of "racial dictatorship" (from the days of slavery through the period of so-called Reconstruction) that required de jure segregation, state-backed violence, and strict color lines. Today, although the Voting Rights Act and the Civil Rights Act brought about momentous and substantive changes, we live in a time of de facto racial and class segregation. True, many people of color have attained the American Dream, but many more struggle to make ends meet.[22]

Immigration from Asia, Latin America, and Africa have made our everyday color lines much more confusing, especially when highly educated and Westernized immigrants easily hobnob with wealthy whites. We do not see water fountains marked "white" and "colored" anymore, but our public schools and prisons clearly demonstrate the difference that being white and middle-class can make in the life chances of twenty-first-century youth. This is a hegemonic racial order because the structural and discursive sources of white supremacy are diffuse and decentered, and because most people voice no qualms with the way things are. To top it all off, the mass media has manufactured our consent to—and simultaneously, our apparent ignorance of—this highly nuanced racial order. Many people may strive toward junior whiteness, but only a few people from any given group will actually get there: whiteness retains its privileges.

Racial distinctions have shifted tremendously but they have not disappeared, and with the exception of Dinesh D'Souza hardly any scholar that I know of would say that racism is entirely a thing of the past. It is a much more common practice simply to undertheorize, or to ignore altogether, the racial dimensions of the post-1965 immigrant or refugee experience. Having no notion of spatial scale and no concept of racism's platial dimensions enables that ignorance. To put it differently, thinking in spatial and platial terms gives us levers and buttons with which to dismantle racism. Doreen Massey and John Allen remind us:

the full meaning of the term "spatial" includes a whole range of aspects of the social world. It includes distance, and differences in the measurement, connotations and appreciation of distance. It includes movement. It includes geographical differentiation, the notion of place and specificity, and of differences between places. And it includes the symbolism and meaning which in different societies, and in different parts of given societies, attach to all of these things. (1984, 5)

Racial formations in the post–civil rights context have taken a seemingly random, chaotic spatial form; but those formations have not disappeared into spacelessness. Indeed, to understand race and racism in the twenty-first century, we need to trace racial formations as they traverse spatial boundaries, jump scale from mini- to macrounits and back again, and morph into ideas and practices that organize and drive community, regional, and national identities. For example, newly racialized ethnic minorities may be spatially enclosed in ethnic ghettos; spatially dispersed, upwardly mobile, and living at some distance from their ethnically marked enclaves; or inserted into close quarters with whites as their domestic service providers. In every case, the plain fact is that racialized ethnic minorities are demarcated, disciplined, and controlled at multiple and simultaneous levels of spatial scale not only by the racial state but also by community leaders themselves.

A major contribution of this study is that place-making allows people to "stay Vietnamese" even when they move away from Little Saigon or take on many of the attributes of white, middle-class existence such as speaking English, voting Republican, praying in a Christian church, treating their elders as equals, or driving to the shopping mall. Their efforts to stay Vietnamese occur against a backdrop that legitimates a certain kind of heroic, anticommunist Vietnameseness, and ignores other kinds. The Vietnamese I have met are proud of who they are, but they (like the rest of us) are also in important and subtle ways marked and controlled by a racial and platial status quo that is not of their own making. What does this imply for other groups? Basically this: containment is only a tiny piece of the story about race and place. We need to work out more clearly and more expansively how racial formations are changing at various levels of spatial scale and in varying platial contexts.

Cuban refugees provide the number one comparison group to Vietnamese Americans because they were similarly established as refugee settlements in the aftermath of the cold war.[23] Like the Vietnamese, their "ethnic archipelago" has had a focal point, Miami, to which political expatriates have flocked. Over time, Cubans seem to be leaving Miami for suburbs in more affluent counties. Only the most disadvantaged Cubans are staying in place. Still, the headline for Cubans usually reads "successful Hispanic entrepreneur," just as many Vietnamese are stereotyped as "valedictorians."

Maybe, for some orientalist researchers, the fact that many Cubans may pass as "white" ends the comparison with Vietnamese. Perhaps Vietnamese as "Asians" would be considered by leaps and bounds more "foreign" to U.S. society than any Cuban, even a working-class Afro-Cuban, could possibly be. Remember that one Vietnamese leader told me she could never be "blonde or blue eyed" and so she could never qualify as "American." Her statement presents a very narrow phenotypic definition of the nation, one that Holly-wood films export daily around the world. The persistent question of the construction of whiteness and white institutional privilege vis-à-vis access to resources and identity in U.S. society requires thoughtful and critical examination. A comparative analysis of the role of whiteness in racial for-mations among U.S. Latinos and Asian Americans would illuminate this problem.

The issue of racialization and place pans out so differently for Cubans than for Vietnamese not only because of real and perceived ties to Europe but also because of the contemporary context in which Spanish-language use has become both widely accepted and also highly politicized, especially along the U.S. borderlands. If Samuel Huntington had his way, all native Spanish-language speakers would go home, no matter how red, white, and blue their political views might be![24] He did not bother to target Asian-language speakers because no one will never see the day when Vietnamese is widely spoken anywhere in the United States outside of Little Saigon. That is because of numbers and geography, not racism. But what is com-mon to both Cubans and Vietnamese is that native-language use and place-making can go hand in hand, and when street signage or other aspects of architectural design become salient, the question of "who owns speech, and where" easily takes on racist undertones.[25]

The erroneous and biologistic idea that over time racial distinctions in the United States will disappear because people will intermarry across racial lines to produce multiracial or "blended" children has emerged again in recent sociological literature on immigration and ethnicity. Lee and Bean, for example, refer to offspring of marriages between Asians or Latinos with whites as indicative of a "reduction of social distance and racial prejudice" (2004, 236). This "contact theory of race" was popular too in the 1930s when Robert Park and his Chicago School colleagues were trying to figure out whether Asians (especially Japanese, Chinese, and Filipinos) who were considered "inassimilable" to white society would ever become assimilated. The odd thing about then and now is that "race" continues to be treated as a heritable matter of genetics, even though gallons of scholarly ink has been spilled since World War II debunking this very thought. More importantly, people marry across race usually with someone *who shares their same socioeconomic background.* This might be one of the few cases where money does lead to happiness. When it comes to small-scale intimate encounters between groups in the United States, it would be rash to assume that "race" is going to disappear just because all the new immigrants seem to be getting along with—either striving to mimic or to marry—whites.

The contact theory of race suggests that more contact between racial groups will lead to more positive and understanding interactions between them. But one of the requirements is that the groups encounter each other as equals, for example, as teammates on a playing field. Meetings between groups that are clearly unequal will not do much to improve "race relations" and if anything will probably exacerbate and harden racial tensions. In a fascinating study of a contemporary gated community in Orange County, California, Kristin Hill Maher (2004) shows how racial borders and other lines of social distinction are drawn when whites are in close quarters with Mexicans who work for them as nannies, cooks, gardeners, and drivers. As we might expect, those daily interactions serve to elaborate upon racial inequalities—not to dismantle them. It would not be hard to imagine other circumstances in which, for example, rich Vietnamese and poor Mexicans are similarly ensconced. The point is not to hate on elite Asians or anyone else as much as it is to underscore the trump card that wealth can sometimes represent, and to highlight the minute spatial scale in which racial formations and class domination may be generated and preserved.

The narrative of the "ethnic entrepreneur," uplifted as it is with visions of upward mobility, is in actuality loaded down with a big responsibility for disciplining and controlling racialized ethnic minorities in part by platializing them. The Vietnamese Americans I spoke with were primarily community leaders rather than business people, but the places they built were often attributed with the positive qualities of "ethnic enclaves" in which self-sufficient and selfless refugees sacrifice and toil for the well-being of their families, grateful for the chance to "make it" in America and with not the slightest idea about public policies that might advance their futures. Asian ethnic places—regardless of the ethnic tag or platial contours— seem always to be stamped with this idea.[26]

This notion of absolving government of the need to take care of its citizens was present in the earliest versions of the model-minority myth propounded by journalists in the 1960s: those portrayals juxtaposed the industrious and apolitical inhabitants of Chinatown with the highly organized masses of African American workers in other marginal parts of the metropolis who demanded affirmative action in the workplace and civil rights at home.

Today, thanks mostly to decades of domestic political backlash and a massive concentration of global corporate power, most of us are hard put to distinguish between the "right" and "wrong" sides of racial or ethnic mobilizations. But thinking regionally in southern California brings to mind the contrast between images of the "enterprising immigrant" (who is sometimes Vietnamese) and images of the "illegal" and therefore criminal migrant laborer (who is often Mexican). In the latter example, *colonias* all along the U.S. borderland in general are treated as a priori unlawful places despite the honest blood and sweat given by individuals and families to make ends meet. One could argue that in the international context of corporate free trade agreements such as NAFTA and GATT, labor migration is a highly rational choice. What could be more "enterprising" than sending members of your family, or even your whole province, to defy death by drowning in the Rio Grande in the hopes of better wages and the chance for a better future?[27]

My point is that the categories of "entrepreneur," "drug addict," and "illegal alien," like so many other racially coded terms, are tools for marking, manipulating, and surveying groups and places—and ultimately, for preserving the dominant logic of whiteness that informs U.S. national identity. Whether we are talking about seaport cities that attract refugees and immigrants, pocket-size ethnic shopping and eating districts that have reversed urban blight, or the barbed wire zones of the U.S.-Mexico border, we are still gesturing to huge geopolitical issues that are intricately grafted via "race" onto people's bodies, homes, and neighborhoods. What looks like the personal decision of one refugee turns out to be part of an international battle between the First World and the Second World. What looks like the personal decision of one migrant laborer turns out to be part of a global trend to open up markets in developing countries. Global North and Global South reposition themselves by minute actions in the lives of ordinary people. By opening up new ways to connecting racial formations with spatial and platial processes, we expose that complex and global grafting process.

Platial and Glocal: Paths to Other Futures

Platial is not merely another way to think about space. The word has even more potential to open our eyes and widen our imaginations to tie global processes down to their most intense and specific effects. Indeed, "platial" should pair up with "glocal" as descriptors for widely occurring processes, practices, and events that have important and particular geographical consequences. According to the Glocal Forum, "glocalization" is a "new strategy for international relations" that attends to the "interests and identities" of those who have been left out by recent economic expansion.[28] Glocalization means something extra special to people who "think global, act local" because glocal is a hands-on term tied to a project with practical intentions. In contrast, platial is more of an abstract concept. Platial links spatial and local together in order to emphasize the specific contexts in which space matters. If we understand the platial effects of globalization, we can more assuredly support glocalization.

In *Planet of Slums* Mike Davis (2005) excoriates the devastating effects of neoliberalism and structural adjustment on metropolitan regions around the globe. Neoliberalism creates extreme wealth as well as pockets of poverty. Significantly, poverty is platial because the corporate-led agenda to privatize natural resources and to deregulate trade has wrought particular, localized concessions from people and the earth. The intensity of these concessions manifests at multiple levels of geographic scale, from the individual body ravaged by HIV/AIDS-related diseases to entire towns, villages, and regions that have been hollowed out, ransacked, and abandoned by profit-seeking industries. Treating the epidemic of slums as platial and not only as global brings to the fore the actual, concrete, and lived dimensions of the neoliberal project.

Ultimately, the displacement into exile of Vietnamese refugees and the subsequent creation of a Vietnamese diaspora around the world has both platial and glocal dimensions. The two communities this book examines have sibling communities around the United States and in many other Western nations, especially Canada, Australia, and France. Thinking platially means looking at place-making and community-building in their local contexts, attending especially to the demands made upon Vietnamese refugees and immigrants by the prevailing notions of citizenship. Thinking glocally would mean framing these Vietnamese places and communities in broader international terms and looking at Vietnamese efforts to rebuild their own lives amidst the big sweeps of wealth and inequality in a region.

But if we do not stop shoving Vietnamese American successes into racially coded master narratives about assimilation, we will be hard put to arrive at any platial or glocal insights, and those barren narratives will continue to dominate our thoughts and research.

Notes for the Future

So many other pressing issues and questions remain. Throughout this book, I did not theorize gender or sexuality. As a result, I provide no frame for understanding the gendered and sexualized dimensions of Vietnamese American community-building and place-making and therefore I avoid making some obviously necessary comments about community and place. I can, in retrospect, at least forward some questions. For example, the Westminster War Monument is a tribute to soldiers as men. What role do women have in Vietnamese American strategic memory projects? Queer artists and organizers have spoken out in Little Saigon and perhaps, although I do not know from firsthand experience, also in Fields Corner. How do places accommodate or internalize these emergent voices? To what extent do Vietnamese American national narratives depend on conventional notions of masculinity and heteropatriarchy, and how do the actual experiences of men and women—as parents, laborers, refugees, businesspeople—challenge those notions?

The voice of the second generation is relatively weak throughout this book, although I interviewed a handful of college and university students in both regions. Often their perspectives helped me to see the impact of a generation gap within Vietnamese America. A couple of these students had great difficulty articulating the issues that shape their community, probably because their only source of relevant information is their parents, and their parents see the world through a much different lens. As a second-generation immigrant I understand this problem; it is the reason I did not choose to research community and place among Filipino Americans. I would have found myself to be shamefully inarticulate, and my elders would have lost no chance to correct and edify me. As a consequence of the relatively subdued presence of younger Vietnamese American voices in this book I perhaps overemphasize an elder's exile perspective on staying Vietnamese. On the other hand, the whole project of staying Vietnamese is by definition of greater concern to the older generation.

By restricting my research to English-language sources, I capture only a very small slice of what staying Vietnamese really means to Vietnamese Americans. Even the people I did interview surely would have conveyed many more nuances if they could have spoken with me in their own languages. Because I am not familiar with Vietnamese accents or customs, important details were definitely lost on me, such as the presence of northerners or ethnic minorities in the communities I studied. I take small comfort in the fact that prior to this one most social scientific investigations of Vietnamese Americans have been conducted by non-Vietnamese researchers who make no apologies as far as I know about their English-only methods. Furthermore, they do not talk about orientalism, much less eschew it. I hope that future researchers who are fully multilingual will carry out a better approach to race and U.S. racial formations.

My scholarly inattentiveness to religion and religious affiliations is most certainly a loss. Although I interviewed two Catholic priests, several Buddhists, and at least one Cao Dai worshipper, I did not consider the many ways that religion and spirituality inform Vietnamese American life. A multimillion-dollar Catholic center in Westminster and a series of formerly Irish, now Vietnamese, parishes in Boston, not to mention dozens of Buddhist and other kinds of temples, would be excellent sites for the study of Vietnamese American platiality.

My findings would have been greatly enriched had I benefited from a team of researchers who could help me include other major communities and places in my comparative framework; for example, Falls Church, Virginia; San Jose, California; Houston, Texas; or New Orleans, Louisiana. In the aftermath of Hurricane Katrina in 2005, the implications of racism and displacement loom large over the nation, with very little public discussion about the fate of black people, not to mention the Vietnamese. For those Vietnamese who left the Gulf to resettle in Houston, what aspects of place—locality, built environment, and narration—now shape their new lives? Is a twice-displaced refugee still a refugee in the conventional definition of that word?

For all my emphasis on race and racism, I did not attend deeply to "race relations" between Vietnamese Americans and other groups in Boston or Orange County. To do so would have required a more prolonged and more complex immersion in each region. The payoffs would have been worthwhile. For example, Stephen Steinberg asserts that "Immigrants are implicated in America's race problem through the very act of immigration" (2005, 43). By this, he means that immigrants benefit from the placement of native-born blacks at the bottom of the race "totem pole." Previous research on Vietnamese Americans does not provide much of a direct challenge to Steinberg's assertion. Under what conditions do Vietnamese

Americans benefit from America's already existing racial hierarchy? To what extent does Vietnamese American community-building and place-making reinforce this hierarchy? What examples of Vietnamese Americans working in solidarity with other nonwhites should be surfaced so as to counter the idea of a white-supervised racial food chain?

Many years of studying Vietnamese American community-building and place-making in Boston and Orange County have allowed me to address some very basic themes of community and place. I offer explanations for what I think is going on in those two regions, with the hopes that my method of comparison and analysis may be applicable to other communities and places. I would not go so far as to say that whatever is happening in Boston is the same as what is happening in Chicago, for example, but I would point out that those two cities share some common characteristics: nineteenth-century growth and expansion based on manufacturing, neighborhoods known for their ethnic identities, racial segregation, rapidly changing demographics due to post-1965 immigration, and a unique regional "personality." Those characteristics likely have a strong impact on the parameters for community-building and place-making among Vietnamese refugees or other groups. Similarly, I would not equate Orange County with Houston or San Jose, but I would expect suburban sprawl to play an important role in the shape and character of community and place. I take seriously the idea that local context matters and that we cannot erase the distinct features of place when we seek to explain the nuances of culture and identity for refugees or immigrants.

This book is particularly bent on promoting an active view of space and place. I emphasize the mesounits of place: cities, suburbs, communities. At this level of scale, I aim to reveal the hopes and struggles of a racialized ethnic group as emplaced, embodied demands. I make some gestures to national identities and global capitalism, but a more serious transnational scholar would probably advise me to interrogate more carefully those moments when I or my informants "jump scale" from single monuments to huge, worldwide events and back again. I do not delve into the very interesting microdimensions of place: families, homes, personal life. Surely the things that happen to construct and produce community and place at this micro-scale are crucial to Vietnamese American life, and it is quite possible that even this small scale of social interaction is influenced by local contexts and cultures. For example, whether refugees and immigrants attempt to "stay Vietnamese" in southern California or in the Gulf Coast or in Texas must have implications for relationships within the family, notions of home or personal belonging, and bodily space. The devastation wrought by Katrina—a regional storm that forced people to cling to their roofs and their refrigerators for fear of drowning, and thousands did drown—made brutally clear the connections among micro-, meso-, and macrodimensions of social and spatial life.[29]

I also want to expose and dismantle the assumptions behind the narratives of immigrant assimilation and American exceptionalism. This work of exposing and dismantling happened prior to my interviews in the sense that I made up questions that would help me get at those issues, but this work also occurred in the analytical process, long after the interviews were recorded and transcribed. I see Vietnamese American community-building and place-making as material and discursive efforts to stay Vietnamese, within and sometimes against these persistent and entrenched narratives. By putting the voices of Vietnamese American leadership at the forefront, I hope the idea of Vietnamese refugees as tragic and passive victims is finally dead.

Conclusion How Do You Stay Vietnamese in America?

I WENT TO VIET NAM TWICE IN 2006: first in January on a group tour, and a second time in November by myself and as part of a longer personal journey that concluded in the Philippines.

During the first visit I joined a group of scholars, trade unionists, and Vietnam War–era peace activists made up primarily of North Americans but also including individuals from Ireland, Greece, and Palestine. Most of us were curious and concerned about the policies and practices that the government of Viet Nam has followed since *doi moi,* the series of economic reforms instituted in 1986. My own purpose was to gather some initial impressions of life in Viet Nam that would broaden my understanding of Vietnamese culture and of the Vietnamese American experience. This was also a step in my broader, more creative exploration of what it means to be Asian American in this era of global capitalist expansion.

Over nearly three weeks we toured the country, spending several days in Ha Noi, Hoi An, Hue, and then Ho Chi Minh City. Besides the typical sites that most tourists see, we also visited the Vietnam Women's Union, the Ford Viet Nam plant, the national Confederation of Trade Unions, and the Ho Chi Minh Political Academy. The highlight of our trip was a two-day conference on Culture and the Changing Global Economy held at the Academy, the government's official training center.

At the conference, I was the only nonwhite U.S. representative and the only person addressing the issues facing Vietnamese living in the diaspora. We alternated with the Vietnamese scholars in taking the podium to deliver the main point of our papers, which were simultaneously translated and circulated in printed form to all the participants. When my turn came, I shared ideas derived from this book, mostly from chapter 4. In very abbreviated language, I described the significance of racism—particularly white privilege—for Vietnamese American place-making and community-building. I explained what I meant by the dominant collective memory of the war, and the impact I believe that memory has had on Vietnamese Americans. Then I talked about marketplace multiculturalism as an impulse that requires Vietnamese to sell their culture and identity in order to gain recognition and resources for their communities.

By attending this conference, we were introduced to many officials of the ruling Communist Party. One afternoon, a few other members of my tour delegation and I were invited to meet briefly with the Vice Chairman of the Central Committee of the Communist Party, the equivalent of our nation's Vice President. Interestingly, I cannot imagine any circumstance in which anything I do would lead to a visit with him. But at the Presidential Palace in Ha Noi, I gave a two-minute version of my research, and in response, the Vice Chair asked me what I thought Vietnamese Americans were going to do to "help Viet Nam."

I don't remember my answer exactly but I do remember the feeling of a gap or a hole, a "present absence" of the Vietnamese Americans I have interviewed. I know that the government of Viet Nam, like its counterparts throughout Asia and Latin America, wants to get its hands on the dollars of Viet Kieu, or overseas Vietnamese. By comparison with their relatives who are considered wealthy if they own a water buffalo and a motorcycle, most Vietnamese Americans might as well be billionaires.

Most of the people I interviewed for this book would rather die than help Viet Nam. In fact, at least one told me that he sends money to support terrorists in the jungles of Thailand who he hopes will eventually overthrow the Vietnamese government. Surely he would be shocked and horrified to know that not only did I travel to Viet Nam with a bunch of lefty antiwar peaceniks but that I also willingly spoke with officials of the Communist Party. I worry what he, and other Vietnamese Americans, would think about my travels.

Gisele Bousquet (1991) tells of the meticulous safety precautions she took in interviewing Vietnamese in Paris who were either staunchly communist or staunchly anticommunist, their lives divided by a metaphorical "bamboo hedge." Her research project more directly confronted this hedge, and she was probably wise to take those measures. On the other hand, throughout the period in which I was doing my fieldwork in Orange County and Boston, I never intended to address international politics head-on or to take sides. I did not knowingly ever dispute anyone's political or ideological orientation. That was not the point of my research, and I was able to gather enough interesting data about community-building and place-making without broaching those tough issues.

But in traveling to Viet Nam and reporting on my visits in this book, I crossed the hedge. As a result, I have sharp new insights into the notion of "staying Vietnamese" that I would not have come upon had I not experienced Viet Nam briefly for myself, and then continued on to the Philippines where I could judge how much of my second-generation Filipino American self was "pinay pa rin," still Filipino. Now, I imagine and understand the production and construction of Vietnameseness (and Filipinoness) as a complex and ongoing global and historical project that is mitigated by many forces and dynamics, including activities in the United States. I also have a comparative international framework within which to consider two very different kinds of purported "Asian American" identities. This is not the venue to elaborate upon the many fascinating layers of that comparison. Suffice it to say that Viet Nam and the Philippines look like "bookends" of U.S. empire, starting with the mock battle in 1898 with Spanish troops in Manila Bay and ending with the rushed departure of U.S. troops from Sai Gon in 1975.

One common result of that imperial relationship is the condition of dispersal and exile that faces Filipinos and Vietnamese, especially but not exclusively in the United States. I suspect, but have no hard proof, that the results of that condition vary widely between and within the groups.

In November, I had a coffee in Ha Noi with a member of the National Assembly. Although he seemed to relate to the nuances of my American way of talking and thinking, when I got to the topic of racism in the United States, I lost him. Then, when I added that young Asian Americans often need to create anew a positive ethnic identity, he saw the dilemma that might pose for Vietnamese Americans. They would have to "go back" to Viet Nam to look for their roots, but for many that trip is difficult or forbidden.

The same can be said of all the Filipinos I know who left the Philippines during the turbulent years of martial law, only to be stuck in a permanently frozen condition of nonconnection all the way around. In this case, as with Vietnamese, travel back and forth between the two places is sometimes impossible. But even when one does have the opportunity to physically return to "the homeland," such a trip does not necessarily help to resolve a historical and political rupture that has deep, psychic, and multigenerational consequences.

This is not to overlook all the U.S.-born Vietnamese who, like me, are exploring their roots in part by visiting the land of their parents' and grandparents' birth. I simply mean to acknowledge that going to Viet Nam as I did is not achievable—or desirable—for many Vietnamese Americans. Besides, Vietnamese American community-building and place-making has its own, mostly separate, agenda from whatever is going on in Viet Nam. No matter what, it seems a good idea to widen the options for how to be or stay Vietnamese in the United States, especially for the next generation.

Appendix   Research and Methodology

Characteristics of Interviewees

Many issues discussed in this book are highly contentious, and many people have spoken frankly with me about them at great risk to their relationships with and reputations in the Vietnamese American community. To protect their anonymity and to minimize any harm done, I describe people loosely, use pseudonyms, and sometimes disguise their gender or affiliations. However, when a person I have interviewed is described or quoted in a public document such as a newspaper or an organizational brochure, I use their real names and identifiers.

To locate possible interviewees when I first entered the field, I culled names from a variety of sources, including newspapers, business directories, and names of board members of key organizations. With the help of key informants, I sorted through and ranked this list. This reputational technique is meant to determine "who runs the show," although that would require knowing in advance what the show is.[1] More often, speaking to a new person gave me additional insights into the different kinds of ongoing "shows" in the community and who is running them.

Ultimately, this book focuses on three shows—race, memory, and marketplace multiculturalism—each run in their own way by three groups: first-wave refugees, ex–political detainees, and second-generation Vietnamese Americans. Because my sample was limited, the perspectives of ethnic Chinese (with the exception of a few very successful entrepreneurs), Amerasians, and pre-1975 immigrants or refugees are particularly absent.

The idea of leadership is so controversial in the Vietnamese American community that hardly anyone would agree that all the people I interviewed qualify as "leaders" or even "movers and shakers." Some would label others mere "mouthpieces"—or worse, "self-appointed chiefs." To expand my list of interviewees, I also used the snowball method (asking people for their suggestions of other people I could speak with) and the quota method, for which I developed categories of social actors whose perspectives I hoped to include in this book. These categories included ethnic entrepreneur, public official, social service provider, community spokesperson, newspaper/ TV/radio editor or producer, clergy, white-collar professional, college/university professor, college/university student. I then sought to fill "quotas" for each category. Of the fifty-two people I interviewed, nearly half fit into the social service provider or community spokesperson category, reflecting the impact of funding and programs designed to resettle refugees and to create leadership in the refugee community.

Open Interviews

I entered the field in 1994 armed with a set of open questions designed to guide a conversation about place and community. I sought to obtain the main details of each person's personal biography and then to explore their perspectives on themes I thought they would be knowledgeable about. By eliciting each person's interpretation of their experience, I intended to apply my own version of feminist "standpoint theory" to the activities I later defined as Vietnamese American community-building and place-making.[2] Over the years, I revisited Orange County and Boston several times, making repeated contact with about a dozen individuals who made themselves available to me. Those individuals guided me toward an ever more nuanced understanding of what is going on in Vietnamese America. Because only a small group of people made themselves available to me over the entire course of this study, their views may have swayed me more than those with whom I met only once.

As one outside observer remarked when I visited in 2005: "Some things have changed, but many things stay the same."

Sample Questions

Would you tell me about your personal story, when you and your family left Viet Nam, when you came to the United States, and so on?

Where do you live now?

What is your occupation?

In your opinion, who are the most important or influential people in the Vietnamese American community in Orange County/Boston?

Where is the "center" of the Vietnamese American community?

How would you describe your position in the community?

Have you ever gone back to Viet Nam? If yes, why? If no, why not?

Do you identify with the term Asian American? Why or why not?

What are the most important issues facing the Vietnamese American community?

Is there anything particular to your community that you think I should know?

These questions allowed me to elicit a broad base of information about general issues from the perspective of various individuals. Over repeated interviews, I was able to probe more deeply about topics that seemed central, especially racialization, memory, and the commodification of culture.

A Note about Method and Methodology

This book includes photographs and tables as illustrations or elaborations of points that I make in the text. I feel compelled to comment on my creation and use of these visual elements, because so often "visualizing difference" is an undertheorized and underexamined activity. If nothing else is clear, I hope my use of photographs is not interpreted as an effort to add "factual" evidence so as to evade argument. What I say about photographs extends also to maps, though I have not included any maps in this book.

Photographs and maps add a powerful visual dimension to the analysis of social and spatial relationships presented in this book because those images circumvent, and in a sense operate beyond, words.[3] Yet, as social activities, photography and mapping are far from obvious, innocent, or benign. In both mapmaking and photography, the selection and presentation of information involve a chain of important decisions that are intended ultimately to enhance the message behind the image. Inevitably, reality is distorted so that a specific idea may be conveyed. While these distortions are necessary, they are not always good. The potential uses and abuses of maps and photographs have been underexamined—if they are examined at all—in the scholarly literature on Vietnamese Americans. In the course of my fieldwork I uncovered many examples of visual images that use Vietnamese American experiences to articulate or support certain familiar narratives of assimilation, difference, individualism, or cultural consumption. Many of these images make misleading or deceptive claims to truth and objectivity. By deception I do not mean to suggest that the authors of these images were purposefully lying; instead, I mean simply that the persuasive elements of such images probably go unnoticed by the less-experienced viewer.

For the naïve viewer, the appeal of maps and photographs lies in their vigorous claims to reality. Sociologists, like journalists, often take advantage of these claims. For example, including a map and a series of photographs along with an ethnography of a little-known community helps to verify the location and appearance of the group in question. Depending on how they are presented, the apparent veracity of these visual images may allow the author to present a world that seems to require no argument. Thus, images may allow an author to skip out on a broad set of intriguing and necessary epistemological questions: What expertise does the author bring to this topic? How do we know what she is saying is true? Do insiders view their community differently from how the author does? What other arguments about community might others put forward based on the same information?

Posing these questions is not to say that maps or photographs should not be used because they are inherently bad or dangerous; I would hate to encourage a phobia of visual media. I intend merely to point out that we often allow the cartographer and the photographer full rein of the visual images they produce, without thinking twice about what those images were intended to accomplish. There is no such thing as a map or a photograph that is opinion-free.

Other writers explain how maps and photographs contribute to the West's imperialist enterprise and to the elaboration of Westerners' sense of superiority and entitlement.[4] One of the Vietnamese Americans I interviewed was once a mapmaker for the CIA. Maps and photographs have played a practical role in state surveillance and the control of movement and migration in Viet Nam and in America. It would follow that in the cultural realm, mapping and photography, along with video and film, have played key roles in producing and constructing Vietnamese bodies and Vietnamese spaces as sites of political liberation or repression, moral recuperation or depravity, and racialized difference.[5]

As an aspiring photographer, I would have liked to explore the visual dimension of Vietnamese American community-building and place-making further. For example, it would have been fascinating to create a photo essay in which the leaders I interview portray with their own cameras what community and place mean to them. Architects might be more impressed with my spatial analysis had I been able to attend to the visual aspect of design, the shape of roofs, signage, placement of landmarks, and so on.

I have been influenced by critical scholarship in sociology, Asian American studies, and women's studies to see "method and methodology" as much more than a set of techniques for finding and handling data (such as interviews, statistics, maps, or photographs) but as an arena rich with urgent and necessary questions about power and knowledge. C. Wright

Mills (1971–72) impressed on me the notion that by using the "sociological imagination" we can see the otherwise invisible cords connecting personal biography to collective history. No person is an island or an individual hero; each of us is the product of broad social and historical forces that extend far beyond our own horizons. Charles Lemert (1997) labels our everyday activity of getting through the day as "practical sociology"; even ordinary individuals can be seen as very knowledgeable about the world they navigate daily. Henry Yu (2001) makes clear the Orientalist leanings of traditional social science by tracing the development of research on Asian immigrants by early Chicago School sociologists. His study makes me ultra-aware of the complex inside/outside boundaries that circumscribe our communities and of the various conditions under which I might be seen as having "insider" bias. Nancy Naples (2003) provides many concrete examples of feminist research that explores and explains what people do not know and cannot see because they/we are immersed in our own lives. From all of these scholars, I have taken away the message that one of the most important methodological contributions of a researcher is to lay bare the social relations of power and inequality that pervade the world.

In 2005, I was invited to the home of Mr. Hien Dang; his wife made an elaborate meal and generously allowed Mr. Hien and me to have an extended conversation about the Vietnamese American community in Boston. When I asked him about the one thing he thought it was most important for me to say in this book, he told me:

> In your book you need to understand the culture, what the Vietnamese feel. Even the Vietnamese read it, they think you are Vietnamese. That is a true book.

Years of academic training have instilled in me a deep skepticism about the possibility of putting forth any perspective as "true." Yet, I am very moved by Mr. Hien's wish that I portray the Vietnamese American community as they would also portray themselves. I take it as a sign of his hope in me that I might be so faithful to the stories that people have told me that in my analysis "even Vietnamese" would think I was Vietnamese. In an ideal world of real multiculturalism, perhaps I could truly see the world from other people's eyes. For now, I can offer only what I know, based on the information many people have so generously shared with me.

Acknowledgments

Dozens of people in Orange County and Boston spoke to me with candor and generosity about their hopes, dreams, anxieties, and nightmares during the past decade. Though you may disagree with things that I have written here, I hope you see the value of this project. Your efforts to make a rewarding and meaningful life in this country, for yourselves and for others, deserve our utmost attention.

Without editors and publishers, professors like me could not keep our jobs. I am lucky to have found Jason Weidemann and his colleagues at the University of Minnesota Press, whose professional insights added legibility and credence to this project.

Many years of persistent and supportive mentors and colleagues in graduate school and long afterward allowed me to start—and finish—this project. In 1994, Peter Nien-Chu Kiang from the University of Massachusetts, Boston, pointed me toward Fields Corner. At the sociology department of Brown University, David Meyer expressed an ambivalence about my interest in place that inadvertently led me to develop the notion of "platializing race." Hilary Silver and José (Pepe) Itzigsohn gave me useful and lasting sociological advice; Professor Silver clarified and underscored the paradox underlying my Orange County–Boston comparison, and Professor Itzigsohn freely shared with me his discoveries about Latino immigrants in New England. As former director of Asian American studies at the University of California at Irvine, Ketu H. Katrak took it upon herself at a crucial moment to get me back on track. For those two pivotal hours, she has my everlasting gratitude. While we cruised Sunset Boulevard, Jan C. Lin, a sociologist at Occidental College, gave me professional advice in a fun-loving and brotherly manner.

Numerous times over the past decade I visited the Southeast Asian Archive of the University of California, Irvine and (like so many other students and scholars) I benefited enormously from the guidance and generosity of Anne Frank. She pulled books and articles aside for me before I even knew I needed them, and she kept me informed of the latest developments. Giving me entrée to Boston's history of antiwar, peace, and social justice movements, Elizabeth Mock and Dale Freeman, the archivists at the Healey Library at the University of Massachusetts, pleasantly entrusted me with boxes and boxes of yellowing papers and news clippings. I swear that librarians are truly a researcher's best friends.

In 1997, then chair of American studies at the University of Minnesota, David Roediger told me to "think about Minnesota." Eventually I did even more than that: now I live here and consider it my home. Since 1999, Janet Carlson, Galo Gonzalez, Peter Rachleff, Duchess Harris, and Kathie Scott have cheered me on at Macalester College, never voicing any doubts in me. Jane Rhodes congratulated me for each minute step toward the completion of this project and at the eleventh hour lent me a book that helped me polish off an important point. One hot summer afternoon, Joi Lewis and Joan Ostrove delivered a frozen chocolate confection to my door. No subsequent act could match theirs in timing or intention. On the other side of the Mississippi River, the Asian Americanists at the University of Minnesota have always been kind and collegial; I am especially thankful to Cathy Ceniza Choy and Greg Choy (now in Berkeley, California), Erika Lee, Jigna Desai, and Josephine Lee.

Over the years, I received several grants and fellowships that allowed me to embark on and then complete this project. A University Fellowship from Brown University supported my first year in graduate school, and a Predoctoral Minority Fellowship from the American Sociological Association got me through three more years. A Humanities Fellowship from the Rockefeller Foundation in 2002 allowed me to spend four months as a scholar-in-residence at the William Joiner Center for the Study of War and Social Consequences at the University of Massachusetts, Boston. There, Kevin Bowen and Nguyen Ba Chung introduced me to the world of Vietnamese history, poetry, and literature. I'm sure this book does not reflect half of what I am still learning from that experience. To support my 2003–4 junior sabbatical at Macalester College, I received a generous Career Enhancement Fellowship for Underrepresented Minorities from the Woodrow Wilson National Fellowship Foundation. Generous travel and research funds from Macalester College allowed me to travel twice to Viet Nam in 2006, bringing this project full circle around the globe.

While in Boston, I reconnected to friends and fellow scholar/activists who showed interest and enthusiasm for my work: Susan Moir and Harneen Chernow; Cynthia Peters, Loie Hayes, and the South End Press collective; Estelle Dische, Rita Arditti, Connie Chan, and Marie Kennedy, my feminist scholar role models; Chris Tilly and John Miller (and the rest of the *dollars & Sense* collective); Boone and Peggy Schirmer (practically grandparents to me, now in memoriam). Every once in a while, I receive a postcard from Cynthia Enloe with a message that keeps me intact and whole. Thank you all for your unforgettable examples of commitment to a lifetime of activism.

A few great friends made my memories of southern California particularly fond with their hospitality, friendship, conversation, and culinary escapades: Alice Y. Hom, Gisele Fong, Dean Toji, baby Evan Fong-Toji, Alice Tuan, Susan Tuan, Patrick X. Rousseau, Eric Estuar Reyes, Theo Gonzalves, June F. Kurata, and Mariam Beevi Lam. With Gina Masequesmay, I continue a wondrous sociological and spiritual journey into and around Vietnamese America.

Here's a nod to the Next Generation Leadership program, an initiative of the Rockefeller Foundation now associated with the Robert F. Wagner Graduate School of Public Service at New York University. At our first NGL reunion in Boulder, Colorado, Rickie Solinger, a guest lecturer and feminist historian I had never before met, introduced herself, read my mind, and then helped me to recover a writing voice I thought I had lost forever in graduate school. That is a debt I'm sure I can never repay.

For their camaraderie and insistence on deep theorizing, a huge thank-you to NGL's Changing Racial Realities Cluster Group 2005–6 for keeping me on my toes. The independent filmmaker Liz Canner is so in tune with the creative process that even in the last grueling weeks I looked forward to answering the one question that writers ordinarily dread: "How's the writing going?" I hope all writers have friends like her.

My parents, Delia D. Aguilar and Sonny San Juan, read drafts of chapters and provided assiduous comments. In the midst of a writing frenzy during the summer of 2005, my brother Eric San Juan and his partner Jack Davis visited from Washington, D.C., and made themselves useful by refilling my birdfeeder, mowing my lawn, and reminding me of the joys of queer life in the Twin Cities.

In two separate conversations, Susan Moir and Tracy E. Ore each came up with the phrase "staying Vietnamese" to describe the enduring attachments to place and identity in Orange County and Boston that I had described to them. Every now and then, Susan gives me a gift by asking when

I am coming "home" to Boston. I'm lucky to have so many people and places say they miss me.

What teacher does not, deep down inside, love her students? I love and appreciate mine, especially the ones who fearlessly question me. Their persistence but also their patience, kindness, and belief that they make a difference remind me that scholarship matters.

One day in St. Paul, my sixteen-year-old, destined-to-be-a-professor friend Ian Koller asked me what this book was about. When I told him it was about how two Vietnamese American communities deal with place, he replied, "Now *that's* making a mountain out of a molehill!" Shouldn't we all have a clever teenager to crush our egos and put our biggest worries into perspective? During the final months of my completing this book, a team of wonderful people looked after my physical, emotional, and spiritual health: Sharon T. Haire; Sandy Agustin; Karen Belling; Colet Lahoz; Heather Burke; Marina Proudfoot; Sifu Ray Hayward, Sifu Paul Abdella, and my friends at Twin Cities Tai Chi Ch'uan; and all my dharma brothers and sisters at Dragon Gate Zen and Clouds in Water Zen Center. To all, a bow—and my thanks.

Notes

Introduction

1. See Vo (2000) for an excellent and brief overview of Vietnamese American community formation.

2. For two enjoyable journalistic accounts of the significance of place, see Hiss (1990) and Gallagher (1993).

3. Well aware of the issues I describe here, scholars and activists in the Vietnamese American community put their heads together years ago to create an innovative curriculum for high school students in Orange County called *Vietnamese Americans: Lessons in American History* (Vietnamese American Curriculum Project Committee 2001).

4. See Almaguer's account of the historical origins of whiteness in California (1994).

5. See Gayk (1990) for the demographic side of Orange County's changing image. See Lamb (1974) and Baldassare (1998) for the political side of whiteness in Orange County.

6. Schirmer (1975) gives a fascinating account of the anti-imperialist league's Bostonian roots.

7. Yu (2001) provides a complex and nuanced analysis of the early Chicago School's forays into Chinatowns, Japantowns, and Manilatowns in Chicago and California in the 1920s through the 1950s. During this period, sociologists constructed Asian Americans as racial others who remained "Oriental" so long as they occupied distinct social and physical spaces from whites. Chinatowns were seen as exotic and foreign places, even though they were located in U.S. cities. White scholars were "outsiders" who could not "penetrate" these places, so they made use of Chinese or Chinese American graduate students who ventured bravely inside and thus helped to elaborate upon what more established white sociologists had already defined as an "Oriental problem."

8. Spatial-assimilation theory (Massey 1985) continues to be a central component of the ethnicity paradigm, encapsulating the ecological tradition of the Chicago School by equating residential mobility—specifically suburbanization—to

acculturation and to an advanced phase of "structural" assimilation; see M. Gordon (1964). This said, it is still true that social scientists have observed, in recent years, the appearance of nonwhite immigrants in suburbia at, or near, the beginning of their trajectories of assimilation; in particular, two researchers have described the emergence of suburban Chinatowns, more generally termed "ethnoburbs" (Fong 1993; Li 1999). However, this "hallmark" event evidently has not been treated as a cue to revise or reject spatial-assimilation theory (Alba et al. 1999). Despite an emerging literature tying the growth of suburbs to a possessive investment in whiteness (Lipsitz 1998), the privatization of community (McKenzie 1994), and a widespread culture of fear (Zukin 1995), scholars influenced by spatial-assimilation theory promote a view of suburbs as desirable and normative spaces for all immigrants.

9. For an interesting attempt to intervene into the normalization of whiteness in spatial-assimilation research, see Wright, Ellis, and Parks (2005) and the negative response to it from Logan, a more established scholar (2005).

10. For key moments in the ethnic enclave/economy debate, see Portes and Jensen (1987), Portes and Jensen (1989), Portes and Manning (1986), Nee and Sanders (1987), and Waldinger (1993).

11. Steinberg (1981) points out that authenticity is not possible once culture is removed—or in the case of refugees, forced away—from its "original matrix." Canclini (1995) describes the "hybridity" of postmodern culture in Latin America, suggesting that no culture today, even Vietnamese culture in Viet Nam, can remain pure or untouched by developments in the larger global economy.

12. Two groups of students presented term papers on Harmony Bridge to Professor Beheroze Shroff in Asian American studies (Malia Cong 1997; Nguyen et al. 1996). These papers were then archived at the Southeast Asian Library.

13. Two journalists writing about Dorchester in the 1980s describe the struggles of early Vietnamese refugees, many of them ex–political detainees, just to make ends meet. See Weiss (1994) and M.-L. Pham (1992).

14. See the Weblog at http://www.platial.com for an intriguing definition of neogeography.

15. For the examples of www.platial.com and two scholarly articles on landscape research, I am indebted to a personal communication with Professor Daniel Trudeau in the geography department of Macalester College, May 2, 2008.

16. For a clear and succinct discussion of place, see Gieryn (2000).

17. My father, Professor E. "Sonny" San Juan, helped me to develop this insight.

18. N. Chung argues that, "There may be a unified country called Vietnam today . . . but in actuality, there are many 'little Vietnams'" (2002, 38–39). Rather than simply blaming today's factions on the inability of groups to overcome divisions arising as a result of post-1975 events, he traces these "cultural discontinuities" all the way back to fifteenth-century Viet Nam.

19. This idea of an equilibrium state is a gesture to a Parsonian, functionalist view of society in which parts shift and change in order to restore balance to the

whole. I owe Professor Tracy E. Ore, a sociologist at St. Cloud State University, for this important insight.

20. The cost of losing those connections is higher than most of us imagine: one Finnish Canadian friend offered me her personal view. As she put it, when she crossed the border into Minnesota and became a U.S. resident, she exchanged her Finnish community and culture for the chance to become white and shop at the Mall of America. While whiteness is often theorized in terms of its possessive investment (Lipsitz 1998) and property value (Harris 1993), in fact systems of racial domination exact a high price from everyone involved.

21. For the original discussion of institutional completeness, see Breton (1964).

22. See the Appendix for a discussion of the treatment of maps and photographs as "evidence."

1. Producing and Constructing Vietnamese America

1. For community, see Lyon (1987). For place, see Relph (1976).

2. For the classic Marxist elaboration on the production of space, see Lefebvre (1991). For postmodern space, see Soja (1989). For the experience of space and place, see Y. Tuan (1977).

3. For the nostalgia associated with community, see Bellah et al. (1996). For the increasing habit of Americans to isolate themselves and "bowl alone," see Putnam (2000).

4. Wirth (1995) famously linked cities with alienation and a loss of community; in contrast, Suttles (1968) contributed to the idea of order and community in cities.

5. Saunders (1986) argues that urbanists should study patterns of consumption and production, which ultimately determine the spatial arrangement of cities, instead of studying space as a category unto itself.

6. In gravitating away from spatial metaphors, I do not mean to deny their ability to reframe dominant frameworks and narratives of citizenship and belonging. For example, the idea of a lost "homeland" (*que huong*) for Vietnamese exiles has the potential to challenge the assimilation paradigm because the attachment to the homeland metaphor suggests that something is still missing for the Vietnamese community despite structural integration into the U.S. labor market and suburbs. However, as Smith and Katz (1993) insist, metaphors can also create unquestioned, hegemonic space: in other words, the homeland metaphor might imply that "home" is the site of universal belonging rather than just another contested, in this case, national and ideological, space.

7. Sayer (1985) points out one important aspect of space that is absolute: relationality. For example, betweenness is something that describes the relationship of objects to each other and is not explained more adequately through reference to larger patterns of social relations.

8. See Anderson (1991) for the role of imagined communities in sustaining

bourgeois nationalism; see also Noble (2000) for an important discussion of visions of the nation that exclude or marginalize "people without history."

9. Social mobility and geographic mobility are often linked; thus, socially upwardly mobile groups can afford to ignore the perspectives and concerns of those who are socially, and spatially, trapped.

10. Boggs (2000), citing Dirlik (1999), calls place-consciousness the "radical other" of global capitalism.

11. For analyses of suburbia as community gone awry, see McKenzie (1994), Jackson (1985), Teaford (1997), and Low (2003).

12. I learned this term from a Los Angeles native, for whom Orange County exists as a separate country that requires a special visa. Her attitude was prevalent among others I met in southern California. While a map includes both counties as if it were all one huge terrain, the lived reality is that Los Angeles County and Orange County have distinct histories, cultures, and reputations. These social distinctions are so laden with meaning that they produce a "curtain" that many people actually never go past.

13. Describing Eden Center, the counterpart to Asian Garden Mall in Falls Church, Virginia, geographer Joseph Wood writes: "Eden Center serves an 'epiphoric' function: it is more important and less tangible than itself. . . . Now it is a symbol with complex, contested meanings" (1997, 70). The Asian Garden Mall is similarly epiphoric.

14. My research into the SEARAC training leaves several questions unanswered: Who chose the person who would be a "sparkplug" in the community? Was this specific model of transitioning from services to community-building as influential in Orange County as it was in Boston? My point in mentioning the training is to suggest that "leadership" in Vietnamese America is not a matter of charisma or skill alone.

15. I borrow the phrase "jumping scale" from Smith (1993).

16. The earliest study of Chinatown that one might consider to be in the Asian American studies tradition would be Nee and Nee (1986). For more recent studies, see Fong (1998), Saito (1998), and Zhou (1992). I refer to Kwong (1996) and Lin (1998) elsewhere in this book.

17. For example, see A. Chung (2007), J. Lee (2002), and C. Kim (2000).

18. For the phrase "humanistic epistemology" I must credit Dan Trudeau at Macalester College (personal communication, May 2, 2008).

19. Pham (2003) citing Rumbaut (1995).

20. I owe this insight to a talk by Ramón Grosfoguel at Brown University (November 15, 1994) based on his article (1994).

21. This quote is taken from a clipping from the *New York Times* (March 26, 1975), "Torrent of Refugees in South Vietnam Laid to Fear of War, Not of Communism: Panic Is Believed to Dominate Flow," accessed March 2004 at the Healy Library, Archives and Special Collections, University of Massachusetts, Boston.

22. Nixon is quoted in an article in the *Manchester Guardian Weekly* (April 12,

1975), no title available, accessed March 2004 at the Healy Library, Archives and Special Collections, University of Massachusetts, Boston. Migration to the cities was pushed by forced-draft urbanization and by Operation Phoenix, a program to kill forty thousand Vietnamese in the countryside. One of my informants told me her father was in charge of Operation Phoenix.

23. In the *New York Times,* April 7, 1975, Premier Pham Van Dong says the U.S. plan to evacuate Vietnamese children is a crime. In the *New York Times,* April 10, 1975, the PRG says it would treat the children left behind by American soldiers "without hatred or discrimination." Both articles accessed March 2004 at the Healy Library, Archives and Special Collections, University of Massachusetts, Boston.

24. Quote from the *Manchester Guardian Weekly* (April 12, 1975), accessed March 2004 at the Healy Library, Archives and Special Collections, University of Massachusetts, Boston.

25. Quote from the *Boston Globe* (April 8, 1975), no title or author available, accessed March 2004 at the Healy Library, Archives and Special Collections, University of Massachusetts, Boston.

26. Smyser (1987) provides an important insight into the varying perspectives on "persecution" and "protection" that Europeans, Africans, and the United Nations High Commissioner for Refugees (UNHCR) brought to the table in the 1950s and 1960s. Westerners saw totalitarianism, represented by the figures of Hitler and Stalin, as the cause of persecution. Africans, on the other hand, saw the West itself as a potential problem. As Smyser puts it, "For them, the West itself could be and had been a source of violence. It had enslaved them, seized their lands and treasures, and imposed itself upon them. They needed to fight against it to gain their own freedom" (19). The UNHCR concept of refugees had "no fixed boundaries," reflecting instead the need to respond to situations that might not fit in any preset language.

27. For more of the story of Vietnamese Amerasians, see Bass (1996).

28. The idea that spatial assimilation is seen as a way to domesticate and deracinate Asian immigrants is put forth in a legal framework by Hing (1993), and also touched upon as part of an intellectual history of the Chicago School by Yu (2001).

29. See Rutledge (1992) for an anthropological account of the first Vietnamese arrivals to these centers.

30. For now-classic discussions of the relationship between physical proximity—"propinquity"—and the formation of community, see Webber (1963) and Wellman (1979).

31. Using the CMSA instead of county or city data captures the important patterns of commuting across city or county boundaries for work and thus more accurately depicts the region a certain population inhabits.

32. See Wood's analysis of place-making in Falls Church, Virginia (1997).

33. These 2000 census figures are cited from Max Niedzwiecki and T. C. Duong, *Southeast Asian American Statistical Profile* (2004), Washington, D.C.: Southeast Asia Resource Action Center (SEARAC).

34. Those populations are about one-sixth the size of Vietnamese Americans.

35. From the Survey of Minority Owned Enterprises 1987 and 1997.

36. Disidentification is a term I borrow from queer theorist José Esteban Muñoz (1999).

37. The model of "segmented assimilation" acknowledges that the path to white middle-class society is not available to everyone (Rumbaut 1996). Asian ethnic groups become racialized in the historical and contemporary context of the genocide of indigenous peoples and the enslavement of Africans—not to mention the neocolonial and imperialist expansionism that forced Mexicans, Puerto Ricans, Filipinos, and Hawaiians into spheres of U.S. authority and control. As Gary Okihiro notes, Asians have been "near white" or "near black" according to the needs of the U.S. labor market and political climate (1994, 34).

38. For an important intervention into the assumption that Asian Americans shun blackness, see J. Kim's proposal that Asians reconsider the racial subversiveness of seeing themselves as "black," or at least not as model minorities (1999). Palumbo-Liu (1999) provides an extended argument about the historical and contemporary impact of Asian migration on U.S. national and racial boundaries.

39. For an extended and scary account of Los Angeles as a city of fascist social control, read Davis (1990).

40. Quote from "Exploring Costa Mesa," in *Where: Orange County* (Costa Mesa, CA: Tourism Development Corporation, Summer 2001), 24–27.

41. For discussions of Orange County as an extreme suburb, see Kling, Olin, and Poster (1991), Lamb (1974), and Maher (2004).

42. Quoted from Riegert (1996, 199).

43. For more on Irvine's development visions, see Schiesl (1991).

44. On Orange County's bankruptcy, see Baldassare (1998).

45. For moving accounts of Boston's most turbulent times, see Lukas (1986) and Formisano (1991).

46. For some brief insights into Orange County's Chinese American history, see Vo and Danico (2004) and J. Liu (1998).

2. Q: Nationality? A: Asian.

1. I do not mean to dismiss the important and complex arguments within mainstream social science about ethnicity and upward mobility. I intend only to point out a disturbing conceptual gap between the insights into race by such sociologists as DuBois (1994), Winant (2001), and Bonilla-Silva (1999) versus the insistence on ethnicity and assimilation—and the simultaneous displacement of race—by others, such as Portes and Rumbaut (2001) and Alba and Nee (2003). I cannot be sure, but I suspect that other social sciences face similar contradictions.

2. For example, Steinberg (2005) argues provocatively that U.S. racism against blacks is facilitated by non-white immigration. Essentially, he posits racism as a force against blacks but not against native/indigenous people, Chicanos, Puerto

Ricans, Filipinos, Vietnamese, or any other groups who have also been racialized in the course of U.S. expansionism and imperialism. This is not to say that "race" operates in a commensurate way for all groups, or that "race" is necessarily the best lens with which to examine the history of each group.

3. How can racism exist while most whites claim to be "color-blind"? For the arguments and the evidence on racism in public policy and among progressive whites, see Prashad (2001b) and Bonilla-Silva (2003).

4. For a useful discussion of the model minority myth as it applies to Asian Americans in southern California, see Cheng and Yang (1996).

5. I do not intend to dismiss or belittle the hugely important contributions of sociologists and other social scientists to the literature on race, for example, Michael Omi and Howard Winant, Eduardo Bonilla-Silva, and Yen Espiritu. Yet the impulse to bury race, to marginalize the experiences of racialized minorities, and to ignore altogether the construction of white privilege is strong within the traditional disciplines, requiring constant intervention from the interdisciplinary fields oriented specifically toward race/ethnicity. In my own field of American studies, the turn toward a race-cognizant approach owes much to ethnic and women's studies.

6. Omi and Winant define racial formation "as the sociohistorical process by which racial categories are created, inhabited, transformed, and destroyed" (1994, 55). For an excellent online primer on the scientific, historical, legal, and social dimensions of race, see "Race: The Power of an Illusion" http://www.pbs.org/race/000_General/000_00-Home.htm.

7. See Hannaford (1996) and Smedley (1999) for two illuminating discussions of the origins of race as a core idea for Western empire-building and expansionism.

8. For book-length treatment of U.S. racial formations in a global context, see Winant (2001). Unfortunately, the author makes no comment on Asia or Asian Americans.

9. See Zuberi (2000) for a necessary analysis of race as an *effect* rather than a *cause* of racial policy.

10. The literature on "ethnicity" is profuse and multivaried: ethnicity may refer to ethnic boundaries (Barth 1970; Nagel 1994), emergent or resilient ethnicity (Portes and Rumbaut 1990), and symbolic ethnicity (Gans 1979). For an important critique of ethnicity from an anthropologist, see Zelinsky (2001).

11. In their scathing indictment of ethnicity as the preeminent, and wrong, paradigm for race since World War II, Omi and Winant (1994) point out that the ethnic framework portrays minority groups as if each one interacted with the dominant group only. In my view, this is another way of saying that the ethnic framework hides from view the larger context in which white privilege is first and foremost *relational,* and then also *invisible,* a seemingly inevitable feature of society.

12. In his review of *Growing Up American,* Shiao tactfully notes, "although race relations set the stage, they vanish from the script, returning only in the director's notes" (1999, 858).

13. Waldinger (1993) points out that the interest in "ethnic enclaves" as a mechanism for immigrant advancement has to do with the fading possibilities of upward mobility through the manufacturing industries due to the decline of manufacturing since the 1980s.

14. Smyser (1987) makes an important observation that in defining the characteristics of a refugee in the 1950s and 1960s, the Western nations emphasized persecution by a totalitarian state and saw themselves as sites of refuge. Meanwhile African states saw the West as a potential source of violence and danger, from which civilians ought to be granted refuge.

15. Lipsitz (1998) argues that white people benefit from identity politics because they are able to cash in on whiteness in a variety of ways: for example, buying homes and accumulating wealth, getting jobs with stable incomes, and seeing themselves represented in popular culture.

16. Alba and Nee (2003) exemplifies this mirage-making in the treatment of Asians as near-whites.

17. "Vietnam" is the common U.S. term to describe the war and the country. Elsewhere in the book, I use "Viet Nam" to refer to the country, as a gesture of respect to the Vietnamese people and language. I have left out important diacritic marks to simplify publication.

18. Whiteness is a category that has been analyzed critically by scholars in a variety of fields. See Lipsitz (1998), Harris (1993), and Roediger (1991).

19. For a historical perspective on white supremacy in California, see Almaguer (1994). Strangely, I know of no widely recognized scholarly history of white supremacy in Boston; however, for a small pamphlet/book circulating in black bookstores, see Apidta (2003a).

20. Alba and Nee (2003, 211–13) note the hostility Vietnamese refugees faced upon arrival to this country.

21. For more about Vincent Chin, see the documentary film *Who Killed Vincent Chin?* (Tajima 1988) and also Zia's chapter on Detroit in *Asian American Dreams* (2000).

22. McIntosh (2002) lists ordinary things like "I see people who look like me on TV" among the tools that are tucked into white people's "invisible knapsacks." I am assuming that not being the target of a white supremacist killer could be among those tools.

23. Steinberg (1995) makes an important and forceful argument about the political left's retreat from racial justice.

24. See Bonilla-Silva (1999) for a social scientific rebuttal to the argument that race no longer exists.

3. Like a Dream I Can Never Forget

1. I use "Viet Nam" to refer to the country and nation. To refer to the U.S. War in Viet Nam, I use "Vietnam." I acknowledge in this small way a crucial distinction

between the dominant collective view of the war and a less well-recognized and much more complex perspective on the Vietnamese people and culture.

2. For a stunning example of Anglocentric assimilationism revived for the twenty-first century, see Huntington (2000). For an illuminating postmortem on American exceptionalism, see Noble (2000). Zinn (2005) points out that American expansionism, thought to be divinely ordained, usually involved "dealing harshly" with the people who resist American occupation. Ignatieff (2005) notes that "American freedom aspires to be universal, but it has always been exceptional because America is the only modern democratic experiment that began in slavery."

3. The literature on the role of the United States in Viet Nam is voluminous. Some entry points are Allen and Long (1991), Berman (1982), and McNamara (1995).

4. In Alba and Nee's newly retooled version of assimilation, the idea of assimilation, though contested, remains a "master trend" (2003, 101). Throughout their book, American exceptionalism is never named, nor are the realities that the exceptionalism myth is intended to hide: U.S. colonialism, expansionism, or interventionism abroad. The authors write: "The aim of this book is to . . . [provide] new ways of theorizing assimilation as a social process stemming from immigration" (9). But in the absence of an explanation for why immigrants and refugees end up in the United States, students of immigration are left to rely upon the dominant prevailing narrative of exceptionalism. The index does not list the terms "history" or "memory," following the conventional understanding of immigrants as having no past to speak of or, in Noble's words, of non-Anglo-Protestant males being "people without history" (2000, 7).

5. The idea of the settlement of Vietnamese refugees providing a "substitute victory" for the U.S. government was forwarded by Yen Le Espiritu in her brilliant and incisive keynote address at the conference, "30 Years Beyond the War: Vietnamese, Southeast Asian, and Asian/American Studies" held on April 19–20, 2005 at the University of California, Riverside.

6. The literature on the impact of the war on American culture is enormous. For starters, see Christopher (1995) and Rowe and Berg (1986).

7. See Erikson (1970) for a classic discussion of sociology's historical perspective.

8. Here my take on the past is presentist and instrumentalist, as I am interested in the past primarily as it serves the social uses of the present. However, I do not mean to ignore aspects of the past that somehow do not change over time, or that resist reconstruction through discursive or spatial means.

9. Other aspects of the war are also omitted from the dominant memory. According to Appy (1999), a "muffling of public memory" has erased from consciousness many aspects of the past, including a discussion of why the war was so divisive to begin with. The U.S. war in Iraq is often compared to Vietnam, in part because of its divisiveness; see Purdum (2005).

10. See A. Gordon (1997) for an innovative analysis of the relationship between haunting and the sociological imagination.

11. Maya Lin is the subject of a feature-length documentary film (Mock 1996). The Vietnam Veterans Memorial draws no explicit conclusion about the war (Wagner-Pacifici and Schwartz 1991). However, Lin's concept of a timeline forces history into a linear format that conforms to a dominant view of the past (Abramson 1996).

12. For Stanley Karnow's brief biography of Ho Chi Minh, see http://www.time .com/time/time100/leaders/profile/hochiminh.html.

13. The most important difference between Adolf Hitler and Ho Chi Minh is that Hitler was not a Jew. He declared Jews to be an inferior race and exterminated them. Ho Chi Minh, on the other hand, was a Vietnamese nationalist and is today considered the national hero of Socialist Viet Nam. This is not to disregard or diminish the intense hatred harbored by exiled Vietnamese for Ho or for socialism.

14. For more information about Vietnam War memorials, see Strait and Strait (1988).

15. Christian Appy, a native of Dorchester, points out that working-class men from Dorchester were four times more likely to die in Vietnam than their counterparts from Boston's "fancy suburbs" (1993, 12).

16. The Joiner Center "promotes research curriculum development, public events, and educational, cultural, and humanitarian exchanges which foster greater understanding and innovative means of addressing the consequences of war" http://www.joinercenter.umb.edu/.

17. A description of the memorial site and a biography of the artist are provided by the Westminster Chamber of Commerce: http://www.westminsterchamber.org/tourist/vietnam.php.

18. Joseph Trinh offered his remarks at a roundtable entitled "Political Intimidation of Vietnamese Media" at the conference, "30 Years Beyond the War: Vietnamese, Southeast Asian, and Asian/American Studies" held on April 19–20, 2005 at the University of California, Riverside.

19. I am thankful to Nina Ha for providing me with the text to Professor Viet Nguyen's editorial.

20. The relationships between whiteness, nationhood, history, and a collective past are complex. Noble (2000) comments that the purveyors of American exceptionalism saw white, Anglo-Protestant males as the agents of history and, more significantly, of Western civilization. Indigenous peoples, and people of color, were seen as "people without history." But the critical white studies literature suggests that whiteness remains unmarked and normative so long as individual white people do not see themselves as connected via a shared racial history. David Roediger has written several foundational texts: for starters, see Roediger (1991).

4. What's Good for Business Is Good for the Community

1. For an interesting discussion of postmodernism and consumer culture, see Featherstone (1991). For a powerful critique of multiculturalism as it is debated in the academy, see Rieff (1993). Where Rieff is talking about capitalism's multicultural

imperative—the endless need to expand markets and exploit new pools of labor—I am talking about the multicultural imperative of place within a capitalist economy.

2. See Smith (1984) and Lefebvre (1991) for well-recognized discussions of uneven development and the capitalist production of space. See Zukin (1993) for the distinction between market and place, and for the purposeful construction of landscapes of power.

3. The innovative Orange County high school curriculum on Vietnamese American history is a great example of the impact of multiculturalism as a discursive intervention into exclusive narratives of U.S. national identity (Vietnamese American Curriculum Project Committee 2001).

4. At the end of the war, ethnic Chinese in Viet Nam were considered a "classic example of a state within a state" (Osborne 1980, 41). By the end of the 1980s, the government of Viet Nam had taken several important measures to acknowledge and support the language and culture of the Hoa (ethnic Chinese) along with other minorities (Ungar 1988). Viet Nam has "scientifically" classified its population into fifty-four ethnic groups with the Kinh or Viet people being the majority and the Hoa or Chinese people being the third largest minority group (Keyes 2002).

5. Perhaps the United States has never achieved the scale of empire seen in prior epochs, yet the term imperialism aptly describes the U.S. impulse for economic, cultural, and military domination in the Philippines, Viet Nam, and now Iraq. For contemporary and widely respected discussions of empire in the U.S. context, see Hardt and Negri (2001) as well as C. Johnson (2000; 2004).

6. I find Karnow's nostalgic tour of Little Saigon, accompanied by journalistic photographs, to be a fascinating example of the colonial gaze (1992).

7. See Prashad (2001b) for a journalistic criticism of race-blind social policy; see Steinberg (1995) for a sociological discussion of the liberal left's retreat from racial justice.

8. See Hakim (2005) for a glimpse of layoffs at General Motors—a giant in the manufacturing industry—and the impact of its decline on families who have worked at GM over many generations. Waldinger (1993) offers a useful overview and analysis of the ethnic enclave literature. Portes and Manning (1986) and Zhou (1992) argue for the ethnic enclave as an "apprenticeship" where immigrants gain the skills and capital for upward mobility. Nee and Sanders (1987) argue that employers benefit more than workers from an enclave economy. Kwong (1996) elaborates on the multiple dimensions and consequences of class conflict within New York's Chinatown, the quintessential ethnic enclave. Lin (1998) bridges many conceptual divides by illustrating the role of overseas capital in shaping New York Chinatown's ethnic economy.

9. The lack of human, social, and financial capital in native-born communities of color has deep, structural roots and cannot be simply pinned on "race" or cultural deficiencies: see, for example, Squires (1994) and Oliver and Shapiro (1996).

10. For discussions of internal colonialism, see Allen (1990), Blauner (1972), and Savitch (1978).

11. Quoted in Spiller (1994).

12. From *Westways*, the lifestyle magazine of the Auto Club of Southern California, January/February 2005, 24.

13. I owe political scientist Nhu-Ngoc Ong for the insight regarding the financial incentives behind the CFZ resolutions. The rest of the interpretation is my own.

14. For these quotes, see Dizon (1996), Do (1996), and Pope (1996).

15. Boston's Main Streets Program seeks to revitalize nineteen areas in the city through a combination of commercial and technological development. See http://www.cityofboston.gov/mainstreets/.

16. Massachusetts Association of CDCs 2004 Annual Report.

17. Quoted by Michael Kane in the newsletter of the Pioneer Institute, http://www.pioneerinstitute.org/pdf/ps2_1cf.pdf (accessed January 2, 2006).

18. The mayor's New Bostonians program summarizes information on neighborhoods by "race," which does not indicate the significant ethnic and cultural boundaries within each racial group, such as between and among black/African Americans and immigrants from Haiti or Cape Verde. Citywide, the population of Vietnamese (10,818) is overshadowed by Haitians (18,979) and by Cape Verdeans (11,060). Puerto Ricans alone number 27,442 and there are 19,783 "unspecified Latinos." See "New Bostonians Demographic Report" at http://www.cityofboston.gov/newbostonians/publications.asp.

19. That is to say that as an agenda for getting rid of structural and economic inequality, marketplace multiculturalism is definitely toothless, a point made forcefully in the heat of the culture wars by Rieff (1993).

20. Viet Nam is searching for ways to attract investments from foreigners, including Viet Kieu, or overseas Vietnamese, and some Orange County Vietnamese are looking for places to invest. See Flanigan (2006) and Paterniti (1997).

5. Implications for Community and Place

1. Meena Alexander's book, *The Shock of Arrival* (1996), speaks to the experience of immigrants in America.

2. Alba and Nee assert that despite the many arguments against assimilation, "Assimilation is nonetheless the master trend, and for the majority of whites and Asians descended from the earlier era of mass immigration, ethnicity does mean considerably less than it did a generation or two ago" (2003, 101). Later, they add: "But even as we underscore the continuities in spatial assimilation, we are aware that, as a totality, the residential picture is more mixed: that elements of persisting segregation appear alongside those of integration. . . . Thus, the spatial assimilation of some will not dilute the patches of racial and ethnic colorations on future social mappings of U.S. metropolitan regions, but by the same token the visibility of those patches should not obscure the occurrence of such assimilation" (260). In many sections of

their book, Vietnamese provide supportive examples. By theorizing space and place, I am offering an explanation for the spatial assimilation they observe to exist concurrently with what they term "patches of racial and ethnic coloration." I do not hope to embrace or reinforce assimilation as a "master trend."

3. For example, these are important themes in the work of Montero (1979), Rutledge (1992), Gold (1992), Zhou and Bankston (1998), and Portes and Rumbaut (2001).

4. Okihiro (1994) makes the compelling argument that Asians in the United States have been treated as "near-black" or "near-white" depending on the economic and political needs of the nation. The term "junior white" describes the fact that even when Asian Americans are celebrated as model minorities and therefore close to white, they will never play on the varsity team. I owe the term to Tarso Luis Ramos and my colleagues in the Next Generation Leadership "Cluster Group on Changing Racial Realities." To me, "junior whites" captures more accurately than "honorary whites" the secondary status of Asians as white wannabes; see also M. Tuan (1998).

5. Sociologists have always been aware of the double-edged sword of community. See Joseph (2006) for a new and extended warning on the dangers of romanticizing community from a women's studies perspective.

6. See Bonilla-Silva (2003) for an important analysis of the four frames that whites use today to veil their racism in color-blind terms: abstract liberalism, naturalization, cultural racism, and minimization.

7. Okihiro (1994) describes the history of Asian Americans as going back and forth along a spectrum of near-white and near-black depending on the political exigencies of the time. In a startlingly different way, Prashad (2001a, 9) draws lines between Asian and African cultures such that political struggle, not skin color, connects Asian Americans to African Americans. Mainstream social science has yet to make any serious connections between or among the "darker" nations.

8. This is not to overlook completely the suburban Koreatown in Garden Grove that lies adjacent to Little Saigon. According to Vo and Danico (2004), many Koreans moved from Los Angeles to Orange County in the aftermath of the 1992 riots. However, Garden Grove is primarily a Korean shopping district, whereas Little Saigon is a shopping district in which a bulk of the Vietnamese population also resides.

9. Ethnic Chinese in Viet Nam have had different experiences of exclusion depending on whether they lived in the north or south. Ethnic Chinese dominated commerce in South Viet Nam since the French colonial period. In the 1950s, Diem forced ethnic Chinese to become citizens of Viet Nam despite their loyalties to China. In 1978–79, Viet Nam purged ethnic Chinese; many fled, leaving a much diminished population in the south. Since the 1980s, ethnic Chinese have been "undisputed citizens" of Viet Nam. See Osborne (1980) and Ungar (1988).

10. See Gold (1994). I am not aware of any other scholarly treatments of the role of ethnic Chinese in Vietnamese America. Smith-Hefner (1995) provides an excellent analysis of the role of Chinese ethnicity in the business culture of Khmer in Boston.

11. As far as I know, Masequesmay (1991) was the first person to borrow the term "community of memory" from Bellah et al. (1996) and apply it to Little Saigon.

12. Some prominent individuals have not embraced the Vietnamese American strategic memory project or the taboos against Viet Nam. One person I interviewed will never set foot in a Vietnamese American place for fear of his physical safety although he is a knowledgeable and in some eyes influential scholar of Vietnamese history. His profile as a visible antiwar activist during the 1970s excludes him from the circles of Vietnamese American leadership. For different reasons, Nguyen Cao Ky—former prime minister and vice president under Nguyen Van Thieu—once told the *Los Angeles Times* that he is not a "social worker" and does not need to be seen as a leader in Little Saigon (1988). In 1990, he and other expatriates led a call for easing relations with Ha Noi, much to the consternation of the most bitter refugees, many of whom are former political detainees (Awanohara 1990).

13. See Krieger, Cobb, and Turner (2001) for a fascinating mapping of Boston's history.

14. This strange, exotifying phrase is common in Orange County's booster literature describing Little Saigon.

15. See King (1981) for a discussion of the phases of black community development in Boston; see Gastón and Kennedy (1987) for an analysis of the displacement of Roxbury's poor residents.

16. See http://www.platial.com/about.

17. This debate would pinpoint the origins of the term "platial" to the publication of Stuart Elden's book *Mapping the Present: Heidegger, Foucault and the Project of a Spatial History* (2001). In his argument for the English word "platial," Elden would limit its use to discussions of the work of Martin Heidegger; see Elden (2003) and Malpas (2003).

18. Ginwright, Noguera, and Cammarota (2006) offer an important critical intervention into scholarship on school reform and youth organizing. Two basic principles behind their analysis are that youth are integral parts of communities and that youth are capable of changing their communities in positive ways.

19. Zhou and Bankston make perfectly clear that their emphasizing "the role of the ethnic community in promoting the adaptation of Vietnamese American young people . . . does not stem from any desire . . . to glorify Vietnamese community life or to engage in ethnic boosterism" (1998, 20). But without accompanying conceptual analyses of the experience of the racialization of black youth and of the historical social neglect that Americans in the Gulf Coast region of the country have suffered, Zhou and Bankston end up contributing to the prevailing expectations that immigrants can move up but racial minorities cannot.

20. Lee and Bean provide an illustrative example of this seemingly race-aware approach to immigration. Their principal finding, that "America's changing color lines could involve a new racial/ethnic divide that may consign many blacks to disadvantaged positions qualitatively similar to those perpetuated by the traditional black/white

divide" (2004, 237), is certainly bad—and unfortunately, believable—news. But at no point do the authors analyze the policies or practices of white people or the racial state in redesigning the race/color line. Instead, the authors suggest that twenty-first-century immigrants will probably blow their chance to fix racism in the United States and, moreover, that Latinos and Asians will "fall into the nonblack category."

21. My attempts to bring race, ethnicity, and place together here owe much to both the successes and shortcomings of the twentieth-century theory of internal colonialism as presented by Allen (1990), Blauner (1972), and Gutierrez (2004).

22. In Viet Nam, some people argued with my claim about racism in the United States. "But you have Condi and Ophrey!" they said, incredulously. "After the South was liberated," one Vietnamese social scientist explained to me, "black people moved to the North for jobs. They remained poor because they were not educated." One person looked sick when he finally took in my message about the deep structural racism that people of color, including young Asian Americans, face despite high levels of schooling.

23. For two portrayals of Cuban Americans, see McHugh, Miyares, and Skop (1997) and Portes and Stepick (1993).

24. I am referring to Huntington's famously racist tract, "The Hispanic Challenge" (2000). By privileging the Anglo-Protestant origins of the first settlers, Huntington claims everyone else needs to quiet down, or get out.

25. For an important discussion of language and power in ethnic enclaves, see Mari Matsuda's essay, "Who Owns Speech?" (in Matsuda 1996).

26. Even the Hmong on University Avenue in St. Paul, Minnesota are treated with this frame, which seems ironic given that they face the highest poverty rate of all Asian ethnic groups and face many of the same problems as their African American neighbors (Kaplan 1997).

27. For a moving journalistic account of indigenous Mexicans crossing the border to find a better life, see Martinez (2001).

28. For information on the term glocal, I owe the students in my Fall 2007 course, "U.S. Racial Formations and the Global Economy," who labored collectively on a Working Glossary and identified the term for me. See http://www.glocalforum.org.

29. Racialized absences in specific places are telling. Spike Lee's moving 2007 documentary, *When the Levees Broke* (2007), describes the tragedy in four brilliant acts. Despite a Gulf Coast Vietnamese community of about twenty thousand, to my knowledge not one scene in the documentary shows the drama of Vietnamese people who fled the storm. A well-received sociological examination of Vietnamese in New Orleans, *Growing Up American* (Zhou and Bankston 1998), makes no mention of the regional culture of the Coast or of any positive influences of black people on Vietnamese. Blackness seems to signify nothing more than cultural deficit, the negation of whiteness. Consequently, the book treats "ethnic ties" as one of the most valuable assets in the Vietnamese community and inadvertently adds to the invisibility of Vietnamese in the Katrina context.

Appendix

1. The reputational technique is described by Trounstine and Christensen (1982).

2. See Naples (2003) for a discussion of feminist methodology and standpoint theory in particular.

3. A fully elaborated commentary on the significance, power, and danger of maps and photographs especially in relation to the construction and production of racialized Others such as Vietnamese Americans is beyond the scope of this Appendix. My comment should signal, if nothing else, that I am aware of the problems involved by making maps and photographs. In addition, I hope to steer the interested reader toward the vast literature on critical approaches to visual culture.

4. For a practical discussion of the relationship between mapmaking and political propaganda, see Monmonier (1991). For a persuasive argument that *National Geographic's* prolific images of non-Western people are more important for constructing the identities of white, Western readers in the United States than they are for teaching about life in the non-Western world, see Lutz and Collins (1993). For an extensive discussion of the relationship between visuality and colonialism in Africa, see Landau and Kaspin (2002). I am not aware of a similar discussion of visual images and colonialism in Asia although surely that literature is prolific.

5. See Christopher (1996) for a discussion of Vietnamese in U.S. films.

Works Cited

Abramson, Daniel. 1996. "Maya Lin and the 1960s: Monuments, Time Lines, and Minimalism." *Critical Inquiry* 22:679–709.

Abu-Lughod, Janet L. 1991. *Changing Cities: Urban Sociology.* New York: HarperCollins.

Alba, Richard D., John R. Logan, Brian J. Stults, Gilbert Marzan, and Wenquan Zhang. 1999. "Immigrant Groups in the Suburbs: A Reexamination of Suburbanization and Spatial Assimilation." *American Sociological Review* 64:446–60.

Alba, Richard, and Victor Nee. 2003. *Remaking the American Mainstream: Assimilation and Contemporary Immigration.* Cambridge, Mass.: Harvard University Press.

Alexander, Meena. 1996. *The Shock of Arrival: Reflections on Postcolonial Experience.* Boston: South End Press.

Allen, Douglas, and Ngo Vinh Long. 1991. *Coming to Terms: Indochina, the United States, and the War.* Boulder: Westview Press.

Allen, Robert L. 1990. *Black Awakening in Capitalist America: An Analytic History.* Trenton, N.J.: Africa World Press.

Almaguer, Tomas. 1994. *Racial Faultlines: The Historical Origins of White Supremacy in California.* Berkeley and Los Angeles: University of California Press.

Anderson, Benedict. 1991. *Imagined Communities.* New York: Verso.

Apidta, Tingba. 2003a. *The Black Timeline of Massachusetts: A History of White Supremacy in the Bay State.* Boston: Reclamation Project.

———. 2003b. *The Hidden History of Massachusetts: A Guide for Black Folks.* Boston: Reclamation Project.

Appy, Christian. 1993. *Working-Class War: American Combat Soldiers and Vietnam.* Chapel Hill: University of North Carolina Press.

———. 1999. "The Muffling of Public Memory in Post-Vietnam America." *Chronicle of Higher Education,* February 12, B4–6.

Ascher, Carol. 1981. *The United States' New Refugees: A Review of the Research on the Resettlement of Indochinese, Cubans, and Haitians.* New York: ERIC Clearinghouse on Urban Education, Institute for Urban and Minority Education, Teachers College, Columbia University.

Awanohara, Susumu. 1990. "Reconciling the Past: Vietnamese Expatriates Ease Opposition to Hanoi." *Far Eastern Economic Review*, August 16, 21.

Baldassare, Mark. 1998. *When Government Fails: The Orange County Bankruptcy.* Berkeley and Los Angeles: University of California Press.

Baldwin, James. 1985. "State of the Union: 'Second American Revolution'; Transcript of President's State of Union Address to Congress." *New York Times*, February 7.

Bao, Quong. 1997. "Two Sides of Tragedy in Vietnam." *Boston Globe*, April 12.

Barth, Fredrik. 1970. *Ethnic Groups and Boundaries.* Boston: Little, Brown.

Barthel, Diane L. 1996. *Historic Preservation: Collective Memory and Historical Identity.* New Brunswick, N.J.: Rutgers University Press.

Bass, Thomas A. 1996. *Vietnamerica: The War Comes Home.* New York: Soho Press.

Bellah, Robert N., Richard Madsen, William M. Sullivan, Ann Swidler, and Steven M. Tipton. 1996. *Habits of the Heart: Individualism and Commitment in American Life.* Berkeley and Los Angeles: University of California Press.

Berman, Larry. 1982. *Planning a Tragedy: The Americanization of the War in Vietnam.* New York: W. W. Norton.

Blauner, Robert. 1972. *Racial Oppression in America.* New York: Harper.

Bluestone, Barry, and Mary Huff Stevenson. 2000. *The Boston Renaissance.* New York: Russell Sage Foundation.

Boggs, Grace Lee. 2000. "A Question of Place." *Monthly Review*, June, 18–20.

Bombardieri, Marcella. 1999. "Haunting View: Some Vietnamese-Americans See Image as Daily Reminder of Reviled Communist Leader." *Boston Globe*, November 18.

Bonilla-Silva, Eduardo. 1999. "The Essential Social Fact of Race." *American Sociological Review* 64:899–906.

———. 2003. *Racism Without Racists: Color-blind Racism and the Persistence of Racial Inequality in the United States.* Lanham, Md.: Rowman & Littlefield.

———. 2004. "From Bi-Racial to Tri-Racial: Towards a New System of Racial Stratification in the USA." *Ethnic and Racial Studies* 27:931–50.

Bousquet, Gisele L. 1991. *Behind the Bamboo Hedge: The Impact of Homeland Politics in the Parisian Vietnamese Community.* Ann Arbor: University of Michigan Press.

Boyer, M. Christine. 1996. *The City of Collective Memory: Its Historical Imagery and Architectural Entertainments.* Cambridge, Mass.: MIT Press.

Breton, Raymond. 1964. "Institutional Completeness of Ethnic Communities and the Personal Relations of Immigrants." *American Journal of Sociology* 70:193–205.

Brown, Richard D., and Jack Tager. 2000. *Massachusetts: A Concise History.* Amherst: University of Massachusetts.

Buzzanco, Robert. 1999. *Vietnam and the Transformation of American Life.* Ed. J. P. Greene. Malden, Mass.: Blackwell.

Canclini, Néstor García. 1995. *Hybrid Cultures: Strategies for Entering and Leaving Modernity.* Trans. C. L. Chiappari and S. L. Lopez. Minneapolis: University of Minnesota Press.

Carroll, James. 2004. "A City Known for Peaceniks Stands By Its Roots." *New York Times*, July 25.

Cheng, Lucie, and Philip Q. Yang. 1996. "Asians: The 'Model Minority' Deconstructed." In *Ethnic Los Angeles*, ed. R. Waldinger and M. Bozorgmehr, 305–44. New York: Russell Sage Foundation.

Christopher, Renny. 1995. *The Viet Nam War/The American War: Images and Representations in Euro-American and Vietnamese Exile Narratives*. Amherst: University of Massachusetts Press.

———. 1996. "Images of Vietnamese in American Film." *Viet Nam Generation: A Journal of Recent History and Contemporary Culture* 7.

Chung, Angie Y. 2007. *Legacies of Struggle: Conflict and Cooperation in Korean American Politics*. Stanford: Stanford University Press.

Chung, Nguyen Ba. 2002. "The Long Road Home: Exile, Self Recognition, and the Task of Reconstruction." *Manoa* 14:34–44.

Chung, Tom L. 1995. "Asian Americans in Enclaves—They Are Not One Community: New Modes of Asian American Settlement." *Asian American Policy Review* 5:78–94.

Clark, David B. 1973. "The Concept of Community: A Re-examination." *Sociological Review* 21:397–416.

Cong, Mai. 1995. "Orange County Voices: Refugees Face Identity Crisis Not Unlike That of Rip van Winkle." *Los Angeles Times*, April 16.

Cong, Malia. 1997. "A Survival of Conflict: The Vietnamese American Community's Response to Little Saigon's Evolution." Unpublished term paper thesis, Asian American Studies Program, University of California, Irvine.

Davis, Mike. 1990. *City of Quartz: Excavating the Future in Los Angeles*. New York: Vintage.

———. 2005. *Planet of Slums*. New York: Verso.

Dirlik, Arif. 1999. "Place-Based Imagination: Globalism and the Politics of Place." *Review: A Journal of the Fernand Braudel Center for the Study of Economics, Historical Systems and Civilizations* 22:151–87.

Dizon, Lily. 1996. "Acrimony over Project Called 'Harmony.'" *Los Angeles Times*, June 25.

Do, Quyen. 1996. "Designing Little Saigon's Gateway." *Orange County Register*, April 26.

Doob, Christopher. 1999. *Racism: An American Cauldron*. New York: Longman.

Dreier, Peter, John Mollenkopf, and Todd Swanstrom. 2001. *Place Matters: Metropolitics for the Twenty-first Century*. Lawrence: University Press of Kansas.

DuBois, W. E. B. 1994. *The Souls of Black Folk*. New York: Dover.

Elden, Stuart. 2001. *Mapping the Present: Heidegger, Foucault and the Project of a Spatial History*. London: Continuum.

———. 2003. "The Importance of History: A Reply to Malpas." *Philosophy and Geography*, August 6, 2.

Erikson, Kai T. 1970. "Sociology and the Historical Perspective." *American Sociologist* 5:61–77.

Espiritu, Yen Le. 1992. *Asian-American Panethnicity: Bridging Institutions and Identities.* Philadelphia: Temple University Press.

Featherstone, Mike. 1991. *Consumer Culture and Postmodernism.* Newbury Park, Calif.: Sage.

Flanigan, James. 2006. "Small Business: Little Saigon Exports Its Prosperity." *New York Times,* January 16.

Fong, Timothy P. 1993. *The First Suburban Chinatown: The Remaking of Monterey Park, California.* Ed. S. Chan and D. Palumbo-Liu. Philadelphia: Temple University Press.

———. 1998. *The Contemporary Asian American Experience: Beyond the Model Minority.* Upper Saddle River, N.J.: Prentice-Hall.

Formisano, Ronald P. 1991. *Boston against Busing: Race, Class, and Ethnicity in the 1960s and 1970s.* Chapel Hill: University of North Carolina Press.

Forrest, Benjamin. 1995. "West Hollywood as Symbol: The Significance of Place in the Construction of a Gay Identity." *Environment and Planning D* 12:133–57.

Freeman, James M. 1989. *Hearts of Sorrow: Vietnamese-American Lives.* Stanford: Stanford University Press.

———. 1995. *Changing Identities: Vietnamese Americans 1975–1995.* Ed. Nancy Foner. New Immigrant Series. Needham Heights, Mass.: Allyn and Bacon.

Fusion Pictures. 1998. "Letters to Thien" (brochure for film screening). UCLA.

Gallagher, Winifred. 1993. *The Power of Place: How Our Surroundings Shape Our Thoughts, Emotions, and Actions.* New York: HarperCollins.

Gans, Herbert J. 1979. "Symbolic Ethnicity: The Future of Ethnic Groups and Cultures in America." *Ethnic and Racial Studies* 2:1–20.

———. 1982. *The Urban Villagers: Group and Class in the Life of Italian-Americans.* New York: Free Press.

Gastón, Mauricio, and Marie Kennedy. 1987. "Capital Investment or Community Development: The Struggle for Land Control by Boston's Black and Latino Community." *Antipode* 19:178–209.

Gayk, William. 1990. "The Changing Demography of Orange County." *Journal of Orange County Studies* 1:13–18.

Giddens, Anthony. 1984. *The Constitution of Society: Outline of a Theory of Structuration.* Berkeley and Los Angeles: University of California Press.

Gieryn, Thomas F. 2000. "A Space for Place in Sociology." *Annual Review of Sociology* 26:463–96.

Gilroy, Paul. 2000. *Against Race: Imagining Political Culture Beyond the Color Line.* Cambridge, Mass.: Harvard University Press.

Ginwright, Shawn, Pedro Noguera, and Julio Cammarota. 2006. *Beyond Resistance! Youth Activism and Community Change.* Ed. Greg Dimitriadis. New York: Routledge.

Gold, Steven J. 1992. *Refugee Communities: A Comparative Field Study.* Newbury Park, Calif.: Sage.

————. 1994. "Chinese-Vietnamese Entrepreneurs in California." In *The New Asian Immigration in Los Angeles and Global Restructuring,* ed. P. Ong, E. Bonacich, and L. Cheng, 196–228. Philadelphia: Temple University Press.

Gordon, Avery. 1997. *Ghostly Matters: Haunting and the Sociological Imagination.* Minneapolis: University of Minnesota Press.

Gordon, Avery F., and Christopher Newfield. 1996. *Mapping Multiculturalism.* Minneapolis: University of Minnesota Press.

Gordon, Milton. 1964. *Assimilation in American Life.* New York: Oxford University Press.

Gottdiener, Mark, and Ray Hutchison. 2000. *The New Urban Sociology.* New York: McGraw-Hill.

Grosfoguel, Ramón. 1994. "World Cities in the Caribbean: The Rise of Miami and San Juan." *Review: A Journal of the Fernand Braudel Center for the Study of Economics, Historical Systems and Civilizations* 17:351–81.

Gutierrez, Ramón. 2004. "Internal Colonialism: An American Theory of Race." *Du Bois Review* 1:281–95.

Hakim, Danny. 2005. "For a GM Family, the American Dream Vanishes." *New York Times,* November 19.

Handlin, Oscar. 1991/1969. *Boston's Immigrants 1790–1880: A Study in Acculturation.* Cambridge, Mass.: Belknap Press of Harvard University Press.

Hannaford, Ivan. 1996. *Race: The History of an Idea in the West.* Baltimore: Johns Hopkins University Press.

Hardt, Michael, and Antonio Negri. 2001. *Empire.* Cambridge, Mass.: Harvard University Press.

Harris, Cheryl. 1993. "Whiteness as Property." *Harvard Law Review* 107:1707–92.

Harvey, David. 1979. "Monument and Myth." *Annals of the Association of American Geographers* 69:362–81.

————. 1996. *Justice, Nature, and the Geography of Difference.* Cambridge, Mass.: Basil Blackwell.

Hing, Bill Ong. 1993. *Making and Remaking Asian America through Immigration Policy 1850–1990.* Stanford: Stanford University Press.

Hiss, Tony. 1990. *The Experience of Place.* New York: Knopf.

Hummon, David M. 1992. "Community Attachment, Local Sentiment, and Sense of Place." In *Place Attachment,* ed. I. Altman and S. M. Low, 253–78. New York: Plenu.

Huntington, Samuel P. 2000. "The Hispanic Challenge." *Foreign Policy Review,* 30–45.

Ignatieff, Michael. 2005. "Who Are Americans to Think that Freedom Is Theirs to Spread?" *New York Times,* July 10.

Jackson, Kenneth T. 1985. *Crabgrass Frontier: The Suburbanization of the United States.* New York: Oxford University Press.

Jacobs, Jane. 1961. *The Death and Life of Great American Cities.* New York: Random House.

Jang, Lindsey, and Robert C. Winn. 2003. *Saigon, USA.* NAATA.

Jirasek, Rita Arias, and Carlos Tortolero. 2001. *Mexican Chicago.* Chicago: Arcadia.

Johnson, Chalmers. 2000. *Blowback: The Costs and Consequences of American Empire.* New York: Metropolitan.

———. 2004. *The Sorrows of Empire: Militarism, Secrecy, and the End of the Republic.* New York: Metropolitan.

Johnson, Nuala. 1995. "Cast in Stone: Monuments, Geography, and Nationalism." *Environment and Planning D* 13:51–65.

Joseph, Miranda. 2006. *Against the Romance of Community.* Minneapolis: University of Minnesota.

Kahn, Ric. 2000. "New Logo Won't Erase a Debate: The Boston Gas Tank Carries a New Name, Same Old Controversy." *Boston Globe,* October 29.

Kaplan, David H. 1997. "The Creation of an Ethnic Economy: Indochinese Business Expansion in Saint Paul." *Economic Geography* 73:214–33.

Karnow, Stanley. 1992. "In Orange County's Little Saigon, Vietnamese Try to Bridge Two Worlds." *Smithsonian,* August 1, 28–39.

Kelley, Robin D. G. 1997. *Yo' mama's disFUNKtional! Fighting the Culture Wars in Urban America.* Boston: Beacon.

Keyes, Charles. 2002. "Presidential Address: 'The Peoples of Asia'—Science and Politics in the Classification of Ethnic Groups in Thailand, China, and Vietnam." *Journal of Asian Studies* 61:1163–1203.

Kiang, Peter. 1991. "About Face: Recognizing Asian & Pacific American Vietnam Veterans in Asian American Studies." *Amerasia Journal* 17:22–40.

Kibria, Nazli. 1993. *Family Tightrope: The Changing Lives of Vietnamese Americans.* Princeton: Princeton University Press.

Kim, Claire Jean. 2000. *Bitter Fruit: The Politics of Black-Korean Conflict in New York City.* New Haven: Yale University Press.

Kim, Janine Young. 1999. "Are Asians Black? The Asian-American Civil Rights Agenda and the Contemporary Significance of the Black/White Paradigm." *Yale Law Journal,* 2385–2413.

King, Mel. 1981. *Chain of Change: Struggles for Black Community Development.* Boston: South End Press.

Kling, Rob, Spencer Olin, and Mark Poster, eds. 1991. *Postsuburban California: The Transformation of Orange County since World War II.* Berkeley and Los Angeles: University of California Press.

Krieger, Alex, David Cobb, and Amy Turner. 2001. *Mapping Boston.* Cambridge, Mass.: MIT Press.

Kwong, Peter. 1996. *The New Chinatown.* New York: Hill and Wang.

Lamb, Karl. 1974. *As Orange Goes.* New York: W. W. Norton.

Landau, Paul S., and Deborah D. Kaspin. 2002. *Images and Empires: Visuality in Colonial and Postcolonial Africa.* Berkeley and Los Angeles: University of California Press.

Le, Ngoan. 1994. "Profile of the Vietnamese American Community." National Congress of Vietnamese in America.

Lee, Dong Ok. 1995. "Koreatown and Korean Small Firms in Los Angeles: Locating in the Ethnic Neighborhoods." *Professional Geographer* 47:184–95.

Lee, Jennifer. 2002. *Civility in the City: Blacks, Jews, and Koreans in Urban America.* Cambridge, Mass.: Harvard University Press.

Lee, Jennifer, and Frank D. Bean. 2004. "America's Changing Color Lines: Immigration, Race/Ethnicity, and Multiracial Identification." *Annual Review of Sociology* 30:221–42.

Lee, Robert G. 1999. *Orientals: Asian Americans in Popular Culture.* Philadelphia: Temple University Press.

Lee, Spike. 2007. *When the Levees Broke: A Requiem in Four Acts.* 40 Acres and a Mule Filmworks.

Lefebvre, Henri. 1991. *The Production of Space.* Trans. D. Nicholson-Smith. Cambridge, Mass.: Basil Blackwell.

Lemert, Charles. 1997. *Social Things: An Introduction to the Sociological Life.* Lanham, Md.: Rowman & Littlefield.

Levine, Hillel, and Lawrence Harmon. 1992. *The Death of an American Jewish Community: A Tragedy of Good Intentions.* New York: Free Press.

Li, Wei. 1999. "Building Ethnoburbia: The Emergence and Manifestation of the Chinese Ethnoburb in Los Angeles' San Gabriel Valley." *Journal of Asian American Studies* 2:1–28.

Lin, Jan. 1998. *Reconstructing Chinatown: Ethnic Enclave, Global Change.* Minneapolis: University of Minnesota Press.

Lipsitz, George. 1998. *The Possessive Investment in Whiteness: How White People Profit from Identity Politics.* Philadelphia: Temple University Press.

Liu, Eric. 1998. *The Accidental Asian.* New York: Random House.

Liu, John M. 1998. "Orange Blossoms: Asian Americans in the Life of Orange County." In *Orange County Perspective: One Hundred Years of Transition.* Orange County, Calif.: Orange County Public Library.

Liu, Michael Chung-Ngok. 1999. "Chinatown's Neighborhood Mobilization and Urban Development in Boston." PhD Diss., Public Policy Program, University of Massachusetts, Boston.

Loescher, Gil, and John A. Scanlan. 1986. *Calculated Kindness: Refugees and America's Half-Open Door, 1945 to the Present.* New York: Free Press.

Logan, John R. 2005. "Re-placing Whiteness: Where's the Beef?" *City & Community* 4:137–42.

Logan, John R., and Harvey L. Molotch. 1987. *Urban Fortunes: The Political Economy of Place.* Berkeley and Los Angeles: University of California Press.

Los Angeles Times. 1988. "Vietnam's Once-Fiery Ky Now Just a 'Papa San.'" October 14.

Low, Setha M. 2000. *On the Plaza: The Politics of Public Space and Culture.* Austin: University of Texas.

———. 2003. *Behind the Gates: Life, Security and the Pursuit of Happiness in Fortress America.* New York: Routledge.

Lukas, J. Anthony. 1986. *Common Ground.* New York: Vintage.

Lutz, Catherine A., and Jane L. Collins. 1993. *Reading National Geographic.* Chicago: University of Chicago Press.

Lynch, Kevin. 1960. *The Image of the City.* Cambridge, Mass.: MIT Press.

Lyon, Larry. 1987. *The Community in Urban Society.* Chicago: Dorsey Press.

Maher, Kristin Hill. 2004. "Borders and Social Distinction in a Global Suburb." *American Quarterly* 56:781–806.

Malpas, Jeff. 2003. "On the Map: Comments on Stuart Elden's *Mapping the Present: Heidegger, Foucault and the Project of a Spatial History.*" *Philosophy and Geography,* August 6, 2.

Martinez, Ruben. 2001. *Crossing Over: A Mexican Family on the Migrant Trail.* New York: Picador.

Masequesmay, Gina. 1991. "Little Saigon: An Exploratory Study of an Ethnic Community." Undergraduate thesis, Pomona College.

Massey, Doreen, and John Allen. 1984. *Geography Matters! A Reader.* New York: Cambridge University Press.

Massey, Douglas. 1985. "Ethnic Residential Segregation: A Theoretical Synthesis and Empirical Review." *Sociology and Social Research* 69:315–50.

Matsuda, Mari J. 1996. *Where Is Your Body? And Other Essays on Race, Gender, and the Law.* Boston: Beacon.

Mazumdar, Sanjoy, Shampa Mazumdar, Faye Docuyanan, and Colette Marie McLaughlin. 2000. "Creating a Sense of Place: The Vietnamese-Americans and Little Saigon." *Journal of Environmental Psychology* 20:319–33.

McHugh, Kevin E., Ines M. Miyares, and Emily H. Skop. 1997. "The Magnetism of Miami: Segmented Paths in Cuban Migration." *Geographical Review* 87:504–19.

McIntosh, Peggy. 2002. "White Privilege: Unpacking the Invisible Knapsack." In *White Privilege: Essential Readings on the Other Side of Racism,* ed. P. Rothenberg, 97–101. New York: Worth.

McKenzie, Evan. 1994. *Privatopia: Homeowner Associations and the Rise of Residential Private Government.* New Haven: Yale University Press.

McLaughlin, Colette Marie, and Paul Jesilow. 1998. "Conveying a Sense of Community along Bolsa Avenue: Little Saigon as a Model of Ethnic Commercial Belts." *International Migration* 36:49–63.

McNamara, Robert S. 1995. *In Retrospect: The Tragedy and Lessons of Vietnam.* New York: Times Books.

Medoff, Peter, and Holly Sklar. 1994. *Streets of Hope: The Fall and Rise of an Urban Neighborhood.* Boston: South End Press.

Meyer, Peter. 1993. *The Wall: A Day at the Vietnam Veterans Memorial.* New York: Wings Books.

Mills, C. Wright. 1971–72. *The Sociological Imagination*. New York: Oxford University Press.

Mock, Frieda. 1996. *Maya Lin: A Strong Clear Vision*. P.O.V. PBS Documentary.

Molotch, Harvey, William Freudenburg, and Krista E. Paulsen. 2000. "History Repeats Itself, but How? City Character, Urban Tradition, and the Accomplishment of Place." *American Sociological Review* 65:791–823.

Monmonier, Mark. 1991. *How to Lie with Maps*. Chicago: University of Chicago Press.

Montero, Darrell. 1979. "Vietnamese Refugees in America: Toward a Theory of Spontaneous International Migration." *International Migration Review* 13:624–47.

Moxley, R. Scott. 2000. "Yeah, We Want 'Bush.' " *Orange County Register*, September 22.

Muñoz, José Esteban. 1999. *Disidentifications: Queers of Color and the Performance of Politics*. Minneapolis: University of Minnesota Press.

Nagel, Joane. 1994. "Constructing Ethnicity: Creating and Recreating Ethnic Identity and Culture." *Social Problems* 41:152–76.

Naples, Nancy A. 2003. *Feminism and Method: Ethnography, Discourse Analysis, and Activist Research*. New York: Routledge.

Nee, Victor G., and Brett de Bary Nee. 1986. *Longtime Californ': A Documentary Study of an American Chinatown*. Stanford: Stanford University Press.

Nee, Victor, and Jimy M. Sanders. 1987. "Limits of Ethnic Solidarity in the Enclave Economy." *American Sociological Review* 52:745–73.

Nguyen, John, Kim Khanh Nguyen, Phuong Nguyen, and Son Vu. 1996. "The Harmony Bridge." Paper submitted to course titled Vietnamese American Experience, Professor D. C. Pham, University of California, Irvine.

Nguyen, Tina. 1995. "Vietnam Monument of Freedom Project." *Los Angeles Times*, April 14.

Nguyen, Viet Thanh. 2003. "Behind Flag Fight, Deep Pain." *Orange County Register*, August 17.

Noble, David. 2000. *The Death of a Nation: The End of American Exceptionalism*. Minneapolis: University of Minnesota Press.

Norman, Jan. 1992. "Going Westminster: City Relies on Entrepreneurs for Its Vitality." *Orange County Register*, May 2.

Okihiro, Gary Y. 1994. *Margins and Mainstreams: Asians in American History and Culture*. Seattle: University of Washington Press.

Olick, Jeffrey K., and Joyce Robbins. 1998. "Social Memory Studies: From 'Collective Memory' to the Historical Sociology of Mnemonic Practices." *Annual Review of Sociology* 24:105–36.

Olin, Spencer C. 1989. "Community in Orange County: Historians' Perspectives: Reconceptualizing Community in the Information Age." In *Proceedings of the Conference of Orange County History*, ed. L. Estes and R. Slayton, 138–40. Orange, Calif.: Chapman College.

Oliver, Melvin L., and Thomas M. Shapiro. 1996. *Black Wealth/White Wealth: A New Perspective on Racial Inequality*. New York: Routledge.

Omatsu, Glenn. 1994. "The 'Four Prisons' and the Movements of Liberation: Asian American Activism from the 1960s through the 1990s." In *The State of Asian America: Activism and Resistance in the 1990s*, vol. 2: *Race and Resistance*, ed. K. Aguilar–San Juan, 19–69. Boston: South End Press.

Omi, Michael, and Howard Winant. 1994. *Racial Formation in the United States: From the 1960s to the 1980s*. New York: Routledge.

Ong, Aihwa. 1999. *Flexible Citizenship: The Cultural Logics of Transnationality*. Durham, N.C.: Duke University Press.

Osborne, Milton. 1980. "Indochinese Refugees: Cause and Effects." *International Affairs* 56:37–53.

Palumbo-Liu, David. 1999. *Asian/American: Historical Crossings of a Racial Frontier*. Stanford: Stanford University Press.

Park, Robert E., Ernest W. Burgess, and Roderick D. McKenzie. 1968. *The City*. Ed. M. Janowitz. Chicago: University of Chicago Press.

Paterniti, Michael. 1997. "Saigon: The Sequel." *New York Times Magazine*, January 12.

Pham, Mai. 1996. "Another Senseless Hate Crime." *Newsletter of the Asian American Resource Workshop*, 11.

Pham, Mai-Lan. 1992. "Strangers in Fields Corner: The Formation of a Vietnamese Community in Dorchester." *Boston Review* 17 (September/October).

Pham, Vu. 2003. "Antedating and Anchoring Vietnamese America: Toward Vietnamese American Historiography." *Amerasia Journal* 29:137–52.

Phan, Duong. 1996. "A Distraught Vietnamese Community." Boston, Mass.: Coalition for Asian Pacific American Youth (CAPAY)

Plant, Raymond. 1978. "Community: Concept, Conception, and Ideology." *Politics & Society* 8:49–78.

Pope, John. 1996. "Developer Scraps Plan for Bridge in Little Saigon." *Los Angeles Times*, July 3.

Portes, Alejandro, and Leif Jensen. 1987. "What's an Ethnic Enclave? The Case for Conceptual Clarity." *American Sociological Review* 52:768–71.

———. 1989. "The Enclave and the Entrants: Patterns of Ethnic Enterprise in Miami before and after Mariel." *American Sociological Review* 54:929–49.

Portes, Alejandro, and Robert D. Manning. 1986. "The Immigrant Enclave: Theory and Empirical Examples." In *Competitive Ethnic Relations*, ed. S. Olzak and J. Nagel. New York: Academic Press.

Portes, Alejandro, and Ruben G. Rumbaut. 1990. *Immigrant America: A Portrait*. Berkeley and Los Angeles: University of California Press.

———. 2001. *Legacies: The Story of the Immigrant Second Generation*. Berkeley and Los Angeles: University of California Press.

Portes, Alejandro, and Alex Stepick. 1993. *City on the Edge: The Transformation of Miami*. Berkeley and Los Angeles: University of California Press.

Prashad, Vijay. 2001a. *Everybody Was Kung-Fu Fighting*. Boston: Beacon.

———. 2001b. "The Problem of the Twenty-First Century is the Problem of the Color-Blind." *Z Magazine*, March 31.

Purdum, Todd S. 2005. "Flashback to the 60's: A Sinking Sensation of Parallels between Iraq and Vietnam." *New York Times*, January 28.

Putnam, Robert. 2000. *Bowling Alone: The Collapse and Revival of American Community.* New York: Simon and Schuster.

Relph, E. 1976. *Place and Placelessness.* London: Pion.

Rieff, David 1993. "Multiculturalism's Silent Partner." *Harpers*, August, 62–72.

Riegert, Ray. 1996. *Hidden Southern California.* Berkeley: Ulysses Press.

Roediger, David R. 1991. *The Wages of Whiteness: Race and the Making of the American Working Class.* New York: Verso.

Ross, Andrew. 1997. "The Mickey House Club." *Artforum*, February, 25–26 and 100.

Rowe, John Carlos, and Rick Berg. 1986. *The Vietnam War and American Culture.* New York: Columbia University Press.

Rumbaut, Ruben G. 1995. "Vietnamese, Laotian, and Cambodian Americans." In *Asian Americans: Contemporary Trends and Issues*, vol. 174, ed. Pyong Gap Min, Sage Focus Editions, 47–68. Thousand Oaks, Calif.: Sage.

———. 1996. "The Crucible Within: Ethnic Identity, Self-Esteem, and Segmented Assimilation among Children of Immigrants." In *The New Second Generation*, ed. A. Portes, 119–70. New York: Russell Sage Foundation.

Rutledge, Paul James. 1992. *The Vietnamese Experience in America.* Bloomington: Indiana University Press.

Sack, Robert David. 1997. *Homo Geographicus.* Baltimore: Johns Hopkins University Press.

Saito, Leland. 1998. *Race and Politics: Asian Americans, Latinos, and Whites in a Los Angeles Suburb.* Urbana: University of Illinois Press.

Saunders, Peter. 1986. *Social Theory and the Urban Question.* New York: Holmes & Meier.

Savitch, H. V. 1978. "Black Cities/White Suburbs: Domestic Colonialism as an Interpretive Idea." *Annals of the American Academy of Political and Social Science* 439:118–34.

Sayer, Andrew. 1985. "The Difference That Space Makes." In *Social Relations and Spatial Structures*, ed. D. Gregory and J. Urry, 49–66. London: Macmillan.

Schiesl, Martin J. 1991. "Designing the Model Community: The Irvine Company and Suburban Development, 1950–88." In *Postsuburban California: The Transformation of Orange County since World War II*, ed. Rob Kling, Spencer Olin, and Mark Poster, 55–91. Berkeley and Los Angeles: University of California Press.

Schirmer, Daniel Boone. 1975. *Republic or Empire: American Resistance to the Philippine War.* Cambridge, Mass.: Schenkman.

See, Katherine O'Sullivan, and William J. Wilson. 1992. "Race and Ethnicity." In *Handbook of Sociology*, ed. Neil J. Smelser, 223–42. Newbury Park, Calif.: Sage.

Shalom, Stephen Rosskamm. 1993. *Imperial Alibis: Rationalizing U.S. Intervention after the Cold War.* Boston: South End Press.

Shiao, Jiannbin. 1999. "Review of *Growing Up American.*" *Social Forces* 78:857–58.

Smedley, Audrey. 1999. *Race in North America: Origin and Evolution of a Worldview.* Boulder: Westview Press.

Smith, Neil. 1984. *Uneven Development: Nature, Capital and the Production of Space.* New York: Basil Blackwell.

———. 1993. "Homeless/Global: Scaling Places." In *Mapping the Futures: Local Cultures, Global Change,* ed. J. Bird, B. Curtis, T. Putnam, G. Robertson, and L. Tickner, 87–119. New York: Routledge.

Smith, Neil, and Cindi Katz. 1993. "Grounding Metaphor: Towards a Spatialized Politics." In *Place and the Politics of Identity,* ed. M. Keith and S. Pile, 67–83. New York: Routledge.

Smith-Hefner, Nancy J. 1995. "The Culture of Entrepreneurship among Khmer Refugees." In *New Migrants in the Marketplace: Boston's Ethnic Entrepreneurs,* ed. M. Halter, 141–60. Amherst: University of Massachusetts Press.

Smyser, W. R. 1987. *Refugees: Extended Exile.* Ed. W. Laqueur and A. A. Jordan. New York: Praeger.

Soja, Edward W. 1989. *Postmodern Geographies: The Reassertion of Space in Critical Social Theory.* New York: Verso.

Sorkin, Michael. 1992. *Variations on a Theme Park.* New York: Hill and Wang.

Spiller, Jane. 1994. "Public Places: Little Saigon, 'A Tour of Asia without Air Fare.'" *Los Angeles Times,* October 10.

Squires, Gregory D. 1994. *Capital and Communities in Black and White.* Ed. A. G. Dworkin. Albany: SUNY Press.

Steinberg, Stephen. 1981. *The Ethnic Myth: Race, Ethnicity, and Class in America.* Boston: Beacon.

———. 1995. *Turning Back: The Retreat from Racial Justice in American Thought and Policy.* Boston: Beacon.

———. 2005. "Immigration, African Americans, and Race Discourse." *New Politics* 10:42–54.

Strait, Jerry L., and Sandra S. Strait. 1988. *Vietnam War Memorials: An Illustrated Reference to Veterans' Tributes throughout the United States.* Jefferson, N.C.: McFarland.

Sturken, Marita. 1997. *Tangled Memories: The Vietnam War, the AIDS Epidemic, and the Politics of Remembering.* Berkeley and Los Angeles: University of California Press.

Suttles, Gerald. 1968. *The Social Order of the Slum: Ethnicity and Territory in the Inner City.* Ed. D. P. Street. Chicago: University of Chicago Press.

Tajima, Renee. 1988. *Who Killed Vincent Chin?* New York: Filmmakers Library.

Teaford, Jon. 1997. *Post-suburbia.* Baltimore: Johns Hopkins University Press.

Tran, Mai. 2003. "Statues' Donors Asked to Give Again; Why is still more money needed for the Westminster memorial featuring American and South Vietnamese soldiers, they wonder." *Los Angeles Times,* March 8.

Trounstine, Philip J., and Terry Christensen. 1982. *Movers and Shakers: The Study of Community Power.* New York: St. Martin's Press.

Tsang, Daniel C. 1996. "Twice-Fried Mayor: Westminster's Frank Fry Revisits the Vietnam War." *Orange County Weekly*, December 20–26.

Tuan, Mia. 1998. *Forever Foreigners or Honorary Whites? The Asian Ethnic Experience Today.* New Brunswick, N.J.: Rutgers University Press.

Tuan, Yi-Fu. 1977. *Space and Place: The Perspective of Experience.* Minneapolis: University of Minneapolis Press.

Ungar, E. S. 1988. "The Struggle over the Chinese Community in Vietnam, 1946–86." *Pacific Affairs* 60:596–614.

Urry, John. 1990. *The Tourist Gaze.* London: Sage.

Vergara, Camilo José. 1997. *The New American Ghetto.* Princeton: Rutgers University.

Vietnamese American Curriculum Project Committee. 2001. *Vietnamese Americans: Lessons in American History.* Garden Grove, Calif.: Orange County Asian and Pacific Islander Community Alliance.

Vo, Linda Trinh. 2000. "The Vietnamese American Experience: From Dispersion to the Development of Post-Refugee Communities." In *Asian American Studies: A Reader,* ed. Jean Yu-Wen Shen Wu and Min Song, 290–305. New Brunswick, N.J.: Rutgers University Press.

Vo, Linda Trinh, and Rick Bonus. 2002. *Contemporary Asian American Communities: Intersections and Divergences.* Ed. S. Chan, D. Palumbo-Liu, and M. Omi. Philadelphia: Temple University Press.

Vo, Linda Trinh, and Mary Yu Danico. 2004. "The Formation of Post-Suburban Communities: Koreatown and Little Saigon, Orange County." *International Journal of Sociology and Social Policy* 24:15–45.

Vu, Cam Nhung, and Thuy Vo Dang. 2005. "Competing Images: Anticommunist Protest in Little Saigon." Paper presented at conference entitled "30 Years and Beyond: Vietnamese, Southeast Asian Refugee, Asian/American Studies." University of California, Riverside.

Wagner-Pacifici, Robin, and Barry Schwartz. 1991. "The Vietnam Veterans Memorial: Commemorating a Difficult Past." *American Journal of Sociology* 97:376–420.

Waldinger, Roger. 1993. "The Ethnic Enclave Debate Revisited." *International Journal of Urban and Regional Research* 17:444–52.

Warner, Sam Bass, Jr. 1982. *Streetcar Suburbs: The Process of Growth in Boston (1870–1900).* Cambridge, Mass.: Harvard University Press.

Webber, Melvin. 1963. "Order in Diversity: Community without Propinquity." In *Cities and Space: The Future Use of Urban Land,* ed. Lowdon Wingo Jr., 23–54. Baltimore: Johns Hopkins University Press.

Weiss, Lowell. 1994. "Timing Is Everything." *Atlantic Monthly,* January, 32, 34–36, 44.

Wellman, Barry. 1979. "The Community Question: The Intimate Networks of East Yorkers." *American Journal of Sociology* 84:1201–31.

Whalen, Carmen Theresa, and Victor Vazquez-Hernandez. 2005. *The Puerto Rican Diaspora: Historical Perspectives.* Philadelphia: Temple University Press.

Winant, Howard. 1995. "Race: Theory, Culture, and Politics in the United States Today." In *Cultural Politics and Social Movements*, ed. M. Darnovsky, B. Epstein, and R. Flacks, 174–88. Philadelphia: Temple University Press.

———. 2001. *The World Is a Ghetto: Race and Democracy Since World War II*. New York: Basic Books.

Wirth, Louis. 1995. "Urbanism as a Way of Life." In *Metropolis: Center and Symbol of Our Times*, ed. Philip Kasinitz, 58–82. New York: New York University Press.

Wood, Joseph S. 1997. "Vietnamese American Place Making in Northern Virginia." *Geographical Review* 87:58–72.

Wright, Richard, Mark Ellis, and Virginia Parks. 2005. "Re-placing Whiteness in Spatial Assimilation Research." *City and Community* 4:111–35.

Wright, Talmadge, and Ray Hutchison. 1997. "Socio-spatial Reproduction, Marketing Culture, and the Built Environment." In *Research in Urban Sociology: New Directions in Urban Sociology*, vol. 4, ed. Ray Hutchison, 187–214. Greenwich, Conn.: JAI Press.

Yip, Alethea. 1995. "Enemies All Around." *AsianWeek*, November 3, 17–18.

Young, Marilyn. 1991. *The Vietnam Wars: 1945–1990*. New York: Harper.

Yu, Elena S. H., and William T. Liu. 1986. "Methodological Problems and Policy Implications in Vietnamese Refugee Research." *International Migration Review* 20:483–501.

Yu, Henry. 2001. *Thinking Orientals: Migration, Contact, and Exoticism in Modern America*. New York: Oxford University Press.

Zelinsky, Wilbur. 2001. *The Enigma of Ethnicity: Another American Dilemma*. Iowa City: University of Iowa.

Zerubavel, Eviatar. 2003. *Time Maps: Collective Memory and the Social Shape of the Past*. Chicago: University of Chicago Press.

Zhou, Min. 1992. *Chinatown: The Socioeconomic Potential of an Urban Enclave*. Philadelphia: Temple University Press.

Zhou, Min, and Carl L. Bankston III. 1998. *Growing Up American: How Vietnamese Children Adapt to Life in the United States*. New York: Russell Sage Foundation.

Zia, Helen. 2000. *Asian American Dreams: The Emergence of an American People*. New York: Farrar Strauss Giroux.

Zinn, Howard. 2005. "Myths of American Exceptionalism." *Boston Review*, Summer.

Zuberi, Tukufu. 2000. *Thicker Than Blood: How Racial Statistics Lie*. Minneapolis: University of Minnesota Press.

Zukin, Sharon. 1993. *Landscapes of Power*. Berkeley and Los Angeles: University of California Press.

———. 1995. *The Cultures of Cities*. Cambridge, Mass.: Basil Blackwell.

Index

Abramson, Daniel, 180n11
Abu-Lughod, Janet L., 4
Accidental Asian, The (Liu), 56
African Americans. *See* blacks
Afro-Cubans, 149
Alba, Richard, 20, 23, 24, 172n8, 176n1, 178n16, 178n20, 179n4, 182n2
Alexander, Meena, 182n1
Ali, Muhammad, 43
All-America City Yearbook, 104
Allen, Douglas, 67, 179n3
Allen, John, 147–48
Allen, Robert L., 182n10, 185n21
All-State Foundation, 103, 104, 110
Almaguer, Tomas, 171n4, 178n19
Amerasian Homecoming Program, 20
Amerasians, 20
American exceptionalism, 61, 63, 66, 87, 156, 179n2, 179n4, 180n20
American Legion 555 of Midway City, 79
Anderson, Benedict, 173n8
Anderson, Don, 102
Anglocentric assimilationism, 179n2
Anh Thach, 52, 57
anticommunism, 11, 63; as "disciplinary cultural practice," 83, 131; "heritage" flag as icon of, 84; Hi-Tek incident and, 11, 79–80, 82–83,

84, 85, 105, 121, 128; marketplace multiculturalism and, 121
antiwar movement, 43, 69
Apidta, Tingba, xiv, 30, 178n19
Appy, Christian, 62, 63, 129, 179n9, 180n15
"architecture" of Vietnamese America, 17, 34
Army of Republic of South Viet Nam (ARVN), 67, 69, 76, 117
Ascher, Carol, 21
Asian American(s), 159; changes in traditions to accommodate American society, 66; comparing Vietnamese American socioeconomic status with, 24–26; differential positioning of blacks and, 146; economic mobility and racial distinction among, 143; history of, as near-white and near-black, 126, 176n37, 183n7; as "junior whites," 183n4; misconceptions about, xviii; as "model minority," 38, 66; as "perpetual foreigners," 42; racialization as, 26, 27, 176n37; racial violence directed against, 45–51; soldiers in Vietnam War, 43; tradition of examining spatially bounded communities of, 14–15
Asian American panethnicity, 40–41,

201

Karin Aguilar–San Juan is associate professor of American studies at Macalester College in St. Paul, Minnesota.